REVOLUTIONS

How Women Changed the World on Two Wheels

HANNAH ROSS

WEIDENFELD & NICOLSON

For Cleo, who I hope grows to love cycling too.

First published in Great Britain in 2021 by Weidenfeld & Nicolson
an imprint of The Orion Publishing Group Ltd
Carmelite House, 50 Victoria Embankment
London EC4Y 0DZ

An Hachette UK Company

1 3 5 7 9 10 8 6 4 2

A CIP catalogue record for this book is
available from the British Library.

ISBN (Hardback) 978 1 4746 1136 7
ISBN (Export Trade Paperback) 978 1 4746 1137 4
ISBN (eBook) 978 1 4746 1139 8

Typeset by Input Data Services Ltd, Somerset

Printed and bound in Great Britain by Clays Ltd, Elcograf S.p.A.

MIX
Paper from
responsible sources
FSC® C104740

www.weidenfeldandnicolson.co.uk
www.orionbooks.co.uk

CONTENTS

PART IV: QUEENS OF TRACK, ROAD AND MOUNTAIN

LIST OF ILLUSTRATIONS

PROLOGUE: LA PETITE REINE

The French have long affectionately referred to the bicycle as *La petite reine* – the little queen. Which is ironic, since the impression you might get from most accounts of over a century of cycling is that it hasn't involved many women.

Turn on the TV or look at the sports pages every July and it's hard to avoid coverage of the travails of almost two hundred cyclists battling it out over several thousand miles across France in one of the biggest sports events of the year. Every one of those taking part is a man. Look around you in most cities and towns in the world and you are likely to see more men on bikes than women. On this evidence, cycling would appear to be something of a boys' club rather than anything to do with little queens.

Yet since its inception, cycling has been a feminist issue. The late-nineteenth-century suffragist Susan B. Anthony went so far as to credit the bicycle with having 'done more to emancipate women than anything else in the world'.

When the bicycle emerged in the 1880s it triggered a revolution. Countless lives were transformed by this practical and efficient machine; not only did it allow the rider to cover distances with comparatively little effort, taking them to places they might never otherwise have ventured, it made getting about fun. Even now, when there are so many ways to travel, people still love to cycle. That feeling of pedalling along, the wind in one's hair, the sensation of flying as you make a descent – it never gets boring.

If you ask people what they like most about cycling, the words 'freedom' and 'flying' come up again and again. Yet as I started researching the history of the bike, it was striking how often women had had their wings clipped. Whereas men have never had to think twice about jumping into the saddle and pedalling off, for women cycling has always been politically charged, with society imposing limits on what they can and can't do.

In the 1890s, as the bicycle craze swept the world, around a third of owners in the UK and North America were women. An impressive statistic at a time when women's behaviour was heavily policed, and the sight of a woman cycling was liable to provoke more than just a few raised eyebrows. Female riders had insults and in some cases stones hurled at them. They also had to contend with the hazards of impractical long skirts, petticoats and other cumbersome garments deemed essential to public decency. Undaunted, women embraced this new machine with élan. And they didn't stop when they were told it would ruin their looks, leave them infertile, or lead to promiscuity.

The bicycle was expanding their world and they were determined to seize the opportunity. Some would go as far as circumnavigating the globe on two wheels. But even those who never made it further than the local park were riding over the established view that women were frail creatures, who – if their financial situation meant they didn't need to work – were best suited to a stifling and genteel life indoors, indulging in suitable pastimes such as needlework or flower-pressing. This first wave of female cyclists set a match to such restrictive notions of femininity. Though most cycled for pleasure, it was a political act to be seen using their bodies in this way. It's no coincidence that the suffragists who fought for women to be treated as equal citizens were enthusiastic cyclists; to them, bicycles were feminist freedom machines.

A century after women got the vote, it seems astonishing that we still account for less than a third of cyclists in the UK and North America. How is there still so much gender disparity when women today have so many more freedoms than their Victorian sisters? Whether for sport or leisure, the benefits of cycling are wide and far-reaching – and should be available to all. As those early pioneers demonstrated, gender is no barrier – although unwieldy skirts and corsets might be.

By getting people where they need to go cheaply and easily, the bike has proven itself a powerful tool for change. In addition to providing access to education or employment, it can deliver profound health benefits, both physical and psychological. Asked to list those benefits, most cyclists will say cycling makes them happy, with some reporting they *have* to bike to stay sane. We live in a world where there are bikes to suit every need and preference – featherlight road bikes for the more competitive, electric bikes to provide extra power where it's needed, adapted bikes for those with mobility issues. It's widely recognised that getting more people cycling could transform our cities from poisonous gridlock to quieter, cleaner and happier places with significantly lower carbon footprints. A no-brainer when we are currently tipping over into climate catastrophe.

That there are people who feel cycling isn't for them suggests there is still a long way to go. In countries like the Netherlands and Denmark, where government funding has made cycling infrastructure safer and more inviting, not only do more people cycle but there is an even split between genders. Representation matters. When we see people who look like us doing something, we're more inclined to give it a try. For too long cycling has presented a narrow and exclusive image, making it appear a closed shop.

My aim is to portray a different picture. I want to put women and girls – the queens of cycling – at the centre by telling some of their extraordinary stories. Stories of freedom, empowerment and revolution, which for too long have been pushed to the margins, forgotten or unrepresented. Whether they were going after medals, exploring the world, or spreading the word about votes for women, these female cyclists are an inspiration. *Revolutions* tells the story of over 130 years of women on bikes, from Europe and North America to Afghanistan, India and beyond.

When I told people I was writing this book, many assumed I would be focusing on those engaged in competition at the highest level. These formidable athletes are an important part of the narrative, but there is more to cycling than medals and power meters; to suggest it is all about sport is restrictive and limiting in its own way. You also don't need to have the most expensive bike and most Instagrammable kit. Female cyclists come in all shapes and sizes, from diverse backgrounds and with wide-ranging interests, and they fall in love with cycling for a variety of reasons. That's what I hope to show here.

Part I tells of the revolution that started it all: the emergence of the bicycle in the late nineteenth century, and the early female pioneers who bravely endured the torrent of abuse and misinformation thrown at them. In Part II we meet women who have used their bikes in the name of liberty, equality and sisterhood. Then we go onto the open road in Part III, with those who pedalled roads less travelled (certainly by women), and encouraged their contemporaries to follow. Finally, Part IV turns the spotlight on those who have raced at speeds and distances many assumed impossible for their sex, starting in the days when the bicycle was still a novelty, and women racers even more so. We will end with some of the incredible women who not only compete at the highest level but engage in activism to transform the sport, calling for equal pay, better conditions, more visibility and inclusivity.

The time for a more female-centred version of cycling history is long overdue. This is a story for everyone: those of us riding our bikes today and wondering why it's not as diverse an activity as it should be; those who haven't yet realised that; and those who will come after and hopefully never have to question their place on the road, mountain trail and track.

Part I

THE REVOLUTION

CHAPTER 1

Mad About the Bike

Cambridge Mob Rule

It is 21 May 1897 and a large, raucous crowd of male students – some armed with eggs and fireworks – has assembled in Cambridge's medieval market square. A few women students, looking a bit apprehensive, stand at the edge of the crowd. Above everyone's heads, suspended from the first-floor window of a bookshop facing the university senate house, hangs an effigy of a woman on a bicycle dressed in a blouse and bloomers. Why is she here, and why is there a mob of undergraduates swarming below her?

They had all gathered to await a decision from the university's senate, which had been debating a proposal to grant women studying at the university full degrees. Although they had been permitted to attend the women-only colleges of Girton, Newnham and Hughes Hall since the late 1860s, taking courses (provided the professor gave permission) and sitting exams, women were not entitled to be awarded degrees at the end of their studies. So while they could just about study, they could never be considered full members of the university and they could not graduate. They were still better off than their predecessors in the early 1860s; the university's first five female students had to study thirty miles away, lest their presence upset the male students.

The protesters outside the senate were not challenging the gross unfairness and inequality of the situation, they were outraged at the possibility that the proposal would be passed – even though other universities in the UK were already awarding degrees to men and women on an equal basis. The proposal was so divisive that extra trains had been put on from London to enable graduates to return and cast their vote. Many held aloft placards that made their feelings clear: 'No Gowns for Girtonites' and 'Varsity for Men'.

When the news broke that the senate had rejected the pro-posal, with 661 voting in favour and 1,707 against, the male students' delight was palpable. They tore down the effigy in a frenzy, ripping off her head and tearing her body into pieces before posting her remains through the gates of Newnham College. The women students locked inside – disgusted and possibly terrified – looked on as a mob tried to break down the gates. As far as these men were concerned, they were the moral victors; women needed to know their place and stop making outrageous demands that would encroach on male privileges.

It was another fifty years before women would be granted degrees at Cambridge on equal terms to men – the one re-maining university to hold out against the tide of change. It wasn't until 1988 that the last of its all-male colleges ac-cepted women, and once again the male students protested – less violently this time – by donning black armbands and flying their flag at half-mast.

To understand why the 1897 protest targeted that female cyclist effigy, we need to trace two movements that in-tersected in the run-up to that raucous event. The first of these was the emergence of the 'New Woman', an upsurge in feminism which had been growing in strength since the publication of Mary Wollstonecraft's *A Vindication of the Rights of Woman* in 1792. Determined to break free of the shackles imposed by late-Victorian patriarchy, women began demanding access to education, careers and other activities which had previously been the sole preserve and prerogative of men; this would ultimately evolve into large-scale move-ments for suffrage in the early part of the next century. The second catalyst was the 'bike boom', which saw cycling go from a minority pursuit to a mass activity in Western Europe and North America, thanks to the invention of a new type of bicycle. Women began taking up cycling in droves, but before exploring their fascination with this new activity we must understand the revolutionary potential of the new machine, and why some men were intent on keeping it for themselves.

Two-wheeled Genesis

In 1885, Coventry's Starley & Sutton Company launched a new bicycle called the Rover 'Safety'. It wasn't the first bicycle, but it was the one that would stand the test of time and have the most seismic impact – its basic design forming the blueprint for the machines we ride today. Although the reverberations of this unveiling weren't felt immediately, with some tweaks and refinements it would become the must-have accessory of the following decade.

Looking at pictures of bicycles before the launch of the Safety, it's easy to see why they were superseded. The first was designed by a German inventor, Baron Karl von Drais, who had set out to create a horseless carriage and launched his *Laufmaschine*, or 'Running-machine', in 1817. The key word here was 'running', as that was exactly what the rider was required to do on a contraption which was essentially two carriage wheels joined together by a wooden plank, with a cushioned seat for the rider and a rudimentary steering mechanism. The rider propelled the machine by running along the ground while seated. Apart from looking quite silly, this wasn't an easy thing to do when going uphill, and the absence of brakes didn't make the downhill any more comfortable. But the appetite for a self-propelled wheeled device, pre-motor age, was clearly there; in spite of its drawbacks and its high price-tag, the *Laufmaschine* was soon seen in fashionable cities such as London, Paris and New York. But as a craze it was short-lived; the novelty of running along while seated – wearing quickly through the soles of the rider's shoes – was destined to have limited appeal.*

In the years between Drais's invention and the Rover Safety in 1885, countless aspiring bike builders had a go at improving on the concept. But it wasn't until 1867 that the first pedal-powered bicycle rolled onto the scene.† Designed by Pierre Michaux, a Parisian blacksmith, the velocipede featured pedals attached to the hub of the front wheel – no more running! Dubbed the 'boneshaker' because of the deleterious effect the all-iron frame and wooden wheels had on the rider (air-filled rubber tyres had yet to be invented), the machine enjoyed a few years of popularity with those who could afford it (it cost 250 francs, around £1,200 in today's money). Theatre and circus performers incorporated the machine into their acts, and the more competitive enthusiasts took part in the world's first organised bike races.

As inventors worldwide competed to refine this new-style two-wheeler, patent offices saw a deluge of variations on Michaux's theme. In the early 1870s the craze for the boneshaker was eclipsed by the arrival of the 'high wheel' or 'Ordinary'. Perhaps the most emblematic of all Victorian-era inventions, with the cyclist perched above an enormous front wheel and a diminutive rear wheel providing counterbalance, in Britain it became known as the 'Penny-farthing' because the size discrepancy echoed that between the two coins (the penny being by far the larger). The design now looks so outlandish and impractical it

---

* Drais's design hasn't become entirely obsolete – the wooden balance bikes that children now use to learn to ride bear some similarity.
† Some believe the first ever pedal-driven bicycle emerged as early as 1839, created by the Scottish blacksmith Kirkpatrick Macmillan. Since he never patented his design it was never commercially available, making it impossible to prove conclusively that he was indeed decades ahead of his time with his invention.

seems it must have been invented by someone with a loose grasp on reality. Yet there was something about this strange new beast that stuck, at least for a few decades after 1871 when Starley & Sutton put their 48-inch-wheel bike on the market.

Far cheaper than Michaux's boneshaker, this new bike was also much lighter and remarkably nippy. Even without the luxury of air-filled tyres, the oversized front wheel meant the rider was much further from the lumps, bumps and ruts that – pre-tarmac – were endemic in roads at that time.

As the decade progressed the wheels continued to expand and speeds, along with distances covered, increased. Races drew large crowds, where the first riders to achieve the three-minute mile were cheered over the finish line. Demand grew so great that by 1880 there were over a hundred Ordinary manufacturers in the UK, with consumers in the US – after overcoming some initial scepticism – no less enthusiastic. One convert was Thomas Stevens, an emigrant from the UK, who in 1884 became the first to cross the country on two wheels when he rode an American-made Columbia Ordinary from San Francisco to Boston. (That was just the start of Thomas's cycle adventuring; the following year he set off from London, cycling through Europe, the Middle East, China and Japan, to become the first to pedal around the world.)

You may be wondering why the evolution of the bicycle didn't stop with the Ordinary if it had so much going for it. Firstly, they were dangerous: it was a long way to climb up onto the saddle, and a long way to fall – and falling was an occupational hazard for the high-wheel enthusiast. Even for experienced riders, strong winds, ruts in the road and other obstacles (such as fellow cyclists who'd hit the deck) could prove deadly hazards. Serious head injuries were common enough to acquire colloquial names – 'cropper', 'header', 'imperial crowner' – and to deter most people from giving it a go. Detractors referred to cycling as 'a young man's game', but even young men were liable to be put off by the potentially fatal design quirks. Moreover the price was so steep that only middle- and upper-class men of means could splurge on one. All this meant that cycling's pleasures, as well as its dangers, were denied to sensible, middle-aged and less affluent men – and women.

While some women did take to the machines – a few intrepid female riders even raced on them, drawing large audiences – it's fair to say that female fans of the high wheel were in the minority. Which comes as no surprise, given the additional hazards they would need to overcome. Social norms dictated that women hide their bodies beneath layers of petticoats and long skirts that dragged along the floor behind them; getting into the saddle in that garb would be nigh impossible, and any that managed it would inevitably be sent crashing to the ground the minute their skirts got caught in the spokes.*

Some women – and men – took up the tricycle, a three-wheeled machine propelled by foot levers that gained popularity in the late 1870s. No straddling was required, which accommodated standard Victorian dress, and knees could be kept firmly together, which made riding appropriately ladylike and uncontroversial. So much so that Queen Victoria bought one for herself and her daughters in 1881. But, like the high wheel, they had a few fundamental flaws. Machines were so heavy and cumbersome that going uphill required a helping hand pushing from behind, as pedalling was insufficient against such a weight. And while the rider didn't need much in the way of lessons and there was no

_____

* Implausible as it may sound, Starley did create a side-saddle design featuring a rear wheel offset to one side as a counter-balance. However, it's hard to find evidence that anyone actually rode one.

danger of falling several feet from the saddle, there were still risks, such as rolling over after hitting a bump. The size meant you couldn't exactly store one in your hallway, so if you didn't have a coach-house, you might be a bit stuck. More to the point, if you weren't wealthy enough to own a coach-house, then you probably couldn't afford a tricycle either.*

Meanwhile the high wheel remained accessible to only a few, an exclusive boys' club – which no doubt suited many – and clubs started springing up specifically for them. Some were positively lavish: the Massachusetts Bicycle Club (financially supported by the Pope Manufacturing Company) was housed in an imposing four-storey town-house in Boston, where members could cycle straight into the building via a ramp to make use of its washroom and library before settling down in the parlour to enjoy post-ride drinks and cigars in front of roaring log fires. While not all clubs were quite as grand, with many taking whatever space they could find, such as a room above a pub, they all placed high importance on uniform. Members turned out in caps and jackets in their club colours, emblazoned with the club's badge. There was a sense of pride in being part of this elite group of young men who adventured, raced and diced with death, so it's no surprise that the students of Oxbridge formed their own clubs, with Ivy League universities in America soon following suit.

However, caps, badges and deadly giant wheels would prove no defence when this elitism was challenged by the arrival of a new type of bike that would democratise cycling. It was long overdue.

---

* Tricycles have since made a comeback, albeit with far lighter and more user-friendly versions, to enable older people or those with disabilities to cycle. Many users find getting around on them easier than walking.

Safety First

John Kemp Starley got straight to the point back in 1885 when he named his successor to the high wheel the Safety. With its two standard-size wheels it was exactly that: a safe choice. Unlike its absurdist predecessor, it was low enough for the rider to place their feet on the ground when they stopped. While early designs featured a slightly larger front wheel, there was only a small disparity, so anyone who was reasonably mobile could mount one without difficulty. Its iconic diamond frame, still the basis for bikes today, proved the design breakthrough all those aspiring inventors had been hoping to get to first. But, as with most objects that become design classics, it was a few years before it really took off; devoted high wheels initially spurned the Safety, declaring its proximity to the ground to be most undignified. Nevertheless change was a-wheel in the bicycling world, and the Rover Safety was soon being shipped all around the world. Even Starley could not have predicted how revolutionary it would become.

Three years later, another design breakthrough occurred which finally set the wheels turning for a true bike boom. Its creator was John Dunlop, a Scottish vet based in Belfast, who in his spare time had been experimenting with fitting air-filled rubber tyres to his son's tricycle to make it more comfortable. Realising he was on to something, he registered a patent. There were the usual naysayers who thought it would never catch on, and early sightings sometimes attracted a crowd, but a quick spin on a Dunlop was all that was needed to prove that riding on air-filled, shock-absorbent tyres was preferable to a solid wheel. When the tyres were fitted to bikes at a race and the average speed increased by a third, there was no doubt that they would become a permanent fixture. With this winning combination, the Western world was about to go bike-crazy.

Boom Time

My great-grandfather, Samuel Moss, a printer on London's Fleet Street, was one of those who was bitten by the cycling bug in the 1890s. By the middle of the decade he was competing regularly at the newly opened Herne Hill Velodrome in London; the trophies he had won for his efforts were proudly displayed on a side-table in my grandmother's house.

While racing was a big thing by then, most people were content with the novelty of going for a sedate spin around the local park. The enjoyable sensation of coasting along with little effort would have been unlike anything most had experienced before, and if they wanted to go further, what was to stop them? We live in a time when people think nothing of covering hundreds of miles a day in a car, but our pre-motor-age ancestors were dependent on horse-power and steam trains. Many people who lived in villages or small towns with no train line would never have travelled further than they could walk in a day. Even those who could afford to keep a horse would have been restricted in the distance they could hope to travel; in an average day of cycling, it's possible to cover twice the distance compared to travelling on horseback. While trains were more efficient, they couldn't take you everywhere.

As bicycles became affordable, the world began to expand dramatically for *fin-de-siècle* Victorians. They now had access to new experiences and opportunities, and perhaps even new romantic liaisons. Sociologists in the UK credit the bicycle with a decrease in genetic faults associated with inbreeding, while in 1900 the US Census Bureau identified the invention as a game-changer: 'Few articles ever used by man have created so great a revolution in social conditions as the bicycle'.

The late Victorians embraced the Safety with feverish enthusiasm, making the end of their century the most significant period in the history of the bicycle, taking it from minority activity to mass pursuit in the course of a few years. In 1890 there were 27 bicycle factories in the USA making around 40,000 bicycles a year; by 1896, upwards of 250 factories were producing over 1,200,000, with many factories working through the night to meet demand. Pope, then the largest US cycle maker, was producing one bike per minute by the middle of the decade. The UK meanwhile had established itself as the world capital of cycling with 700 factories.

Early models were expensive, but as the decade progressed new mass-production techniques brought prices down from around $150 in the early 1890s – six months' pay for a worker at a Pope factory – to an average of $80 by 1897, with some models priced much lower. In addition, options to pay by instalment and a growing second-hand market fuelled by wealthy consumers upgrading to the latest model soon put the machines within reach of all levels of society. By the end of the decade, bicycles were a common sight on the streets of Western Europe, North America and beyond. No longer a plaything for the elite, they were widely used for both recreation and transport.

Copenhagen and Amsterdam, today's great cycling cities, were early adopters and by the beginning of the 1890s were buzzing with bikes. Toronto also became a cycling city at this time; the city's governors promoted bike use, convinced it would help identify their growing city as urban and modern. In the UK, pedal-powered machines were the most fashionable thing to be seen on in the royal parks of London in 1895; by 1896 as many as 3,000 cyclists were parading along the paths of Hyde Park each day. That same year, one of the pioneers of British cinema recorded in grainy black and white the continuous flow of smartly dressed men and women cycling along one of the park's grand avenues, watched by onlookers lining the thoroughfare. The twenty seconds of footage, entitled *Hyde Park Cyclists*, offers an extraordinary glimpse into the world of those fashionable park cyclists.

France too was identifying itself as a cycling nation and dictating what the well-dressed cyclist should be wearing, with the Bois de Boulogne in Paris as the epicentre of *le cyclisme à la mode*. Enthusiasts would meet daily at the park's Brasserie de L'Espérance or Chalet du Cycle, hand their machine to the cloakroom staff in exchange for a numbered ticket, so they could sit and enjoy a coffee or glass of wine before cycling its tree-lined avenues. It was a mixed crowd, with waiters on their lunch break sharing the boulevards with the likes of President Casimir-Périer, who rode a tandem with his wife and children; stage-actors like Sarah Bernhardt; and artists and writers such as Fernand Léger. The Italians were also busy putting themselves on the cycling map, but riding for leisure wasn't quite so compelling to them – it was all about the racing.

In Australia, the bike wasn't so much a fashionable accessory as a practical tool for coping with the challenging climate and geography. During the gold rush it was taken up by prospectors who needed to travel long distances across inhospitable terrain, and it rapidly became an economical alternative to horses for many working in the country's remote mining towns, as well as itinerant shearers travelling between farms.

Germany, in contrast, took a dim view of cycle-mania. Some regional authorities tried to repress the seemingly unstoppable rise of the new velocipede by insisting that cyclists must pass an examination, while others required cyclists to attach a clearly visible identification number to their bikes.

In Berlin, Dresden and Munich, bikes were banned from the city centre. Each region of this recently unified country seemed to have its own regulations, and with plainclothes policemen lurking ever-ready to catch offenders. Such measures could prove challenging for foreign travellers but failed to stem the rise of this practical and pleasurable machine; by 1896 half a million Germans identified as cyclists. Though Tsar Nicholas was a fan, Russia also went through a phase of setting exams for cyclists – and women who wanted to cycle weren't entitled to sit the exam until 1897.

Around the world, manufacturing industries began to complain that their profits were suffering as consumers spent their money on bicycles. Some companies tried to get in on the act: Tiffany & Co., the New York jewellers, produced an amethyst-studded, gold-plated machine with pearl handlebars. Valued at $10,000 (around $230,000 today), it was commissioned by businessman 'Diamond' Jim Brady as a gift for his girlfriend, the performer Lillian Russell. This high watermark of cycling-related conspicuous consumption in America's 'gilded-age' would only have added to the Church's deep suspicion of cycle-mania. A number of prominent members of the clergy decried the activity as profane, outraged that increasing numbers of their flock were choosing to go out cycling on a Sunday instead of sitting on a hard pew to be chastised for their sins.

Clergymen weren't the only ones who feared cycling could be morally ruinous. Even some cycling enthusiasts expressed the view that it was an inappropriate activity for a certain sector of society, namely women.

Why the outrage? This was a time when women were too often denied agency and had few rights. The majority led lives that were decidedly unfree, both socially and physically. They were not supposed to be independent, to pursue an education at elite universities or take off on two wheels.

CHAPTER 2

Wild Women on Wheels

Ladies Who Pedal

It was Starley, the same visionary who invented the original Safety bicycle, who had the foresight to design a bike that would specifically appeal to women. Released in 1887, the 'Psycho Ladies' Safety' featured a frame with a sloping top bar – a step-through – so that that the rider didn't have to straddle a crossbar in cumbersome long skirts, and a chain guard to prevent the layers of fabric getting mangled and causing an accident.[*]

One year later the members of Harriette H. Mills' women's cycling club placed an order, even though it meant shipping the Psycho all the way from the UK to their home town, Washington DC. Harriette owned a US-produced 'Ladies' Dart' bicycle, but the company couldn't produce them fast enough to meet demand. Another company called their ladies' model 'The Witch' – a seemingly counter-intuitive piece of marketing strategy, considering the term had yet to be reclaimed by feminism. Despite the dubious choice of names, it's clear that on both sides of the Atlantic manufacturers were beginning to realise they could sell more bikes if they were specifically adapted to women.

My own family history hasn't revealed whether, while Samuel Moss was winning racing medals, his wife, my great-grandmother, had also caught the cycling bug. But statistics show that by the middle of the 1890s women's bikes accounted for one-third of the market in the UK and North America. This would have seemed an impossibility a decade before when the high-wheel craze was in full swing.

---

[*] Admittedly 'Psycho' seems an odd choice of name if you want to attract a new sector to your market, but it didn't have quite the same connotations as it does now, largely thanks to Alfred Hitchcock's film of the same name.

The popularity of women's bicycles was given a boost by the enthusiasm with which certain members of the upper echelons of society embraced the sport. The Duchess of Somerset, for instance, often hosted fifty or so of her friends for breakfast in Battersea Park's lake house before pedalling circuits of the park together. They also enjoyed night rides through the city, with Chinese lanterns lighting their way, before dismounting for a grand supper. Bicycles could be spotted gracing the marble halls of the aristocracy across London and each morning they would be carefully placed in carriages to be driven to the local park along with their lady owners. Boys in uniform waited on the steps of grand houses ready to polish the cherished bike on its return.

For society cyclists, it wasn't just about being seen on a bicycle, it was also about whether you had the latest model and the clothes you wore to ride it. Daisy Greville, Countess of Warwick (mistress of the Prince of Wales, the future King Edward VII), was described as having caught the 'rabid disease commonly known as cyclomania'. Her devotion to the pursuit led to her becoming the inspiration for the music-hall staple 'Daisy Bell', who according to the observer will 'look sweet upon the seat of a bicycle built for two'. The press fixated on the countess's attire, eagerly reporting the changing colours of her mount and coordinating outfits to match the seasons – moss-green for autumn, all-white for summer, brown and gold for spring – with tailors poised to copy whatever she wore.

The cycling press at the time was filled with interviews with these society ladies – as well as some famous actresses – who were so taken with their new hobby that they had incorporated it into many of their favourite pastimes. Guests to weekend parties at the best country houses were urged to bring their bicycle so they could go on picnic rides and partake in gymkhana-style games and fancy-dress bicycle parades. Some even abandoned their usual equine mount for two wheels in order to follow the local foxhunt.

The ladies of New York society were equally enthusiastic. In 1894, *Cycling* magazine reported: 'as early as five o'clock in the morning, a large number of ladies are seen riding with their maids or footmen upon Upper Fifth Avenue and the Boulevard'. Some of them might have joined the rarefied Michaux Club based on upper Broadway, which catered to the likes of the city's elite 'Four Hundred' group, led by the doyenne of the social scene – Caroline Astor – with Rockefellers and Roosevelts in their number. In 1896, *Harper's* magazine reported that the club comprised 'many of the fashionable folk of the city, and quite as many women as men are enrolled'. With an upper limit of 250 members, the Michaux quickly established a long waiting list. Their premises boasted a library, a lounge for taking high tea, and an indoor school for the winter months, where members cycled to music and performed synchronised routines – like a nineteenth-century equivalent of today's Peloton or Soul-Cycle spin classes.

A reporter from *Munsey's Magazine* was spellbound by the sight, declaring that 'the intricate figures performed by the cyclists, as they follow their leader around the spacious hall, to the music of the band, make one of the prettiest sights in all Gotham'. In spring and summer, group rides were organised to scenic destinations like Riverside Drive, where they would stop for lunch. The city planners responded to the craze by creating a bicycle path that went all the way from Prospect Park to the resort town of Coney Island on the Atlantic. It was so popular that within a month it had to be repaired from overuse and widened to accommodate the high number of users.

In Italy, Queen Margherita of Savoy was a convert, with gossip columns reporting that she rode a bicycle with solid gold wheels. Queen Amélie of Portugal was encouraged to take up cycling by her husband, who worried she was spending too much time reading books about physics. She embraced the pastime enthusiastically, though I hope she still found time to pursue her interest in science.

The impact of the aristocracy's fervour for cycling could be felt as far away as China, where Shanghai's Sing-song girls (the Chinese equivalent of the geisha), who were always first to adopt the latest fashions, could be seen cycling around the city's parks.

By the close of 1896 society cyclists in London, New York and elsewhere had started to let their bikes gather dust. The fad was over for them almost as soon as it started – once the boom reached the point where bicycles became affordable for the masses, the sport became less rarefied and lost its appeal to the elite. It was far from the end of the road in wider society though.

By this point the Church was beginning to accept that cycling was here to stay. Some forward-thinking clergymen installed bike racks so their congregation could combine the two activities. There were even bicycle weddings: in 1897 an Italian couple married in a church in London's Leicester Square, with the wedding party pedalling up the street followed by the bride and groom in wedding dress and with their mounts covered in flowers. The scene attracted so much interest that the police were dispatched to deal with the crowd. And it wasn't just holy matrimony being celebrated a-wheel; in 1896 *Lady Cyclist* magazine reported a christening where the baby and nurse arrived on a tandem, with the rest of the party on as many as eighty bicycles bringing up the rear.

Cycling honeymoons became a thing, often with the newly married couple on a bicycle made for two. Tom and Helen Follett were one such pair, spending two months riding from New Orleans to Washington DC in 1896 after being gifted a tandem by an uncle. While bemoaning the deplorable state of roads in the South, Helen was smitten with life on two wheels, describing it as the 'grandest' of experiences. She felt free as 'a bird, sailing over flower-covered prairies; you fancy yourself a greyhound bounding after a breathless and frightened jack-rabbit; you even compare yourself with a flash of lightning or a whizzing cannon-ball. You realise how Monte Cristo felt when he climbed upon that rock and declared that the world was his'.

In France the previous year, the physicist Marie Curie and her husband Pierre celebrated their nuptials with a cycle trip. The wedding was a simple affair, stipulated by Marie, with no white dress, gold rings or wedding breakfast, and certainly no religious element. Their daughter, Eve, wrote in her biography of her mother that the couple's only indulgence was the two 'glittering' bicycles they had bought with money sent as a wedding gift. Immediately after, 'at the cost of some thousands of pedal strokes and a few francs for village lodgings, the young couple attained the luxury of solitude shared between them for long enchanted days and nights'. She goes on to record that 'during these happy days was formed one of the finest bonds that ever united man and woman'. Cycling would remain a fixture in Marie's life, a way to unwind from her demanding work and the research that would lead to her becoming the first woman to be awarded a Nobel Prize. Each summer Pierre and Marie would explore some part of rural France on their bicycles. Eight months pregnant, she was still cycling: the couple travelled to Brest, covering distances no different to those of her pre-pregnancy days. The trip was only cut short when Marie returned to Paris to give birth.

You Can't Ride Side-saddle on a Bicycle

Before high society made bicycling fashionable in the mid 1890s, albeit in a distinctly genteel way, women cyclists were liable to encounter resistance and disapproval. This ranged from mild harassment – often in the form of questions about their femininity, or supposed lack of it, and suspicions about their sexual morality – to outright violence.

Helena Swanwick, a suffragist and writer, described her experiences when biking in London in the early 1890s: 'bus drivers were not above flicking at me with the whip, and cabmen thought it fun to converge upon me from behind. I was once pulled off by my skirt in a Notting Hill slum.' Undeterred, she carried on cycling; for her the benefits outweighed the prejudice, her life had been 'greatly enlarged' by the activity. She and her husband enjoyed exploring the countryside together on their bikes from their home in Manchester, as well as touring other parts of the UK and France. Helena was educated at Girton College, Cambridge, so it's possible she may have helped inspire that infamous effigy.

The writer Evelyn Everett-Green, like Helena, found that her cycling seemed to offend cab drivers, who regularly called her a 'hussy', while some women called her 'disgusting'. Friends and family tried to discourage her from riding her bike in London as they felt it was 'not quite nice'. They may have changed their tune a few years later, judging by Evelyn's comment: 'in April of 1895 one was considered eccentric for riding a bicycle, while by the end of June eccentricity rested with those who did not ride'.

Other women cyclist pioneers faced physical violence. Lady Dorothea Gibb had stones thrown at her when she started riding her Safety in York, but she wasn't thrown off her pedal strokes and even encouraged her daughter to have a go. Emma Eades, reputedly one of the first women to cycle in London, was pelted with bricks by both men and women and told to go home. Like many others, she carried on regardless. When she took up performing cycling tricks before an audience at the Alhambra, a music hall on Leicester Square, her family were so scandalised they refused to speak of it.

Those female students on lockdown in their Cambridge college and the braying mob of men outside with their cycling effigy are a good analogy for how gender norms in the nineteenth century were constructed. Men and women were supposed to exist in separate spheres, with women confined to the home, tending to their families rather than gadding about for all to see; the social and public world of work, politics and learning was an exclusively male domain. This was a time when a woman could cause a disturbance simply by walking alone down the street; women who did so risked being arrested for prostitution. With their new bicycles, women were escaping the domestic prison and visibly taking space up in the streets – men's territory. Like the women attending Cambridge University, they weren't always welcome.

In their role as 'the angel in the house', preoccupied with domestic issues and with no political power or complete freedom of movement, women were much easier to control. As the 'weaker sex', they were told they risked complete disintegration should they exert themselves mentally or physically. This construct of femininity made many women prisoners in their own homes. So far as the law was concerned, while single they belonged to their fathers and upon getting married they were required to give their property and body over to their husbands, as well as their wages if they worked.

The display and use of their own bodies was similarly

curtailed. Women who were brought up 'properly' concealed their figures with long skirts and petticoats and stayed indoors as much as possible; women who revealed their bodies or walked the street were prostitutes, making a spectacle of themselves. While it was acceptable for working-class women to toil away in drudgery, the daughters of polite society were considered too fragile and precious to break a sweat. In Jane Austen's novel *Pride and Prejudice* (1813), arch-conservative Caroline Bingley is scandalised by Elizabeth Bennet walking three miles to nearby Netherfields to nurse her sick sister, deeming her a social pariah for going out alone in her muddy skirts.

As a physical activity which takes place in public, cycling fell foul of this code of femininity. Before the Safety bike came on the scene, if women of the moneyed classes engaged in sport at all it had to be genteel and 'ladylike'. Croquet, archery, golf and lawn tennis were considered permissible because these were activities that took place away from prying eyes, behind walls or in private gardens. Swimming remained segregated until the 1920s; although women's swimming apparel at this time more closely resembled a burkini than a bikini, with knee-length woollen bathing dresses worn over bloomers and black stockings (not an outfit that could facilitate swimming lengths of the lido), the sight of a woman in bathing costume was considered too risqué for polite society. When women's football matches began in the mid 1890s they were rapidly shut down by protests (only to be revived in the First World War, when they proved hugely popular).

There were, of course, women who successfully undertook arduous feats – such as scaling Alpine peaks and glaciers – in defiance of these restrictive notions, but they were few and far between.

Helena Swanwick and her ilk, taking up space on the

streets on their new machines, no longer hiding the fact that they were in possession of a pair of legs in good working order, were putting a rocket under the rules that sought to contain and control them. To many Victorians, these were dangerous, wild women who were disrupting the established order. Many believed they should be kept under surveillance, and local newspapers did their bit by running stories about the first women to cycle in their town.

Ethel Smyth, a composer of numerous orchestral works and operas, described how the London papers in the early 1890s were full of pictures of 'wild women of the usual unprepossessing pioneer type' riding their bicycles. As someone who would go on to compose the women's suffrage anthem, 'The March of the Women', and spend two months in Holloway Prison for breaking an MP's window, it makes sense that she was attracted to these non-conformist and independent women. Encouraged by her mother, she immediately decided to buy a bicycle. Other family members told her it was an 'indelicate' activity, unsuitable for 'nice' women. Their pleas fell on deaf ears. Why should men be the ones having all the fun?

While an interest in women's suffrage wasn't a prerequisite for these early women cyclists, there is evidence that the type of woman who was attracted to the independence and excitement offered by a bicycle would also have more than a passing interest in gender equality. Kate Shepperd was a shining example of the 'New Woman', the term coined by the writer Sarah Grand in her 1894 essay. A prominent New Zealand women's suffrage campaigner whose work was key to the country becoming the first to establish universal suffrage in 1893, Kate also found time to set up its first women's cycling club.

New Women wanted an education, the right to pursue a career. Some thought they too deserved the right to vote.

In short, they wanted autonomy over their lives. They weren't the first, but this was a period of transition in society, and a groundswell developed that would prove impossible to contain. Intent on disrupting restrictive ideas of Victorian womanhood, these New Women promoted empowerment, freedom and change. No wonder the movement came to be associated with cycling by the press. Hence the effigy of a female cyclist outside the Cambridge senate house; in the eyes of the mob, a bicycling woman was as much of a threat to the established order as a Cambridge-educated one.

In 1896, *Munsey's Magazine* declared that for men the bicycle was 'merely a new toy', but for women it was 'a steed upon which they rode into a new world'. Marguerite Merington, who had once taught Latin and Greek at a women's-only college in the US before going on to become a playwright, would have agreed. In an article written in 1895, she prescribed cycling as the best means for women to break the chains of domesticity: 'now and again a complaint arises of the narrowness of the woman's sphere. For such disorder of the soul the sufferer can do no better than to flatten her sphere to a circle, mount it, and take it to the road.'

The following year, Susan B. Anthony, the American women's rights campaigner, described the bicycle as a 'freedom machine'. She went on to say: 'I rejoice every time I see a woman ride by on a bike. It gives her a feeling of self-reliance and independence the moment she takes her seat; and away she goes, the picture of untrammelled womanhood.'

In the same way that university education opened the door to new opportunities outside of the home, the Rover Safety, with its promise of movement and new worlds to explore, was so much more than a fashionable hobby. It symbolised and actualised the exact opposite of the life of confinement and enforced inactivity many women endured. Is it any wonder they were so eager to publicly embrace this 'freedom machine', with the suffragist and writer Elizabeth Haldane calling for a national memorial to honour the inventor of the new bicycle on behalf of the women whose lives had been revolutionised by it.

But as we have seen, not everyone shared this enthusiasm for the new female freedoms.

Call the Doctor

In an era when women's bodies were heavily policed by the patriarchy, it's hardly surprising that cycling became the focus of intense debate, bad science and misinformation. Out in the open, removed from the watchful gaze of their families and guardians, who knew what morally reprehensible things women might get up to?

In America, the Women's Rescue League was in no doubt that cycling would have a negative moral impact on female enthusiasts. The League's leader, Charlotte Smith, petitioned Congress to get the activity banned, condemning it as 'the devil's advance agent'; if allowed to continue, it would lead to moral and religious demise, 'swelling the ranks of reckless girls who finally drift into the standing army of outcast women of the United States'. In other words, it would turn decent women into prostitutes.

The view that cycling wasn't decorous or ladylike was shared by many.*

Women had been riding horses for centuries by this point, so why was exchanging four legs for two wheels so

---

* In 1891 a letter to Washington's *Sunday Herald* described a woman on a bicycle as 'the most vicious thing I ever saw in all my life . . . I had thought that smoking was the worst thing a woman could do, but I have changed my mind'.

controversial? It all came down to the way you sat on your chosen mount. A woman on horseback would have been expected to ride side-saddle (it would take a world war to kill off this tradition); thus both legs would be demurely draped to one side, hidden by her long skirts. But long skirts weren't practical on a bike, and side-saddle simply wasn't an option. Those who subscribed to the prudish and misguided notion that, for a woman, the mere act of sitting astride a saddle, be it on a bike or a horse, was overtly sexual behaviour, saw this as perilous both to a woman's morals and her reproductive organs.

Some men – and a few women – who considered themselves medical professionals (I use the term loosely, bearing in mind that some doctors at this time thought travelling in fast steam trains might cause brain damage) felt science was on their side. Dr Robert Dickinson, an American gynaecologist, believed that women cyclists went to great lengths to set up their saddles so as to 'bring about constant friction over the clitoris and labia' and that the 'pressure would be much increased by stooping forward, and the warmth generated from vigorous exercise might further increase the feeling'. I think this says more about the state of Dr Dickinson's mind than anything else. He was certainly wrong about many things – not least his endorsement of eugenics and his opinion that homosexual women were a threat to society; he devoted much of his career to trying to 'cure' them.

Others claimed that cycling led to promiscuity, a misconception that persists to some extent now in more conservative cultures, and perhaps also explains why women in supposedly liberal countries report being subjected to more sexual harassment when they ride a bike than when they are walking.

Victorian manufacturers cashed in on the controversy by producing new types of saddles that they claimed prevented sexual stimulation. Labelled 'anatomical' or 'hygienic', most models featured a seat with a deep groove down the middle and a shortened nose. Whatever the design, they all claimed the result was elimination of 'perineal pressure' or of 're-lieving the sensitive parts of the body from pressure of any kind'; in short, lady riders wouldn't be getting off on using one of their new saddles. One company proudly declared, 'You do not straddle the Duplex saddle'.*

Frances Oakley, a doctor who was both a woman *and* a cyclist, had no truck with the saddle-stimulation myth. In 1896 she told readers of *Harper's Bazaar* that the 'freak' saddles being marketed in response to this misinformation were constructed on entirely 'wrong anatomical premises' and their proliferation was a confusing and distressing dis-traction. Sadly, this didn't shut down the argument, with some doctors going beyond genitalia and on to the repro-ductive organs. One thought cycling increased painful periods and others insisted it could cause infertility. The dominant, though entirely incorrect, medical discourse at this time was that the nature of the female reproductive system made women the 'weaker sex' and any exertion would put their reproductive ability at risk. Physical activity such as cycling, where the saddle was in direct contact with female genitals, was a matter for grave concern.

---

* This argument seems ironic now, given that many female cyclists, even with today's technological advances, consistently report that their saddles cause huge discomfort, despite there being a plethora of designs on the market which are supposed to combat this. At the extreme end, Paralympian pro-cyclist Hannah Dines recently revealed she had to undergo surgery on her vulva due to trauma from hours spent training, leaning forward in the race position, which puts pressure on that sensitive area. She decried the level of resources being spent on developing designs to make women more comfortable as 'laughable', another example of women's needs not always being taken seriously in the industry.

According to some, there was no part of a woman's anatomy that might not be ruined by riding a bike, from the head
down to the toes. Cynthia, an anxious would-be cyclist,
wrote to the *Lady Cyclist* magazine in 1896 to ask for help.
She wanted to know if it was true that cycling would make
her feet grow. The respondent assured her there was no possibility of that happening, though there would doubtless be
a stack of periodical articles arguing the opposite. Indeed,
there was a doctor in New York who thought he could detect
something he called 'bicycle walk' in his cycle-mad patients.
He described this as the feet moving in a circular instead
of a forward motion. Others were worried that the act of
leaning forward to reach the handlebars might give them an
unsightly 'bicycle hump'; accordingly, women's bicycles at
this time were designed with high handlebars to ensure an
upright position, an acceptably ladylike riding posture. Any
angling down towards the frame, despite being far more
aerodynamic, was discouraged.

When it came to the perils of cycling for women, the
head aroused as much debate as the reproductive organs.
Concern focused on so-called 'bicycle face'. In 1899, Dr
Arabella Kenealy, another eugenics fan, claimed her patient, Clara, was afflicted. Clara's face had once possessed
a subtle feminine charm, but since she had taken up cycling
and other sports she felt it had been disfigured by 'muscular
tension': 'the haze, the elusiveness, the subtle suggestion of
the face are gone; it is the landscape without atmosphere'.
Another doctor suggested that women over forty were most
likely to be afflicted by the 'ravages' of cycling: 'I have seen
them rapidly decline in the "good looks", become thin and
wrinkled, and quickly lose any freshness of appearance
they might have had previously.' *Harper's Magazine* recommended chewing gum to keep the effects at bay.

Men could also develop the condition, with a *New York*

Herald journalist describing how he saw 'bicycle face' among most of the members attending a meeting of the League of American Wheelman in New Jersey. Doctors were more concerned about how it affected women because their femininity was at stake; cycle-mad women risked becoming indistinguishable from men. Dr Kenealy also claimed that cycling had made Clara a domestic slattern, given her a manly gait and, worst of all, would result in her 'squandering' the 'birth right' of her future children.

So if cycling wasn't sending women freewheeling into a life of prostitution, it was making them barren or, worse, turning them into men by robbing them of their femininity, grace and fertility. The future of the nation was surely at stake.

This belief that cycling would make women sick in mind and body seems all the more ironic in light of the fact that many doctors at that time were treating mental health issues such as depression and a range of symptoms generally labelled as 'hysteria' or 'neurasthenia' by prescribing the 'rest cure'. The treatment is famously critiqued in 'The Yellow Wallpaper', Charlotte Perkins Gilman's feminist short story of 1892. The narrator, described as exhibiting signs of 'temporary nervous depression', is confined to her bed by her doctor husband. She is not even permitted to write, her one true pleasure. Trapped and inactive, she says he 'hardly lets me stir without special direction' – behaviour we would label today as coercive control rather than a necessary medical intervention.

As a result, the narrator progressively loses touch with reality, obsessing over the design of the bedroom wallpaper and encountering visions of a woman crawling on all fours behind the pattern, and 'all the time trying to climb through. But nobody could climb through that pattern – it strangles so'. In her mania, she tries to free the imagined woman by tearing the wallpaper from the walls, but the trapped woman is a projection of the narrator's own psyche – and the author's. For Charlotte Gilman had herself been prescribed a period of complete inactivity – or domestic imprisonment – by Dr Silas Mitchell, the architect of the rest cure, to treat her postnatal depression. A 'treatment' she describes as having nearly driven her to mental breakdown and which she decided to stop, against doctor's orders. She also left her husband, rejecting suffocating Victorian domesticity to become a full-time writer, describing the decision to leave as the only way to keep her sanity.*

Dr Mitchell would have strongly disapproved since he was opposed to women working or indeed doing anything that would make them equal to men: 'The woman's desire to be on a level of competition with man and to assume his duties is, I am sure, making mischief. She is physiologically other than the man'.† The treatment echoed a wider culture

---

* The writer Virginia Woolf was also subjected to Dr Mitchell's rest cure to treat her depression in the early twentieth century. Initially, she too was forbidden to write, a diktat which seems unimaginably barbaric, not to mention absurd. Eventually, though, she was permitted to work on her novel for a few hours a day. She later used her fiction to lampoon his methods.

† If it's not obvious by now, Dr Mitchell had a ludicrously binary approach to gender. At the same time as he was prescribing bed rest to his female patients, he was promoting the benefits of the outdoors and exercise to male patients who were deemed, according to the rigid gender expectations of the time, to be overly intellectual and effeminate. His 'West' cure packed them off to Midwestern ranches to do stereotypically 'masculine' activities like hunting and cattle herding. Patients included Theodore Roosevelt, described at the time as resembling Oscar Wilde (years later, as US president, he was seen as epitomising a more rugged masculinity), and the poet Walt Whitman, who is now widely considered to have been gay; I only hope he had more of a *Brokeback Mountain* experience with the cowboys on the ranch.

that wanted to clamp down on women's physical and intellectual independence, with Dr Mitchell (wilfully) blind to the reality that it was in fact women's lack of political, social and physical enfranchisement that was ailing them.

If only the doctor had listened to the many women who stated that, since they had started cycling, they had never felt better. It couldn't fail to, if the alternative was staying at home to stare at the same four walls. One woman writing to the *Cyclists' Touring Club Gazette* held that her new pastime was the cure for all her ailments, including headaches and vomiting, for which her doctors had been unable to find the cause. When she took up cycling with her daughter and husband, she was delighted that not only did her strength increase but her previous ailments disappeared. She was now convinced all women could benefit similarly from exercise in the outdoors. Another enthusiast described how she had previously suffered poor health and fatigue, but since taking up cycling had been energised and could manage up to seventy miles a day.

Within the medical establishment there was an opposing faction to the Kenealys and Dickinsons, who were convinced that cycling could be of benefit in all manner of afflictions. A Dr Albutt started prescribing moderate cycling to his patients and claimed there was a distinct improvement in all who followed his advice. A woman doctor writing in a cycling magazine in 1897 was unequivocal about the impact the activity had on women's mental and physical health: 'when women began to understand the needs of their own organisms and to bring those disused and unvalued members, their muscles, into action, the whole being responded with a joy born of its new freedom. Derision and croaking availed not; the wind tossed their hair, the sun kissed their cheeks, the blood warmed and reddened on their leaping pulses, and they grew strong in body and refreshed in spirit.'

A French physician, Dr Jennings, countered the idea that cycling led to infertility by suggesting it might have the reverse effect, prescribing it to patients who suffered with reproductive disorders. A Dr Fenton lambasted his peers for spuriously telling women that cycling was harmful: 'there is nothing in the anatomy or the physiology of a woman' to stop her getting on a bike, he insisted, she can 'cycle with as much impunity as a man'. He stuck the boot in the misguided medicalisation of Victorian women and the rest cure by claiming that 90 per cent of cases were a result of ennui and the lack of opportunity to work off energy, and reported that 'already thousands of women, qualifying for general invalidism' had been 'rescued by cycling'. Women weren't so frail and helpless after all, exercise wasn't going to kill them or make them infertile, but only make them stronger – which came in useful if you were going to rise up and demand better conditions and opportunities for your gender.

Cycling on Prescription

Dr Fenton was on to something. The benefits of exercise are now backed up by extensive scientific research, not least a 2017 study published in the medical journal *The Lancet*, which reported that people are as likely to die early from inactive lifestyles as they are from tobacco – an outcome that, albeit unknowingly, patriarchal Victorian culture was willing to force on the female population to keep them under control.

Scientists have also discovered that regular biking, particularly daily commuting, can nearly halve the chance of early death. Research published in the *British Medical Journal* outlined that cycling to the office, as opposed to commuting by car or public transport, is linked with a 45 per cent lower risk of developing cancer, and a 46 per cent lower risk of cardiovascular disease, as well as reducing the risk of a stroke, type 2 diabetes and other life-threatening conditions. While you might skip a workout if you don't feel like it, if cycling is your way of getting to work then you're liable to keep doing it. For many people it's also more pleasurable than hitting the treadmill or lifting weights in a gym, which goes a long way in motivating us.

In another study, cycling was shown to slow down the ageing process, keeping the immune system young and preserving muscle mass. Certainly, the man and woman in their eighties I recently saw happily cycling up a long, steep climb in the South of France looked like they were reaping the health benefits of years in the saddle. According to Cycling UK, the impact is beneficial for schoolchildren too: boys aged ten to sixteen who cycle regularly to school are 30 per cent more likely to meet recommended fitness levels, while girls are seven times more likely to do so. Inspiring statistics compared to the government's figure of one in five children in their first year at primary school in England classed as obese or overweight.

There's a significant impact on mental well-being too, with the psychological health of people who commute by car being far lower than those who pedal to work. While it might not be practical for everyone to cycle, particularly for those commuting longer distances, regular bike-riding has an unarguably positive impact on mental health. The cardiovascular workout results in lower adrenaline and cortisol levels, the stress hormone responsible for spiking levels of tension, and the endorphins released help alleviate anxiety and the symptoms of mild to moderate depression. Numerous studies have also shown cycling to boost feelings of self-worth. All this is evidence that it would have been far more sensible for those doctors to have prescribed cycling rather than confinement in bed.

I know from my own experience that cycling is a mood-booster, and I've come to rely on it. On days when I feel a bit low or stressed, if I can motivate myself to get out on my bike it's likely to help disrupt any negative thought processes I've sunk into and give me time to think in a more expansive way. It is overwhelmingly restorative. Even commuting a few miles to work each day, despite dealing with London traffic, has an undeniably positive impact on my mental well-being. I'm in control of my journey, I won't be held up by crowds or delays, and getting my blood pumping around my system helps start my day with a burst of energising endorphins.

Cycling isn't just making us happier, it also expands our brains, with a study in the *Journal of Clinical and Diagnostic Research* showing people scoring higher on memory, reasoning and planning tests after thirty minutes of cycling. Exercise creates more blood vessels in the brain and stimulates the growth of the proteins responsible for forming new brain cells, suggesting that cycling can improve brain health and might even help reduce the risk of cognitive diseases such as Alzheimer's.

On account of compelling evidence that many incidences of type 2 diabetes, stroke, breast cancer and depression could be prevented if more people cycled, some GPs in the UK have started prescribing cycling to their patients, and health professionals are lobbying governments to invest in cycling infrastructure to enable more people to reap the proven health benefits. If only more of those nineteenth-century doctors had had the same idea, it would have improved the lives of so many women at a time when they were discouraged from any sort of exercise at a great cost to their mental and physical health.

CHAPTER 3

You're Not Going Out Like That

Who Is Wearing the Trousers Now?

If fierce disapproval from late-nineteenth-century reaction-aries and misguided doctors wasn't enough to stop women cycling, then the next problem was how to do so when the clothes they were expected to wear were far from com-fortable – or safe. Dr Fenton recognised this and described women's fashions of the time as a 'handicap', preventing them from doing much in the way of any physical activity.

Lady Harberton, aka Florence Wallace Pomeroy, would have strongly agreed. On 5 April 1899 she brought her years of campaigning to do away with her generation's fashion-staple of long skirts and corsets into the courtroom. The previous October, Florence had been enjoying a bicycle ride through Surrey when she stopped for a caffeine fix at the Hautboy Hotel in Ockham. Making her way to the coffee lounge, she was barred by the hotel's manager, Mrs Sprague, who said she couldn't enter – 'not in that dress'. She was redirected to the public bar, a traditional boozer with spit-and-sawdust floor. A space that was, in Florence's opinion: 'abominable. It smelt of spirits and all the horrors of a drinking bar'.

The hotel would learn that nobody puts a Lady in the bar when they found themselves summoned to court for contravening licensing laws. Though perhaps it would be more accurate to describe the charge as discrimination on the grounds of dress, for the reason why Mrs Sprague had not wanted Florence in her coffee lounge was on account of her not wearing a skirt. To Mrs Sprague, Florence may as well have been naked from the waist down, for she was wearing 'rationals', the same scandalous garment the Cam-bridge effigy had been dressed in.

Rational dress came in various forms, but was chiefly dis-tinguished from any other women's apparel by the bottom half, which consisted of bloomers or knickerbockers instead of a skirt. These were essentially short, baggy trousers tapering to just below the knee.

For many Victorians, women who opted for such overtly masculine attire were at risk of turning into men. In the nineteenth century, only men were entitled to wear the trousers, both figuratively and literally, and many wanted it to stay that way. When the press poked fun at the 'New Woman', whom they generally saw as a threat to the status quo, their satirical features tended to be accompanied by an illustration of a woman in bloomers, either on or posing beside her bicycle. One picture from 1900 – captioned 'Mind the children, finish the washing, and have dinner at 12' – shows a woman in voluminous check bloomers standing by her bicycle while her pinny-wearing husband kneels to tie her laces. In an illustration from *Puck* magazine an oversized, stern-looking woman in rational dress rides a bike with a man half her size perched on her handlebars under the heading 'New Woman takes her husband for a ride'. Cartoonists of the day showed men mistaking women in rationals seen from behind, and even face-on, for men. Their meaning was clear: these women were a grave threat to the natural order of things and they needed to be put back in their place.

The bike industry took a different view. Aware that these liberated women were crucial to their revenue, they ran advertising campaigns that celebrated strong, independent women in rationals. Adverts for Elliman's Universal Embrocation ointment, a muscle rub, featured athletic women in knickerbockers unashamedly speeding ahead of male cyclists, including one showing a male rider taking a tumble as a woman pedals past.

The *Lady Cyclist* magazine, while praising rational dress for contributing to women having more physical freedom, was alarmed by the 'swagger' of some wearers and their ten-dency to 'use boyish gestures and talk', which they thought 'shockingly ungraceful'. It's hard from a twenty-first-century perspective to understand the scandalised reaction to these modest garments, or how they could have been considered a threat to civilisation. One beleagured wearer described the effort to gain acceptance for rationals as a 'great war'.*

Lady Harberton wasn't just experimenting with this risqué fashion, she was the president of the Rational Dress Society, which had been campaigning against the dangerous excesses of Victorian women's clothes since 1881. Cycling had put the issue of women's dress in the spotlight, and her spat with the hotel was an opportunity to make rational dress the *cause célèbre* of the day, the Cyclists' Touring Club (CTC) being the organisation progressive enough to bring the case to Kingston Court on her behalf. While the press was captivated by Florence in her knickerbockers, they came down on the side of Mrs Sprague, as did the British justice system, which concluded that, as the Hautboy Hotel hadn't actually refused to serve her, the charge didn't hold. The jury had also been swayed by photographs of the bar, which had been spruced up for its day in court, with white table-cloths and jugs of flowers. The CTC retaliated by removing the Hautboy from its list of recommended hotels for cyclists and advised its women members to take a skirt to throw on over their rationals when out touring in order to avoid being thrown out of conservative-minded establishments.

---

* A war that continues to this day. In 2019 the Cannes Film Festi-val reportedly turned women away from the red carpet unless they were wearing high heels, while Japan's health and labour minister rejected a petition started by women against dress codes that made heels a requirement in the workplace. His reasoning was that 'it is socially accepted as something that falls within the realm of being occupationally necessary and appropriate'.

Again, it would take a world war before women could wear a bifurcated garment without the risk of having to go to court to get served.

Dying for Fashion

Many women, like Florence, continued to wear rational dress regardless of the opposition and ridicule they encountered. Having experienced the freedom of movement it offered, they weren't about to go back to conventional Victorian women's fashions. The combined weight of skirts and petticoats could be as much as fourteen pounds; they dragged along the floor, picking up dirt and germs and presenting a constant trip hazard. And there were even deadlier risks: in some cases women were burned alive after their skirts brushed against an oil lamp or came too close to open fire; others died after being pulled under the wheels of a passing cart. So it was hardly surprising that women didn't want to wear skirts for cycling. The only purpose they served was preventing the wearer getting very far – perhaps by design; and the richer you were, the more voluminous and impractical your attire.

Writing in *The Rational Dress Gazette*, Florence connected the limitations inflicted by women's clothing with their status as the 'weaker' sex: 'by force of habit, the world forgets that these disabilities are artificial and in consequence the status of women generally, becomes lowered'. She was also forthright about who was responsible for contorting women's bodies: 'the widest part is on the ground, measuring about seven or eight feet in circumference, tapering up to a round waist not so very much larger than a good-sized throat should be . . . in this form, which may literally be called the work of men's hands, not only are the true lines of Nature ignored, but they are positively reversed'.

While it would be some time before common sense prevailed over the fashion for cinching a woman's waist to the size of her throat, many women had taken a unilateral decision to banish the corset – no small thing when corsetry had been considered *de rigueur* since the sixteenth century. Some doctors were ready to back them up, deeming corsets injurious as well as uncomfortable. A Dr Neesen charged the corset with pushing the organs and stomach upwards against the heart in such a way that 'the pressure on the large vessels causes a stagnation of blood in the valve-less veins of the sexual organs – a potent cause of many of the ailments peculiar to women'. I can't attest to whether this is scientifically correct, but it's certainly true that over-tight corsets restricted blood and oxygen flow, causing fainting.

One woman writing to *The Lady Cyclist* magazine in 1895 likened the lives of women who partook in the fashions of the day to 'one long suicide', with corsets responsible for, among other terrible things, 'fainting, hysteria, indigestion, anaemia, lassitude [and] diminished vitality'. In her view, cycling was pivotal in promoting the cause of dress reform: 'Such is the woman of old, now happily dying out. Dress reform is one of the great factors in this result, and the cycle is an aid to this reform', and therefore felt that bicycling should be embraced by 'all thinking women'.

Alarmed at the number of women cyclists abandoning their corsets, the American Lady Corset Company started offering $100 free bicycle insurance with every new corset purchased in an effort to halt the growing trend.

Bloomer Brigade

Florence wasn't the first to start a movement to consign the corset and the crinoline to the bin. The original agitator for the rationalisation of women's dress gave her name to the article of clothing that offended so many: Amelia Jenks Bloomer.

In the 1850s, Amelia, alongside fellow feminists Elizabeth Cady Stanton and Elizabeth Smith Miller, took to wearing billowy Turkish-style trousers which came to the ankle with a knee-length skirt or dress over the top. It was named the 'freedom dress' – much as Susan B. Anthony later referred to the bicycle as a 'freedom machine'. Both items represented independence and autonomy through freedom of movement.

These women had a keen interest in emancipation and had previously been part of the Seneca Falls convention in 1848, the first recorded women's rights gathering. Amelia toured America and the UK, and wrote articles in her women's newspaper, *The Lily*, to encourage others to adopt the costume. Some did, with the actress Fanny Kemble one of the most visible enthusiasts. Further afield, women were wearing versions of the outfit for practical rather than political reasons. Frontierswomen needed garments suited to their harsh lifestyle. One pioneer on a Midwestern prairie farm eulogised about her new style of dress: 'I can do the work for 16 cows, and 18 persons in the family; can walk 7 miles and be none the worse for it'.

Such women were not the focus of the media, who were going wild over the 'bloomer costume', satirising those who embraced the new fashion by featuring caricatures of masculinised women – and their emasculated spouses. Elizabeth Cady Stanton's husband fell victim to media prejudice against his wife's choice of outfit when he ran for a second term in the Senate. Headlines proclaiming 'Twenty tailors take the stitches, Mrs Stanton wears the breeches' undoubtedly helped diminish his majority.

Wearing bloomers in public was attracting the wrong type of attention and Susan B. Anthony had first-hand experience of this on a visit to a post office in NYC. She had to be rescued by a policeman after she was surrounded by a mob of jeering men, forcing her to rethink whether the world was ready for women wearing something akin to trousers.

Before long the original advocates, even Amelia Bloomer, gave up wearing the costume. Much as they valued comfort, they believed it was detracting from the pressing issue of women's rights. It was another forty years before the next generation of women who wanted to ride their 'freedom machines' comfortably would push the idea of 'freedom dress' into the spotlight again. Amelia died in 1894, sadly without seeing the new wave of converts and the controversy they were attracting.

'A Lamentable Incident'

Despite the obvious benefits of rational-style outfits for the cyclist, the debate over whether it was acceptable raged on throughout the 1890s. In 1893, almost five years before Florence's bloomers got her turned away from the Hautboy, Angeline Allen of Newark, New Jersey and her cycling outfit were making the news. One of the most popular US men's magazines of the day, the *Police Gazette*, ran a story under the headline 'She Wore Trousers', which described how Angeline had shocked her neighbourhood when out for a bicycle ride clad in bloomers and black stockings, 'a costume that caused hundreds to turn and gaze in astonishment', with the wearer seemingly 'utterly oblivious of the sensation she was causing'. This was not entirely accurate; interviewed by another journalist, Angeline admitted she wore bloomers *in order* to be looked at. The crowd probably wasn't so unsuspecting either – only a few months earlier she had caused a scandal among her fellow swimmers at Asbury

Park for wearing a bathing dress that stopped several inches above her knees. The shocked, and not unexcited, crowd made such a scene that she was escorted back to the bathing hut to change under police protection. Soon residents of Newark were running to their windows whenever they heard she might be cycling past.

The same year that Angeline was causing curtains to twitch in New Jersey, sixteen-year-old Tessie Reynolds from Brighton, England, became the focus of fierce debate when she attempted to break a new women's cycling record, the 120-mile Brighton to London and back. She achieved a time of 8 hours 38 minutes – an astonishing feat when a woman on a bike was far from universally accepted, let alone one engaging in competition. Afterwards a medical professional examined her and confirmed that it had done no damage, though many might have refused to believe it. Tessie was one of those 'wild women' and had already been cycling for at least three years at this point – with serious intent, if this performance was anything to go by. Her father, who acted as timekeeper for the event, was also cycle-mad; he ran a bicycle shop, raced at the nearby Preston Park Velodrome, and the family home doubled as a boarding house for cyclists.

Newspapers across the country and as far away as the US reported on Tessie's achievement, though many were far from enthusiastic. *Cycling* magazine declared it 'a lamentable incident' that would pain anyone believing in the 'innate modesty and sense of becomingness in the opposite sex'. They were equally fixated on her outfit. Like Angeline and Florence, she chose not to cycle in a skirt, preferring knee-length wool knickerbockers, with a long jacket in the same fabric. One British newspaper called it 'a caricature of the sweetest and best half of humanity'. To its credit, much of the cycling press was more forward-thinking, recognising

the advantages for female cyclists. The women's page of
Bicycling News congratulated Miss Reynolds 'on her courage in being an apostate of the movement'; while a male
writer for the same publication described her as 'the stormy
petrel heralding the storm of revolt against the petticoat'.

Whether people approved or not, Tessie had become a
celebrity. Soon Brighton shops were selling postcards of
her dressed in her rationals. Her unapologetic embrace
of bloomers may have given other women the confidence
to follow suit. Sightings of women in similar outfits grew
common, causing one outraged woman to write to the
Daily Telegraph to 'protest' against 'the shocking and painful spectacle' of women who 'in addition to the degradation
of riding a bicycle, have further unsexed themselves by
doing so in man's attire'. She thought these women were
making her gender even more contemptible in the eyes of
men, and went on to ask whether the law could get involved
on the basis that women wearing men's clothes should be
illegal, as she believed it was for men to wear women's
clothes. Judging by the fan mail Tessie received, including one marriage proposal, not all men found her outfit
repellent.

Tessie would continue to be a vocal advocate of rationals
and may have been the reason why Brighton came to be regarded as the 'home of the bloomer'. One correspondent to
Cycling magazine's letters page in 1894 was unimpressed:
he reported seeing one wearer on Brighton pier drinking
with men in a bar and dismissed the rationals-wearing
women of the seaside city as 'shop girls' wanting to 'create
a small sensation'. In other words, real ladies didn't wear
bloomers.

Meanwhile, across the pond in America, some states had
criminalised 'cross-dressing'. In Paris, where feminist revo-
lutionaries had worn trousers, the end of the Revolution in

1799 was marked by the passing of a law that prohibited women from wearing such attire unless in possession of a permit stating the outfit was required on health grounds. Unfazed by this, the fashionable women of Paris's Bois de Boulogne enthusiastically adopted the bloomer costume. Far from arresting them en masse, the authorities modified the law in 1892 to allow an exception provided the trousered woman was 'holding a bicycle handlebar or the reins of a horse' (otherwise she had to seek permission from the police to 'dress like a man'). Some women wore trousers regardless, risking arrest. The writer George Sand favoured a traditionally masculine outfit that allowed her to move freely around Paris and access places where women were unwelcome or even barred.

The law wasn't formally repealed until 2013, though it had been long since disregarded. It may have been the novelty of the new decree which was behind the sudden popularity in bloomers, but at least the government at the time had recognised that wearing long skirts on a bicycle was neither practical nor safe, even if it wasn't going to go the whole hog and let women wear rationals to do whatever they pleased. The editor of the ladies' page of *Cycling* commented enviously: 'Parisian women are riding and enjoying themselves, blissfully ignorant of the meaning of posing as a pioneer in a rational dress.'

Paris, a city always at the forefront of fashion, was soon inspiring women's cycling fashions around the world. Most of the cycling magazines – and *Vogue* – regularly reported on the latest styles sported in the Bois. Most were enthusiastic about the Parisian women's bloomers, especially when made of fine and delicate pale fabrics, describing them as 'graceful' and 'feminine'. Though the concept may have won a degree of acceptance, it depended on whether the style was deemed ladylike. The less fashion-orientated UK rational wearers, in their practical wool serges and tweeds, still tended to be regarded as perilously close to the male end of the Victorian gender spectrum.

Parisian women in fashionable bloomers weren't enough to convert diehard opponents. Ellen Follett, on her tandem honeymoon in 1896, was warned by a local in New Orleans that a woman would be 'lynched' for wearing bloomers in the Southern states. Helena Swanwick, who described regularly being hurled to the ground as a result of her skirts catching in her pedals, felt unable to wear bloomers except under cover of darkness. The resulting feeling of liberation was such that she found herself bursting into song – a German ditty which included the line, 'what glorious rapture to be a he-man!'

Creative Needlework

While some women believed the benefits of bloomers far outweighed the hostile reception they aroused, others tried to adapt their conventional garments in such a way that they could enjoy improved freedom of movement while still appearing 'respectable'. This might be a matter of simply raising the hem a little and reducing the volume of fabric to create a narrower skirt, or inserting weights into the hem to avoid the fabric flying up and exposing an eyeful of leg. Others used clever devices to create something that could be transformed from a full skirt into a cycle-friendly but uncontroversial garment.

This tension between practical and acceptable meant that bicycle attire for women in the 1890s was a complex puzzle. Countless women were trying to solve it, and many registered their designs with the patent office in the hope of turning their interest into a commercial enterprise.

One such was Alice Bygrave of Chelsea in London, who

had success with her patented Bygrave Convertible Skirt in 1896. The fashion brand Jaeger, then Jaeger's Sanitary Woollen System Co. Ltd, bought the design and produced the skirt in a range of fabrics. Alice travelled to America to promote it. A sophisticated system of weights, pulleys and buttons allowed the skirt to be raised both at the front and the back when mounted, with the material ruched around the hips. The crucial thing for the rider was that it could be, as the advertising boasted, 'instantaneously raised or dropped'. On dismounting, the wearer could seamlessly transition back into the acceptable standard for Victorian feminine dress.

Alice had her sister-in-law, Rosina Lane, a cyclist who raced at London's Aquarium, wear the skirt when she competed to promote the benefits of the design. The new-style garments rapidly grew in popularity, and soon it was possible for those who couldn't afford the Jaeger-produced version to send off for a pattern so they could run one up at home.

The divided skirt, or jupes-culottes as they were called by the fashionable Parisiennes of the Bois, was another popular solution to the problem. These pleated, wide-legged trousers offered freedom of movement without risk of exposing flesh, and best of all they were indistinguishable from a full skirt when the wearer was standing. They also came with the approval of Oscar Wilde, an arbiter of fashion if ever there was one. In an essay entitled 'The Philosophy of Dress', published in the *New York Tribune* in 1885, Oscar argued that women's clothing needed to be simplified – rationalised – and came down in favour of the divided skirt, which gave 'ease and liberty' to the wearer. He was less keen on the idea of using so much fabric in order to 'pass' as a skirt, for he didn't feel that would help the long-term goal of women's dress reform: 'let it visibly announce itself as what it actually is, and it will go far towards solving a real difficulty'.

The fact he had come to dwell on the problem of women's fashions was doubtless down to his wife, Constance Wilde. Constance, who was often pictured in her own elegant divided skirt, campaigned alongside Florence Harberton as part of the Rational Dress Society and was editor of its gazette. Dress reform would have been far from Oscar's thoughts by the time he was tragically imprisoned on charges of sodomy and gross indecency a decade later, though women in trousers, like homosexuality, were still perceived as a threat to Victorian masculinity.

Jupes-culottes enjoyed a comeback as a result of the bicycle, with Parisiennes, those early embracers of the bloomer, considering them the height of fashion for a season at least. For women who longed to be free of their imprisoning garments but weren't quite ready to make a feminist statement with bloomers, the divided skirt offered a neat solution.

Out with the Corsetry, in with the Lycra

Thankfully, women today, in the West at least, are relatively free to decide how they wish to dress. Florence Harberton would have been thrilled by the streamlined and non-restrictive cycle-specific clothing available to twenty-first-century women. Observing London's women cyclists, you will see a wide spectrum ranging from office workers in suits and heels to athletes in head-to-toe Lycra. Sadly, there are still fewer women cycling than men, at least in the UK and US: according to a 2017 Department for Transport study, men make three times as many cycle trips as women in the UK and travel on average four times as far. The lack of safe cycling infrastructure is one of the main reasons, but another significant barrier is the extent to which women feel they are judged by how they look. We may have more options than our Victorian sisters, but our appearance continues to dictate what we feel we can and can't do.

When I was cycling through France in 2018, a male hotel owner made a comment about my bike shoes which exemplified the pressure women are subjected to. The hotelier pointed to my cleated shoes and told me, sarcastically, that they were 'very sexy'. He was making a joke, but one that derives from the assumption that it is a woman's responsibility to look attractive and feminine at all times. The shoes help me pedal more efficiently and, given that I had cycled ninety miles that day, that benefit far outweighed their lack of 'sex-appeal'. Is it any wonder some women don't get as far as putting their workout clothes on when such attitudes are so pervasive?

Insecurity about body image is endemic in Western societies, and pressure from the press and social media plays a huge part in this. People are dying from botched surgery in their quest to look more like a Kardashian. Sport England, whose remit is to encourage greater participation in sport, has found that concerns about body image are cited by many women and girls as a reason for avoiding physical activity. Many feel they don't have the right body shape, that they will look unattractive working out, and are too self-conscious to participate.

The assumption that you have to dress like a Tour de France contender, in skin-tight shorts and jersey, might be enough to stop some women taking up cycling. Many are concerned at being perceived as 'unfeminine' if they appear too sporty. It seems our ideas haven't progressed much since rational wearers were derided as 'unwomanly' or 'ungraceful'. This helps explain why, when girls hit their teens, they tend to give up cycling to school, and why women are less likely to exercise than men.

Happily, body positivity is finally filtering into the main-stream, with ad campaigns featuring models who are more representative. Sport England's 'This Girl Can' campaign shunned celebrities and professional athletes in favour of ordinary women – of all ages, abilities, ethnic backgrounds and body shapes – sharing their positive experiences of working up a sweat. The film celebrates these women – complete with cellulite, sweat and wobbling flesh – as they experience the massive endorphin high derived from getting their blood pumping. The inclusive nature of the campaign challenges entrenched ideas about what women and girls should look like when they are being active, as well as redefining what being athletic looks like. Sport England claims that within a year, 2.8 million women and girls aged fourteen to forty reported that they had done more physical activity as a result of the campaign; 1.6 million of those didn't previously exercise.

There's still a long way to go. Many professional female athletes continue to feel that, in the eyes of both the public and the media, the way they look counts for more than their sporting achievements. In the image-saturated culture of the social-media age, women athletes are expected to look sexy as well as being at the top of their game. In 2018, when Ada Hegerberg, the first-ever female winner of football's prestigious Ballon d'Or Award went up to collect her award, the host asked her to twerk for the audience. She refused.

Countless professional sportswomen have complained of being subjected to derogatory comments from other industry professionals. It seems skinny = good prevails even within professional sport, regardless of achievement. The Olympic cyclist Jess Varnish complained to British Cycling, alleging that its technical director repeatedly insulted her size and shape, among other serious charges. Although he denied any wrongdoing, an internal investigation found in favour of Varnish. In athletics, the Olympic gold-medal-winning heptathlete Jessica Ennis-Hill claimed that a senior figure in British Athletics said she was fat. Numerous female, and even male, professional cyclists have reported developing, or coming close to developing, eating disorders due to the immense pressure to be lean and light, with trainers regularly making digs about their weight.

If women at the top of the game are feeling pressurised to look a certain way, then it's understandable that many non-athletes feel sport is not for them. Without more realistic and representative images of women being active, that's unlikely to change. As a result, people are missing out on the huge proven health benefits; just a few weeks of moderate exercise can help improve someone's body image, even when there's little or no change in their physical appearance. And the good thing about endorphins is that once they start kicking in, they become addictive, with one revolution of the bicycle wheel leading to a different kind of revolution.

CHAPTER 4

Transmission

Pedal Power

It's a blowy day on Hackney Downs in east London. A fore-boding grey sky is offset by a much-needed pop of yellow and red from the autumn leaves. I'm here with a group of female refugees and asylum seekers who have signed up for women-only cycling lessons run by a charity called the Bike Project. They are all at different stages in their learning, with some attempting to master balance as they walk-wheel across the tarmacked ball courts, while others are circling the perimeter, practising hand signals, emergency braking and changing gears. I bring up the rear of a group of riders who have been attending long enough to be able to confidently ride away from the practice court to take their learning to the next level, following their instructor along the park's tree-lined avenue and navigating around dogs, joggers and a group of schoolchildren on a cycle skills lesson. A park-keeper, seeing this crocodile of women cyclists wearing helmets and high-vis, calls out proudly that his daughter is also learning to ride and has just moved beyond stabilisers, a major stepping stone on the way to becoming a cyclist.

Most of the women and girls attending these 'Pedal Power' sessions never had the opportunity to learn to ride as children, so this is a new – and not a little daunting – skill they are hoping to master. When asked why they come and what they get from the experience, they talk about de-stressing, relaxing, learning new skills. One participant says, 'Cycling gives you wings, you're flying. It brings such happiness and joy!' Much-needed positive experiences for anyone, but especially those whose refugee or asylum status means they are denied the right to work and must live in a constant state of uncertainty, wondering if they'll be sent back to the country from which they fled. Not to mention the pressure of having to survive on £37 a week.

An Iranian woman tells me she had been a nurse before she came to the UK. Now, living with her daughter, not allowed to work, she feels she has lost much of her freedom, both financial and personal. She has been in London eight years but is still waiting for a decision from the Home Office on whether she will be granted permission to remain permanently in the UK. Learning to ride a bike is giving her so much more than the physical pleasure of self-propelled movement and speed, and access to an economical form of transport; it's helping to restore a much-needed sense of empowerment.

In the beginners' lesson, an Eritrean woman who is still wobbly on her wheels takes a tumble. Undeterred, and ignoring the instructor's suggestion to take a break, she gets straight back on. Despite the falls, she is one of the group's most enthusiastic learners, telling me that 'every time Friday comes, I am so excited. It's like being in love with a guy and going to see them. I've never had such joy since I came to the UK.' Soon, many of the learners will be expert enough to graduate from the group; each will then be given a second-hand bicycle that has been donated to the charity and expertly restored by its mechanics. Wheels of their own, so these women can enjoy themselves exploring their new home city for free.

For many, learning to ride a bike is a childhood rite of passage. My dad and older siblings were the ones who helped me make the jump from trike to bike. Everyone in my family rode; my mum had used hers to get to work, and my dad used his to de-stress out of the office. My eldest brother had taken up racing, while the other preferred mountain biking. My sister meanwhile had a brown vintage sit-up-and-beg-style bike and she would often sit me on the comfy sprung saddle and pedal me to school. There was no question that at some point I too would be riding around on my own set of wheels.

I can still picture that first bike: acid-yellow with fat white tyres that one of my brothers had found abandoned in a Bristol woodland and had expertly made roadworthy again. He was forever taking apart and reassembling his own growing collection of bikes, so he knew what he was doing. The width of the tyres was an asset when it came to balancing, but I was soon progressing to bigger bikes with skinnier wheels. Later, I would explore the neighbourhood on my pink Raleigh Bianca shopper with friends who had also been bought bikes or inherited them from older siblings. I was jealous of the Raleigh Chopper ridden by the brother of a friend; Choppers were modelled on motorcycles, with very high handlebars and a gearstick, and the large seat had a backrest. For a time I hankered after a BMX, because that's what all the cool kids rode.

Learning to ride was an intrinsic part of growing up, like tying my own shoelaces, and I've been surprised when friends have told me that it wasn't part of their journey to adulthood. Not everyone has someone to teach them and access to a bike, not to mention the motivation.

Many of the learners at Pedal Power were denied the opportunity simply because it wasn't something girls were permitted to do in their country. Others didn't have a bike they could practise on. As an adult learner, it's no easier, and possibly more difficult. It's not like swimming, where you can go to your nearest pool and sign up for lessons. There are cycle sessions for adults, but they are relatively few and far between. Providing bicycles for would-be learners, as well as supplying instructors, is expensive and takes lots of space – though there are some excellent organisations who do just this. It's also physically more challenging as an adult since it's harder to balance, further to fall – tougher on our bodies when we do – and we are inherently more aware of our vulnerability. When you've been riding a bike for years it requires no more thought than walking, but watching the women at Pedal Power go through the stages of mastering balance while propelling themselves with enough speed to keep going, it appears it's more complicated than it may feel to someone who has been doing it long enough for it to be second nature.

When I returned to the sessions after a month, the Eritrean woman who had been unsteady before – falling enough to make someone less determined reconsider whether this was something they really did want to do – was now pedalling around Hackney Downs with confidence. Through grit and determination, something had finally clicked. Her refurbished Raleigh – her 'Lamborghini' as she called it – was going to be coming home with her so she would no longer have to count the days until Friday's cycling session. She is now part of a rich history of women who have been helped by other women to find empowerment, freedom and enjoyment in cycling which stretches back to when women first started taking to two wheels.

Back to School

Learning to ride in the late nineteenth century would have posed similar problems. Many who were keen were long past childhood, and anyway, given that it was considered an adults-only activity, children were generally discouraged from learning. A degree of dedication and bravery was required, not just to conquer the bike but to overcome any qualms about this 'unladylike' activity and what it might do to one's morals, not to mention the disapproval one would have to endure. Vast numbers of women exhibited all these qualities, believing that the effort was a small price to pay for mastering a machine that would bring both pleasure and freedom.

Such was the demand from would-be riders in the bike-mad 1890s, cycling schools took over from ice-rinks as popular venues to while away a few hours. One particularly exclusive school was Kingstone & Co. on London's Sloane Street, described by the *Lady Cyclist* as a 'school for the upper-classes'. Here, novices would start on the 'auto-instructor', a machine suspended on rollers, which allowed them to practise pedalling and balancing without the risk of falling. The magazine was at pains to point out that pupils were fitted with a leather belt with a handle, so male instructors wouldn't actually touch them.

Over in Belgravia, H. G. Thomas's school was housed in a former sculptor's studio. Marble statues filled the waiting room and a grand piano provided musical accompaniment. Not all cycling schools were quite so rarefied; many were attached to bicycle shops, the owners having realised that providing instruction for new riders would boost sales. Just as crowds gathered to watch the cream of London society cycling in the parks, some cycle schools drew spectators who would look on as friends and family tried to get to grips with cycling; Le Petit Ménage on the Champs-Élysées in Paris had a bar so they could keep themselves lubricated while they watched.

Instruction wasn't restricted to cycling schools. Many women penned manuals to share their know-how and encouragement with their sisters. One such author was the American suffragist and president of the Christian Women's Temperance Union, Frances Willard, who in 1893 become a keen cyclist at the age of fifty-three and thought her story might inspire other women.

Frances had been suffering from poor health and had come to recover at Reigate Priory, the English stately home of her good friend Lady Isabella Somerset. Frances describes how she had been on the verge of a breakdown, brought on by the death of her mother in addition to years of working without a break. Instead of a rest cure, she was prescribed an exercise regimen to build her strength. Isabella, a keen cyclist herself, encouraged Frances to learn, gifting her a bicycle which she named Gladys. The two women had a deep emotional bond, with Frances describing Isabella as 'my beautiful picture gallery and library, landscape and orchestra' – and with Isabella calling Frances 'the earthly anchor of my happiness'. It's unsurprising that she followed her advice without hesitation.

Frances was truly taken with her new 'freedom machine', which helped recapture the feeling she had experienced as a child when she 'ran wild' on her Wisconsin farm. That brief taste of freedom had ended abruptly at the age of sixteen when she was forced into the strictures of Victorian female adulthood of long skirts, corsets and a life indoors. In her imprisoning new garments, walking became such a trial that she was deprived of the pleasures of the outdoors – despite being 'born with an inveterate opposition to staying in the house'. She had instead pursued her freedom through education, becoming dean of the women's college of Northwestern University before moving on to the Women's Christian Temperance Union. In addition to promoting sobriety, since she saw women and children as too often victim to drunken husbands who spent all their money on drink, she campaigned for women's education, suffrage, an end to domestic violence, and better prison and working conditions.

Frances had planned to write a novel imagining the life of the first female president of the USA, but her campaigning work was all-consuming and she never got round to it. She would be shocked that, over a century after she had this idea, a female president had yet to exist outside of fiction.*

Frances did, however, find time to write *A Wheel Within a Wheel* (1895). It is dedicated to Isabella, the woman who initiated her into the cycling world, just as she hopes to do in turn for her readers. On the cover and within the pages of my edition are photographs of a serious and determined-looking Frances on her bicycle, almost always surrounded by one or two other women – underlining the message that this is an activity which belongs to women. These supporters are doubtless the series of teachers, 'her devoted and pleasant comrades', who steadied the bicycle while she learned to balance, offering advice and encouragement. She informs her reader that to become an accomplished wheelwoman takes time, patience and strength of will, but she sees these as attributes essential to mastery of life in general. Indeed, she found a 'whole philosophy of life in the wooing and the winning of my bicycle'. She identifies fear of judgement as one of the biggest obstacles in learning this new skill, for 'we are all unconsciously the slaves of public opinion', which is certainly true now and was even more so then, not least for an unmarried woman in her fifties. Frances saw the bicycle's potential for advancing the cause of women, citing the positive impact it would have on rationalising dress, as well as eroding entrenched opinions about what women could or couldn't do. In fact, as a woman in the public eye, one whom so many looked up to, she saw it as her duty to prove that gender was no obstacle.

Frances quotes doctors who were convinced of the benefits of the exercise for women; a sensible tactic when the voices of reason were often drowned out by a chorus of unreason. She also imparts her advice on how to successfully master

* Coincidentally, readers of London's *Evening Standard* in 1913 voted her dear friend Lady Isabella the woman they would most like as a female prime minister.

your own Gladys, including how balance requires more precision than mathematics, that if the mind wobbles then so does the wheel, and how looking down is guaranteed to end in a fall. Within three months of practising for ten to twenty minutes most days, Frances was happily cycling off on Gladys without being propped up by her mentors.

Cycling wasn't a fleeting interest for Frances; her girl-hood love of adventure reawakened, in 1896 she set off on a cycling tour to the South of France with Lady Isabella. The tour was cut short when they decided to go to Marseille to help Armenian refugees fleeing a massacre in their homeland. The women set up a centre in a disused hospital, housing and feeding the refugees, as well as successfully organising resettlement for many in America and the UK.

The same year that Isabella and Frances had temporarily put cycling aside for humanitarian work, Maria Ward, a member of the Staten Island Bicycle Club in New York, published her *Bicycling for Ladies*. A photograph taken the previous year shows Maria (nicknamed Viola) and her sister Caroline standing with their Safety bicycles alongside other members of the club. Unlike most club photos that survive from this period, it shows a group made up of at least as many women as men. Maria is in the centre and seems to be wearing rationals, with the other women mostly in long skirts, puff-sleeved blouses and fancy hats, while the men wear knee-length breeches, long socks and straw boaters. The text on the back invites the recipient to join the club on a ride departing from St George's at 4.30 p.m. on 25 June before returning to the clubhouse for tea. The photo was taken by Alice Austen, a fellow club member and one of the first women documentary photographers. Alice took the many photographs in the book, which feature the gymnast Daisy Elliott illustrating different cycling positions in her knickerbockers.

Maria's book is an instructional primer on everything women would need to know to become an accomplished cyclist. While Frances Willard took a more philosophical approach, this guide is thorough and extensive, covering which type of bicycle to choose; what to wear (bloomers ideally, or a skirt that comes to no longer than halfway between knees and ankles); how to get on and stay on; as well as the rules of the road and how to teach others.

While Maria emphasises the practical benefits of cycling – transport and exercise – she is most rapturous when talking about the opportunities for exploration and discovery. She meditates on how 'the road stretches out before you' with its 'succession of wonderful possibilities' and 'instead of a few squares, you know several towns; instead of an acquaintance with the country for a few miles about, you can claim familiarity with two or three counties; an all-day expedition is reduced to a matter of a couple of hours'. The possibility for adventure, a novelty to so many Victorian women, is the rich reward if you follow Maria's guidance. The sentiment is echoed on the cover of the lavish leather-bound original edition with its gold embossed lettering on deep blue, which features an image of a euphoric woman in rationals coasting down a hill, her feet resting on the foot pegs of her front wheel, hat flying off behind, while on the back cover a little dog dashes down the road after her.

Maria's repeated use of words like 'conquer', 'mastery' and 'achieve' drive home the goal: to become an active agent. While she suggests that female friends can assist each other in learning to ride, she is also adamant that it's possible to do so simply with the support of a fence post. Again and again, *Bicycling for Ladies* stresses the freedom that lies in store for the independent and self-sufficient – radical stuff in an era when women tended to be defined by their very dependence. Though keen on the social aspects of cycling, she also wants her readers to be 'ready to meet any emergency' and not reliant on anyone else to fix or maintain their machines. Those who can accomplish this are, in Maria's view, the most 'keenly alive', and least likely to be stranded helpless on the roadside with a puncture or broken chain.

For where is the freedom of the open road if you must wait for someone else to come along to fix your problem? Maria describes in detail the geometry of the bicycle and how the different parts fit together, instructing her readers to examine each nut and screw to determine its purpose. In a chapter titled 'Women and Tools', she sets out to demystify the idea of working with hardware: 'any woman who is able to use a needle or scissors can use other tools equally well'. Though the reference may date the book for contemporary women readers – I'm sure I'm not alone in being able to mend a puncture but unable to darn a sock – Maria is to be applauded for insisting that hammers and wrenches were no more alien than the staples of domesticity. She takes the reader on a tour of the various uses of the tools required in a bicycle workshop before setting them the task of dismantling a bicycle, cleaning its constituent parts and then reassembling the whole thing – all to be done in a room where the door can be locked to avoid interruptions. It seems that the room of one's own that Maria prized had a workbench and was strewn with bicycle parts, a room she describes in detail, with everything in its proper place. Judging by the confident way in which she imparts her knowledge, this was a room where she had already spent a fair bit of time.

Also in 1896, over in the UK, Lillias Campbell Davidson published the *Handbook for Lady Cyclists*, her contribution to the growing library of cycling self-help books for and by women. Lillias was born in Brooklyn in 1853 but had been living in the south of England for some years by this point. She had previously written a handbook for women travellers, so it's safe to say that Lillias wanted women to get out and see the world. Like Maria, she also wanted them to acquaint themselves with the mechanics of their machines, especially those who yearned to cycle alone in rural areas. Where she may have differed from Maria is in her advice that there is no need for a woman to be 'constantly airing her knowledge in conversation'. Knowledge may be power, but for Lillias it wasn't always advisable to draw attention to the fact that you were in possession of it. She was already practised in hiding things that weren't seen as appropriate to her gender: when she started cycling in the late 1880s as one of those pioneer women, she restricted herself to the early mornings to avoid being spotted.

One thing Lillias refused to compromise on was suitable cycling attire. She insisted it was 'out of the question' for women to wear long skirts and petticoats on a bicycle; her preferred outfit was a shorter, narrow skirt with knickerbockers, which she thought should be adopted for all daily activities. Men's clothing was practical in design, leaving them free to jump on a bike as the fancy took them. They were oblivious to the 'terrible hampering a woman suffers from with a flapping, sail-like mass of draperies' which is the source of a woman's 'most profound anxiety, her deepest sorrow'. For Lillias, having to change outfits to get in the saddle turned the activity into 'a grave affair of premeditation', making it far from the complete 'freedom machine' it could be.

While rationals, or the bloomer costume, seemed to Lillias the most sensible outfits for cycling, she cautioned that they must be cut and tailored for the wearer. For although she was a vocal advocate for women cyclists, in her book, as well as her column in the *Cyclists' Touring Club Gazette*, she hadn't quite left behind her days of swerving into a side street to avoid shocking the vicar. Throughout her handbook she fixates on the need for women cyclists to retain their 'feminine grace and dignity'; those who failed to do so were 'fearsome apparitions'. In her opinion, 99 per cent of women cyclists were 'defective in style', and the blame rested with their fellow women. When teaching an inexperienced friend to cycle, women had a duty to remind them that appearances are everything. According to Lillias, 'if she looks loud, fast and simply a fright, she is doing it [women's cycling] infinite harm'.

This compulsion to encourage women to take up cycling while simultaneously insisting they do so in an appropriately feminine manner was a common trait in manuals and the cycling press at the time. Cycling magazines aimed at women, like *The Lady Cyclist* (edited by a man), stressed the importance of correct deportment and dress on a bicycle. Though they might recommend rationals, it was with the proviso that they be properly tailored so as not to repulse any passing men. Many featured short stories – cycling-based romances featuring well-behaved middle-class heterosexual women – to drive home the message that women who cycle could and should be feminine and desirable. Women's bodies were ruthlessly policed, with commentators pointing out that some items of clothing were unsuited to certain body shapes; one writer opined that women with 'peculiarities of figure and form' would never look good on a bicycle. Though today's women enjoy many rights and freedoms their Victorian sisters were denied, body shaming continues to rear its ugly head in newspapers and magazines. In some respects, it seems we still have a long way to go.

Another contributor declared that there is nothing 'more

distressing to the refined mind than that of a gaudily dressed woman returning travel-stained and untidy after a long day's cycle on dusty roads'. Distress could be avoided by fixing a small vanity mirror to the handlebars for the purpose of checking one's appearance, for 'there is no disputing that one's hair does become disarranged in the course of a long tour, and that smuts do sometimes settle on the nose, and one's hat [is] just a trifle tip-tilted'.

At times it's unclear whether this advice was motivated by a sense that patriarchal norms must be observed, or in the spirit of compromise. By seeming to comply with existing codes rather than flouting them, women would have a better chance of being left to enjoy their cycling in peace. The less fault opponents could find with their appearance and demeanour, the more acceptance cycling would gain as an appropriate pursuit for a woman, which might in turn encourage less socially rebellious women to give it a go. This may seem limiting, but it was an understandable tactic when the UK's first female salaried journalist, the ardent anti-feminist Eliza Lynn Linton, regularly used her column to attack cycling for its role in ushering in 'dangerous' new feminine freedoms to the detriment of Victorian womanhood.

While Lillias couldn't be defined as a rebel – although it's notable she never married, preferring to live alone or with other women – she did want as many women as possible to experience the benefits of cycling. There was safety in numbers; the more it became an everyday occurrence, the less it could be deemed inappropriate. To her, every woman on a bicycle was an 'advocate' – provided they took care to be 'the best advertisement for the sport'. Standards had to be maintained, for 'slovenly' and ungraceful cyclists were letting the side down by frightening rather than encouraging all-important new recruits.

A Club of One's Own

Hackney Downs is an appropriate place for the Pedal Power pupils to be learning to ride bicycles – it was the original home of one of the first cycling clubs, the Pickwick Bicycle Club, formed in 1870, the year of Charles Dickens's death and named in his honour. Uniquely, the club combined cycling with an interest in the author's work. Still in existence today, its members carry on some of the original traditions, including taking on the soubriquet of a character from *The Pickwick Papers*, such as Count Smorltork, Snodgrass or Dismal Jemmy. Members are referred to en masse as The Pickwick Fathers, an appropriately gendered term as this is a men-only institution, even in 2019.

Photographs on the club's website of their annual garden party show a sea of white men filling the grand Connaught Rooms with its crystal chandeliers and vaulted ceiling. It seems fitting that this venue was once the home of another fraternal and exclusive society, the Freemasons. Many of the members wear the club's uniform of straw boater and gold-and-black tie, and are heralded by buglers and other pageantry. The club's stated commitment – to spread 'fellowship and conviviality' – only seems to apply if you are the appropriate gender. You'd think a club like this would have died out with the penny-farthing, but it seems not, so it's only fitting that one of its members is photographed alongside one. It may appear an anachronistic organisation in the twenty-first century, but apparently there is a seven-year waiting list to join its ranks.*

---

* When the former Olympic cyclist Chris Boardman challenged the club about their men-only policy, a member responded on Twitter that 'most real ladies wouldn't want to be on our table #boystalk'. He's probably right – they'd die of boredom. I wrote to the club to ask about the rationale for their men-only policy, but I didn't get a

Even though women accounted for a third of cyclists in the US and UK by the mid 1890s, the Pickwick wasn't the only club to cling to its outdated boys-only rule, though most clubs had the sense to start opening their doors to women members. In Boston, Massachusetts, one club went the other way and voted in 1894 to exclude their existing female members, causing the women in question to form a new club along with male members who disagreed with the ban.

The Cyclists' Touring Club in the UK, the same organisation that had gone to court on behalf of Florence Harberton's rationals, had been open to women since 1880. Even so, many women wanted to form their own clubs, and soon women-only cycling clubs were springing up around the UK and North America. Some were modelled along the same lines as exclusive gentleman's clubs. As in New York's Michaux, members of these high-end institutions would socialise over tea in their clubhouse's lavish dining rooms, perhaps meeting with their tailor on the premises to confer over their new cycling outfit. The Woodbridge Cycle Club in Boston boasted its own bugler. Most clubs, however, were more egalitarian, such as the Ladies' South West Bicycle Club, which would meet by a pond on Clapham Common in London every Wednesday at 3 p.m.

Lillias Campbell Davidson, recognising that many women would prefer to cycle exclusively with members of their own sex, established the Lady Cyclists' Association (LCA) in 1892. Operating as a networking association, the LCA helped connect women cyclists across the UK so they could

---

response. The more I discover about the Pickwick Fathers, though, the more it excites me that a new generation of predominantly non-white women cyclists are falling in love with cycling in the original home of their exclusionary club, helping rewrite the rules of who is allowed to ride a bike.

form their own local clubs to go on social rides. It also published a list of hotels and inns across the country that were hospitable to women cycling on their own, rationals or not. The monthly magazine reassured members that they were far from alone in their interest, and featured exclusive discounts for tailors and bicycles.

It's understandable that many women wanted to carve out a safe space offering female comradeship a-wheel. In most existing clubs they would have been far outnumbered by men, and the more competitive aspects of club life might well have seemed offputting. I belong to a London club that works hard to support its women members, but we account for a fraction over 20 per cent of the membership, which is not unusual today. To arrive at the meeting point on a Sunday morning to a flock of – mostly white – men in Lycra can be daunting, and possibly not an experience that is going to shift the scales the other way without a lot of work towards becoming more inclusive and welcoming to minority groups.

Lillias wasn't keen on club uniforms, arguing that it would be hard to settle on an outfit that suited all members, and this could prove a deterrent for would-be members. But some clubs felt it promoted unity, while others derived their very identity from clothing, such as the Knickerbockers in Chicago and Lady Harberton's Chelsea Rationalists. Lady Harberton's club permitted only rational dress in order to promote and further the work of her society. In contrast, the Countess of Malmesbury led a ride from Richmond Park in Surrey each Wednesday where only women wearing skirts were accepted. This was to encourage more conserv-ative women who might be put off from joining a group in which some wore bloomers. The majority of clubs did not enforce rigid dress codes, allowing members to sport a range of styles depending on their personal preference.

Even so, most did have a badge, and some had specific club colours to identify their cycling crew, just as members of most clubs today, including my own, wear jerseys featuring their insignia and colours.

As an active member of her local (mixed) club on Staten Island, Maria Ward was keen to recommend to her readers the benefits of social rides. She also had some advice about how to start a club, suggesting that the purchase of two bicycles to share among members was a good way to begin – a sort of time-share approach to bicycle ownership. The more members that joined, the more bicycles should be purchased, presumably with membership fees covering the cost. This egalitarian and inclusive approach meant the club was open to those who couldn't afford their own set of wheels. London's Mowbray House Cycling Association – founded in 1892 by Florence Harberton and the aristocratic cycling humanitarian Lady Isabella Somerset, it also received support from the Countess of Warwick, aka Daisy Bell – took egalitarianism a step further. It was specifically aimed at working women, who could never have earned enough to purchase bicycles of their own.

At the outset, Florence and Isabella, with the support of the liberal newspaper editor W.T. Stead, used their own money to purchase a fleet of cycles. Anyone wanting to join paid a modest fee for use of a bicycle for one or two weeks every month. By 1897 they had twenty-four bicycles shared between 150 members. In addition to giving their members some independence by providing them with their own affordable transport, they were also offering much-needed relaxation and pleasure outside the women's long working hours. No wonder the suffragist Millicent Garrett Fawcett was a supporter, and she wrote to readers of the upmarket *Wheelwoman* magazine asking them to donate their old bicycles to the club.

Mowbray House offered training for its inexperienced members. Once they were confident, they could join one of the regular social rides out to rural spots on the edge of London. Members also had the option to take full owner-ship of a bicycle by paying it off in instalments. Additionally, the organisation owned a gypsy caravan, a large canvas tent and a cottage, all located in countryside south of London, giving members the chance to enjoy an economical cycling-based weekend break, the only holiday many could afford. The members met regularly at the club's home in the offices of W.T. Stead's newspaper, the *Pall Mall Gazette* in cen-tral London, where they would discuss club matters and finances, or listen to talks on rational dress and other social and women's issues of the day. With Florence as a founder, many of the members adopted rational dress, and all wore a Mowbray House badge, which featured a butterfly symbol, as well as dressing in the club's colours of blue and white.

This wasn't the only club specifically for working women. London's Guy's Hospital started a club for its nurses in 1896. Miss Nott-Bower, the hospital's matron, said cycling gave 'weary and worn out staff nurses' an opportunity for 'change of thought and exercise after day and night confine-ment in the depressing wards'. It's not clear how long the club was in existence, but its legacy continues today with the newly founded Royal London Hospital Nurses' Cycling Club in east London. This charitable initiative was set up to help female nurses benefit from physical activity. Half of those participating reported that they previously did less than thirty minutes of exercise a week; over 75 per cent were new to riding a bike, with one participant comment-ing that she had been 'trying to find suitable and affordable sessions to learn to ride for the last five years and this is the first group that is regular enough, and where I feel safe and not embarrassed'. A club that is affordable and provides a non-judgemental safe space was core to the foundational principles of Florence and Isabella's project over 120 years before.

Kitchens for Bikes

London's Bike Kitchen in Hackney, with its tools and bicycle parts lining the walls and suspended from the ceiling, and a blackboard showing a bicycle with all its constituent parts labelled, is somewhere Maria Ward would feel right at home. But far from locking its doors to avoid interruptions, this non-profit bicycle maintenance workshop is open to anyone who wants to fix their bike and benefit from extensive know-how and the necessary tools – a way to pass on knowledge and encourage self-reliance, like Maria set out to do, but at the same time providing a place in which to do it. It is particularly important in a city where space is at a premium, with so many living in small flats and house-shares, where the idea of a dedicated space for a bicycle workshop is the stuff of fantasies.

Californian Jenni Gwiazdowski, London Bike Kitchen's founder, says the intention was to demystify the alchemy that happens a bike is handed over for repair, 'pulling back the curtain' on what goes on in a workshop and empowering women to give it a go. The Kitchen runs practical seminars covering a range of skills, from adjusting gears to building a bike from scratch. Inspired by a similar concept in LA, the idea is not only to share know-how but to challenge perceptions about who gets to participate.

The Bike Kitchen has more women mechanics than most workshops, but Jenni is keenly aware of the gender-bias. When she did her training to qualify as a bicycle mechanic, she was the only woman on the course. Despite Maria's *Bicycling for Ladies* having been published nearly 125 years ago, the bicycle workshop remains a predominantly male domain. Gender politics in the toolshed needs overhauling; there's still an assumption that women aren't interested in fixing things, while men are expected to be innately handy with a hammer and wrench. A 2015 study by the Association for Psychological Science indicates that this might go back to childhood development, with boys being encouraged – through marketing and other social forces – to play with construction or complex puzzle games which foster 'spatial reasoning' and cognitive skills that are important in STEM subjects. This normalises the idea of technology and mechanics as a boy's domain and is seen as one of the reasons for the under-representation of women in science and tech, as well as in a bike workshop.

Jenni, undaunted by the prospect of entering such a stereotypically masculine profession, was 'hell-bent' on getting her open-access workshop off the ground. Her first tutor was a woman, a Native American called Therese who had been working in London bike shops for several decades and had achieved legendary status within the industry. She guided Jenni in setting up the workshop, and was keen to help her former student succeed.

When the Bike Kitchen opened its doors seven years ago, there were almost no women using its facilities. That has changed now, in part due to its bi-monthly women and gender-variant – WAG – night. Jenni started these classes in recognition that these are the people least likely to feel confident, able or willing to come to any of their other sessions. Just as women might find joining a cycling club that is 75 per cent male off-putting, many would feel similarly – maybe more so – about entering the stereotypically male environs of a workshop. When I went to one of these sessions there were around ten of us crammed into the intimate workshop for a session on chain care run by Jenni. We were taken through the process, step by step, of getting our chains and corresponding parts in good order and encouraged to ask whatever we wanted, no question being too basic.

Jenni hopes that her WAG sessions will be a 'back door' into – and a way to get comfortable in – an area that may have appeared a closed shop or alien environment. They are about 'getting rid of the idea that it is not something that you're not allowed to do', even if mending a puncture might take you out of your comfort zone. A safe, non-judgemental space where no one will be ridiculed for thinking a cassette was a retro medium for listening to music.

The sessions cover the staples of keeping your bicycle in good working order – as Lillias and Maria Ward argued, the advantages of self-reliance and independence can only be achieved by knowing how to do at least the basic repairs to keep your wheels turning. It's also a lot more economical than taking it to a shop to get fixed each time you have a problem.

Testament to the 'stepping-stone' nature of these WAG classes, the gender split in the Bike Kitchen's other sessions is now much more even. Something to be celebrated when too many still don't feel they are the right 'fit' for the cycling world.

Part II

RESISTANCE AND REBELLION

CHAPTER 5

Fight for Your Right to Bike

Kittie Fought the LAW

It's a fine summer's day in July 1895 and the press has de-
scended on Asbury Park, New Jersey, for the annual meet
of the League of American Wheelmen (LAW). Thousands
of members are arriving from all over the country to take
part, but the press is focused on one particular cyclist,
Katherine 'Kittie' Knox, a twenty-one-year-old seamstress
from Boston. It isn't her gender that is causing a media
sensation, though, it is the colour of her skin. Kittie is mixed-
race, and the previous year the organisation had passed a
controversial 'colour bar', excluding anyone who wasn't
white from joining. As a result, all eyes are on Kittie and
the LAW.

At a time when racial prejudice was ingrained in every
facet of American life, a Southern faction of the LAW led by
Colonel W. W. Watts of Louisville, Kentucky, had successfully campaigned to transform it into a whites-only organisation, overturning a 1892 declaration that 'all races are
eligible for membership'. Colonel Watts had been petitioning
for the exclusion of black people – and for the Californian
branches to refuse prospective Chinese members – for three
years. One Southern member who supported the ban said
it had once been an 'honour' to belong to the organisation,
but that would cease to be the case if non-whites were permitted as members. He wasn't alone in his racists views;
in a secret ballot the colonel got his way by 127 votes to
54, with Southern members voting unanimously for the Jim
Crow-style amendment. The constitution was consequently
changed to 'none but white persons can become members
of the League'.

Not all members agreed with the new policy, and some
of the more enlightened branches refused to implement
the ruling. The Massachusetts division, true to Boston's

abolitionist roots, was one of these groups, and was not averse to ruffling the feathers of Southern racists by showing up with their black members at the annual meet.

In any case, grossly discriminatory though the new ban was, theoretically it didn't apply to Kittie since she was not a new applicant but an existing member of the League when the ban came into force. Despite this, the press, and I'm sure Kittie and her fellow Bostonians, were preparing for a clash of some sort on the day.

As a woman of colour on a bicycle, Kittie was subjected to more scrutiny and moralising than white female cyclists. In addition to her race and sex, her outfits caused a stir; like Tessie Reynolds in Brighton, she'd employed her sewing skills to make herself a rational dress outfit consisting of baggy grey knee-length bloomers with a matching jacket, completing the ensemble with long boots buttoned down the sides. The Chicago cycling magazine, *Referee*, declared her 'a beautiful and buxom black bloomerite'. The outfit was ideal for the men's crossbar bike that she rode, and it won her a prize in a cycle costume competition at what must have been a progressive Massachusetts bicycle event. This being the less enlightened 1890s, there were still murmurings from some quarters about the prize being awarded to a non-white participant.

Kittie also belonged to the Riverside Cycling Club. Founded in 1893, this was one of the first black cycling clubs in the country. She was such a keen cyclist that, again like Tessie, she had ridden in several competitions, including participating in century (100-mile) races. While she may not have been surprised that the press was so interested in her attendance at Asbury, particularly given that she had featured numerous times in newspapers and cycling magazines, she may have wondered why the reports that emerged were so conflicting.

Some sources claim she was prevented from entering the meet, but the *New York Times* reported that Kittie demonstrated some 'fancy cuts' in front of the clubhouse so it seems she must have pedalled into the park along with fellow members. What happened next is much less clear and centres on whether the LAW accepted her membership card when she presented it to them. The *San Francisco Call* reported that her card was refused and she 'withdrew very quietly', though it believed that 99 per cent of members expressed regret. Other papers reported that a member of the executive committee, a fellow Bostonian, demanded they acknowledge her as a member and accord her the privileges to which she was entitled. The *Boston Herald* said Kittie had no complaints whatsoever about her reception at Asbury and was perplexed by the media furore. Further conflicting accounts filtered through to the press from LAW members: not only had she been welcomed at the event, Kittie had been the belle of the ball in the evening, dancing with white men; some witnesses claimed that as a consequence the women members had staged a mass walkout in disgust at her flagrant behaviour.

With the Southern press spewing racist bile in response to Kittie's attendance, this issue wasn't going to go away anytime soon. The *New York Times*'s conclusion that 'this episode will result in temporarily opening the color line question' for the LAW and that some of its members 'will protest against permitting Miss Knox to remain a member' was sadly accurate, even if not much else had been.

Although Kittie's fellow Bostonians had defended her on the grounds that she was an existing member, they were ultimately unsuccessful in overturning the discriminatory new rule for prospective non-white members. Nor did they manage to stem the flow of rising racial discrimination in the cycling world, with more clubs – including ones in Boston – implementing their own ban on non-white members, a policy that would directly curtail Kittie and others from joining clubs and participating in previously open events such as the Boston Wheelman's century ride – a competition she had previously excelled in.

The LAW – today known as League of American Bicyclists – didn't publicly renounce their controversial 'colour bar' until 1999, though the policy had long since been ignored. When they made the retraction, they announced they would be doing more to support diversity in cycling. This was long overdue and continues to need addressing, since women still only make up 25 per cent of cyclists in the US – 27 per cent in the UK, according to a 2008 Department for Transport report – and women of colour represent only a small fraction of that number.

Whatever happened on that day in July 1895, Kittie had been justifiably determined to be part of this event, exhibiting remarkable chutzpah in the face of a rising tide of agitation for segregation in the country. Which is why many Bostonians today call her the Rosa Parks of cycling. She resisted in the face of grossly unfair and prejudiced attitudes and actions that were intended to block her participation for no other reason than the colour of her skin. Kittie remained defiant and holds a place in a long line of women who have continued to ride their bikes despite being told it isn't for them, with some resisting to this day, even when faced with threats of extreme violence. Their fight reveals the extent to which the bicycle remains at the centre of intersecting discourse around the politics of race, gender, public space, climate change, urban planning and more.

Psyco Sisters

A 2019 Women4Climate survey carried out in San Francisco showed that only 13 per cent of cyclists in the city
are women of colour, with Asian and Hispanic women the
least represented. A low figure when you consider that 34
per cent of the population of the city are women of colour.
Many of those interviewed said that 'women like me' don't
bike, that they saw it as a predominantly young, white, male
activity. As ever, representation matters. The problem isn't
isolated to San Francisco, but is an issue across the country
and elsewhere.*

When the African American Monica Garrison started
cycling in Pittsburgh in 2014, she soon became aware that
there were few women who looked like her riding bikes in
the city. In an interview she admitted that she struggled with
the distinct lack of representation in the cycling community: 'I have to admit that I used to have preconceived ideas
about who cyclists were and what they looked like. I was
unsure of where I fit in.'

As a result, she founded Black Girls Do Bike (BGDB),
which she describes as a 'pep rally for black girls on bikes'.
Like Lillias Campbell Davidson's Lady Cyclists' Association, BGDB connects women, though specifically women
of colour, with other cyclists in their area. Now there are
chapters across the country, with more opening all the time,
set up by women who have been supported and inspired
by the organisation. They arrange group rides, support new
learners and share skills such as basic mechanics, creating
a supportive and nurturing community to make cycling

---

* According to research conducted in 2017 by Transport for
London, members of black, Asian and minority ethnic groups – of
both genders – account for only 15 per cent of the city's cycle trips
despite making up 41 per cent of the city's population.

a more diverse and inclusive activity. The aim is for their members to feel empowered and at home, thus helping to change the narrative of who gets to ride bikes that has been ongoing since women first started pedalling.

Lack of diversity in the bike community is a problem in Los Angeles too. In this distinctly cycle-unfriendly city – built for the motor age, with highways bifurcating every neighbourhood – just getting on a bike is an act of resistance. Unsurprisingly, when road safety is frequently cited as one of the major barriers for women's participation, only one in five cyclists in the city is a woman. The number of women on bikes in a particular area is seen as an indicator of how safe it is to cycle; countries with a good cycling infrastructure, such as the Netherlands, have a more favourable gender split. In the east LA neighbourhood of Boyle Heights, a group of predominantly Latina women, like BGDB, are challenging the city's overwhelmingly white male cycling culture, and combining cycling with activism to reclaim the streets.

The Ovarian Psycos Bicycle Brigade, also known as the OVAS (Overthrowing Vendidos, Authority & the State – Vendidos meaning Mexican Americans who have sold out their culture in favour of the dominant American one), are a cycling sisterhood for 'womxn'* of colour from their neighbourhood. Unlike Kittie Knox, they haven't been officially barred from joining other clubs, but they felt they needed to carve out their own cycling space in a way that is representative of their values and daily reality as women of colour in a marginalised community. Though images of the Psycos riding as a group, wearing black bandanas over their faces printed with the group's ovary and uterus imagery,

* The Psycos often use the gender-neutral and non-binary term 'Latinx', as well as 'womxn', which denotes the inclusion of transgender women and women of colour.

may make them look more like a biker gang, they couldn't be further from that.

An overtly feminist and politically engaged crew, the Psycos was founded in 2010 by Xela de la X, a musician and community activist. When Xela's car broke down, and she couldn't afford to get it fixed, she started commuting to her job in downtown LA by bike. In common with women elsewhere, she found that she was subjected to catcalls and other overtly sexist harassment during her daily rides to a degree she had not experienced as a pedestrian. Regardless, she enjoyed being able to weave freely through the city's notorious traffic jams; it made her think, 'This is what freedom feels like, this is what it feels like not to have obstacles blocking your movement.' She wanted other women to have a chance to experience this feeling – not alone and harassed as she had been, but together and supported in a bicycle brigade. Thus the idea for the first Luna ride was born: a full-moon night ride for female-identifying and non-binary cyclists in her community who may not previously have had the confidence to ride out on the streets alone, but who might do if they were surrounded by people like themselves.

Xela's Eastside neighbourhood of Boyle Heights is a stone's throw across the Los Angeles River from the sprawling city's downtown, but a world away from its gleaming skyscrapers and other emblems of capitalism, though creeping gentrification is beginning to change that. The Chicano civil rights movement, a movement to empower Mexican Americans, was centred here in the 1960s and its population is still of predominantly Mexican heritage. The Psycos proudly connect their community's history of fighting for social justice with the activities of the bicycle brigade, referring to themselves as 'warriors', though their focus is specifically on the issues affecting them as women of colour from this area.

Freedom, mobility, autonomy and fearlessness are core to the group's ethos, something Xela felt she was acutely lacking when she was growing up. While her brothers were free to roam, she felt confined indoors – taking up space in the streets with her cycling sisters is an act of defiance. Some of the other members say they weren't encouraged to ride as children because their parents' generation didn't think it was something girls should do; others rode as children but later gave up due to harassment or disapproval. Now they are rewriting the rules and reclaiming control over what they can do with their bodies and where they can go. In the process, they're sending a strong message that through group solidarity they will no longer be scared away from moving freely around the streets, especially at night.

On a Luna ride, they cruise the neighbourhood, riders two or four abreast, chanting 'Whose streets? Our streets!' The power of the group allows them to fearlessly inhabit the space, streets they may have previously avoided alone at night. As Xela says, 'when you are riding with a group of women it feels like, "I'm supported, I got backup." You feel like you could win the war. You feel like nothing, absolutely nothing can stop you. It was women not being scared of riding our bicycles or just claiming space in very dangerous zones.' Another group member says that the feeling she experiences of cycling as part of the brigade, the sense of safety and empowerment it provides, is 'one of the most liberating feelings in the world'.

As part of their activism the Psycos have been known to organise rides to areas where young women from the community have been murdered or kidnapped, to raise awareness of systemic violence against women and reinforce the message that they won't be driven off the streets by fear – much like the gangs of women cyclists in Lizzie Borden's 1983 feminist dystopian film *Born in Flames*, who rescue women who are being threatened or assaulted on the streets. Their physical presence inspires other women to join their movement, women who might not have seen others who look like them riding bikes before. Many of the rides are themed, and they also host talks on issues relevant to their members, such as women's health and self-defence, and undertake activities with a humanitarian focus, such as distributing care packages to the homeless. As an alternative to the popular Critical Mass* rides, which the Psycos see as too white and male, in LA at least, to be fully inclusive, they organise their own alternative annual 30-mile rides, known as 'Clitoral Mass'. No rider is left behind – if someone has a puncture then the whole group waits with them. As member Maryann Aguirre says, 'We're not about who can ride fastest, we're about sisterhood.' By contrast, when the group ride into mostly white and upmarket neighbouring areas like Echo Park and Pasadena, they say they are regularly stared at in a way that makes them feel they don't belong there and which they don't think they would experience if they were all on expensive bikes and kitted out in cycling gear.

When I look through the comment section underneath an online LAist article on one of their recent 'Clitoral Mass' bike rides, it's clear that this group of feminist cyclists is seen as a threat. One anonymous commentator described them as 'Femtards' and 'deluded hysterical females' and suggests people 'throw sticks in their spokes' to 'see how

---

* Critical Mass originated in 1992 in San Francisco; cyclists gathered monthly to ride through the streets, using the safety of numbers to take back the space from motor vehicles, raising awareness about climate change and the safety of cyclists on the road. The event now takes place in cities across the world as both a celebration of cycling and a form of activism to reclaim the streets for greener modes of transport.

tough they are'. But the group is still going strong and has become increasingly active on issues impacting their community, particularly the gentrification of their neighbourhood, which they see as ushering in rent rises and evictions, and the government's policy on the US–Mexico border, which includes the inhumane detainment of migrant children and enforced separation from their parents.

Bicyclists of Bamiyan

Across the world there are still women who are not just discouraged from riding bikes but actively forbidden to do so by their families and community. Some continue regardless, including in Afghanistan, where women who cycle have been labelled 'infidels' and threatened with violence and even death. Though Afghan women gained the right to vote in 1919, only a year after the UK and a year before the US, their country was ranked in a 2018 Thomson Reuters' Poll as the second-worst place in the world to be female, with women and girls facing severe gender-based violence, abuse, illiteracy, poverty, and other human rights offences. It's the legacy of fifty years of instability in a country which has seen Soviet occupation and then years of civil conflict in the 1980s and '90s between Mujahideen groups and government forces, followed by a repressive and violent Taliban rule.

Women's rights under the Taliban were pushed over a cliff. Legislation was introduced banning girls and women from going to school, working, being involved in politics and leaving the house without a male chaperone, as well as requiring them to wear a burqa at all times when out in public. The punishments for non-compliance were violent and, sometimes, deadly. Not surprisingly bicycling, with its connotations of freedom, independence, mobility and pleasure, was not permitted. When the US invaded the country in 2001 to remove the regime, citing its appalling women's rights record as part of their motivation (though the reality is of course more complex than that), the situation began to improve for women in some parts of the country. Education was reinstated and women were even running for parliament, becoming judges, taking a greater role in commerce and generally gaining visibility in public life again.

The adventurer and campaigner Shannon Galpin has spent over a decade visiting and running women's rights projects in Afghanistan. She spoke to me over the phone from her home in Colorado, where she lives with her daughter when she's not travelling. She remembers 2007–08 as a particular high point when it seemed that women's and other important rights in the country would continue to progress unabated. One thing she never saw then, though, despite all the new freedoms, was a girl on a bike; that was still 'too controversial'. Shannon, a keen mountain biker, decided this wouldn't stop her from biking across parts of the country to experience the breathtaking landscapes in ways no other form of transport would have allowed, enabling her to see a country known to foreigners mostly for war, terror and poverty in a completely different way, a country that, far from being monolithic, is in fact one of myriad cultures.

In 2010 Shannon became the first woman to bike the Panjshir Valley in the high mountains north of Kabul and was the first woman most people she encountered had seen cycling. As a foreign woman, she discovered she was exempt from the strict social codes that prevented Afghan women from doing the same; she was viewed as more akin to 'a curiosity, like a circus bear juggling'. Men who would never have deemed it appropriate to approach this American woman had she been travelling in a vehicle as part of a convoy, like most foreigners, came up to talk to her. It was an ice-breaker, she reports: 'whatever that restraint was it had gone. The curiosity overrode the restraint of cultural boundaries.' The open desire to interact often extended to invitations into homes for tea.

In one instance, travelling with a female translator, Shannon was able to have an uninhibited conversation with the women members of a family who felt able to speak freely with no men in the room. The Afghan women started by asking about contraception and women's health, before Shannon took the opportunity to ask them about women's lives in the country. After the fall of the Taliban, women's participation in certain sports was encouraged as the authorities recognised that physical activity was vital to women's health. Football, volleyball, cricket, Tae Kwondo and even boxing were permitted because they could be done behind closed doors. Cycling, on the other hand, remained taboo, because it was largely something you did in a public space. Since Afghan culture has traditionally encouraged women to dress modestly, and in some areas to stay indoors out of sight, women on bikes are considered by some to be too visible and open to the male gaze.

Shannon believes that the other reason cycling remains so controversial in religiously conservative countries like Afghanistan is because the act of physically straddling a bicycle seat is viewed as suggestive of promiscuity and overt sexuality, and is therefore taboo.*

The same is true in Iran, where Ayatollah Khamenei, the Islamic Republic's supreme leader, issued a fatwa in 2016 against women cycling in public on the false grounds that they pose a threat to morality: 'riding a bicycle often

---

* Like the person who commented underneath a 2018 *Arab News* article about women in Saudi Arabia riding bikes who wrote that, as a result of this, they are 'expecting AIDS to enter Saudi soon'.

attracts the attention of men and exposes the society to corruption, and thus contravenes women's chastity, and it must be abandoned'. Many women continue to cycle in Iran, although some have been arrested for doing so; their bikes were then confiscated and they were forced to sign statements promising they will desist. In 2019, authorities in Isfahani, an Iranian city renowned for its high concentration of cyclists due to its extensive network of bike paths, said that women who ignore the ban will be subjected to 'Islamic Punishment'. Apparently they are working on a 'covered bicycle' for them.

Shannon believes that in Afghanistan, where virginity tests are often carried out on prospective brides, many would see cycling as a direct threat to the highly prized intact hymen, though other activities pose a similar risk. One man she met had a different view; he told her that riding a bike takes a lot of intelligence and that's why women couldn't do it.

While Shannon felt that her biking in Afghanistan showed that this was something that women could and did do elsewhere, she recognised that as a foreigner she would never be able to change perceptions about Afghan women and girls doing the same. Unbeknownst to Shannon, while she was biking around the Panjshir Valley there was an Afghan woman a few hundred miles to the west who was risking disapproval and violence by riding her bike, and in so doing helping to normalise the idea of others like her doing the same.

Zahra, now in her twenties, had started cycling at thirteen when she was living in Iran, despite much disapproval. Her parents had died when she was a small child and she was raised by an elder sister who she has described as treating her like a boy in the hope it would give her more freedom and courage than most Afghan girls. It seems to have worked, as Zahra has not shied away from pushing against attempts to prevent her from doing things on account of her gender, including demanding to attend school.

When she was eighteen, Zahra moved to the province of Bamiyan, north-west of Kabul, to study archaeology at the university that had been reopened after the Taliban were removed from the area. She was soon attracting attention for cycling to her classes. Local boys would bike to the university, but there were no other women or girls doing the same, even though there were no buses and it could take as long as two hours a day to walk there and back. Regardless of the risks, Zahra believes that 'girls deserve to have the same opportunities as boys, whether that's education, or the right to ride a bike'.

When I spoke to Zahra down the line from Kabul, where she is continuing her studies, she told me that when she first started getting around this way the religious scholars in the area were so angry that they said she should be stoned. No one would have blamed her for deciding to go back to walking, that it was too dangerous a fight, but Zahra continued. Eventually she convinced them that it was necessary in order to continue her education. She became well known as the woman who cycled, and soon others wanted to join her. The first of these was Zakia, who had learned to ride in Iran and had missed it since she hadn't felt able to continue after returning to her home country.

Zakia's father ran a bike shop and was supportive of women taking part, but understandably she didn't feel confident going it alone, so she stopped Zahra on the street to talk to her and soon they were going on rides together. Before long, other girls wanted to join them and it was at that point that they decided they would start a team, with training sessions and races. Purchasing a bike was yet another barrier to participation – the cost is equivalent to a month's salary – but the father of one team member was so supportive of his daughter's desire to join the group that he borrowed money to buy her one.

The women began meeting regularly, gathering first to chat, eat, warm up, clean and fix their bikes before heading out onto the road. On the busy highways which they share with large trucks and farmers with donkeys piled high with produce they ride single-file, spreading out to ride two abreast on less busy roads, forcing any traffic to slow in order to pass. They often ride past the historic cave complex where the giant sixth-century buddhas of Bamiyan carved into the sandstone cliffs had stood until they were blown up by the Taliban in 2001.

In 2015 the group took part in the Tour of Bamiyan bike race, the first race in Afghanistan to allow women. Yet they still struggle to be accepted, and continue to attract the wrong sort of attention. Some of the local mullahs have labelled them 'infidels' and 'sinners', declaring that what they are doing is shameful and as a result they risk losing their 'honour'. They were told there was no problem with them riding bikes if they did it somewhere private, but they were risking violence by 'parading around in groups'. They were also falsely accused of riding without headscarves and dressing inappropriately (the members all observe the country's dress code for covered arms, legs and hair).

Many of the members were understandably scared, yet Zakia and Zahra remained convinced that they were doing nothing shameful. They organised meetings with the more progressive governor of Bamiyan to obtain his support – and it was gladly offered, though of course he can't protect them from sudden acts of violence that they might encounter. Shannon, who has since biked with Zahra and her team, described her as 'one of the strongest women' she knows, and it's not hard to see why.

Five years later the group is still going strong. Members

are now generally accepted by the community, with some locals proud that this team is part of the identity of the region. Boys who see them out riding tell them that they are going to teach their sisters. Though there are still men who won't let their daughters or sisters take part, Zahra is optimistic that it will become more and more accepted in her country that anyone can ride a bike.

Zahra is now studying full-time in Kabul, so the role of director and trainer has passed to Zakia. The team members, like those of the Victorian Mowbray House bicycle co-operative, share the club's six mountain bikes, their training sessions split between mornings and evenings. On Fridays, when there is no school, they transport the bikes further into the high mountains of the Hindu Kush to the country's first National Park, Bande-e-Amir, to do a longer ride of around 100 km – something that would have been inconceivable before Zahra started defiantly pedalling through the streets of her town.

The group continues to inspire girls and women to have a go and has connected with women's teams in Kabul and Mazar-i-Sharif, arranging race meetings, but there are still many parts in the country where it would be unsafe to cycle. Bamiyan is comparatively progressive and liberal compared to some areas, and has fewer landmines left over from the wars. Elsewhere, the Taliban have regained control, making it impossible for women to demand basic rights such as education – let alone cycle to classes.

While Zahra uses her bike to get to her classes and to visit archaeological sites as part of her studies, as well as for sport, too many others are denied that kind of essential mobility in Afghanistan, especially in rural areas where few have cars and public transport is limited.

There are countries where historically it has not been a cultural norm for women and girls to cycle, but where girls in rural areas are now using bikes to get to school and to access healthcare or job opportunities. Their lives have been transformed by their two wheels; whereas once they would probably have dropped out of education because the journey took too long on foot, they are now getting to school quickly, easily and safely. Among many other benefits, this improves their job prospects and gives them greater control over their own lives.

Shannon believes that bikes are a powerful tool for social justice and if more women in Afghanistan were permitted to cycle then they too would experience similar advantages. It can mean the difference between 'a life fulfilled and a life of oppression'. The charity World Bicycle Relief back this up by reporting that school performance and attendance increase among the girls to whom they have donated bikes.

While the future for women's rights in Afghanistan is uncertain with the resurgence of the Taliban, it is undeniable that there are currently many more girls and women on bikes in the areas where it is safe, many of whom have been inspired by pioneers like Zahra. There is also a women's National Team in Kabul which is rebuilding itself after it was brought down by corruption allegations against its male coach, which he denied. If the team can go on to represent Afghanistan one day in international races, or possibly even the Olympics, then it will be harder to rationalise denying other women the same opportunities.

A Green Bicycle

To the west of Afghanistan, Saudi Arabia, one of the world's most conservative and closed countries, recently granted women the right to drive cars after decades of campaigning. It was the last place in the world to do so, a historic moment for women's rights in a country which has repeatedly sought – and still does – to limit their freedoms in what many regard as a totalitarian dictatorship. Two years previously they were finally granted the right to vote and stand in local elections. Less well known is the fact that in 2013 a ban on women riding bicycles, which had been enforced by Saudi Arabia's Committee for the Promotion of Virtue and the Prevention of Vice – the religious police – was also overturned.

The film *Wadjda*, released in 2012, explored the taboo of girls cycling in Saudi by telling the story of the eponymous heroine's desperate desire to own a bike. The director, Haifaa al-Mansour, was the first Saudi Arabian woman to make a feature film in her homeland and has an intimate understanding of the struggle to pursue a goal that contravenes rigid gender expectations. In the film, Wadjda's best friend, Abdullah, teaches her to ride a bike in secret and she pleads with the local bike shop not to sell the green bike she has fallen in love with until she has saved enough to buy it. Her mother tells her that 'here girls don't ride bikes. You won't be able to have children if you ride a bike', and if she persists she won't be able to marry. Nevertheless Wadjda remains focused on her goal. The news that a Quran recital competition at her school is offering prize money that would pay for the bike turns her into a model student. Wadjda goes on to win the competition. However, when she tells her teachers, whose duties include policing the behaviour of female pupils, how she will spend the money, they are horrified and seize the money, donating it to Palestine on her behalf. Not long after, when her father takes a second wife, Wadjda's mother rebels by buying her daughter the bicycle. As the film closes, we see Wadjda beating Abdullah in a bike race, her face beaming with delight.

While the 2013 decree would have made it legally permissible for women and girls like Wadjda to bike, few did.

The ban may have been lifted but there was a long list of conditions: women cyclists must wear abayas, or modesty robes; they could only ride in certain designated areas; they must be accompanied by a male guardian; and – the most telling stipulation in a country renowned for curbing women's freedom of movement – their bikes couldn't be used for transport, only recreation.

Today, in the east-coast city of Al Khobar on the Persian Gulf, groups of women can be seen riding together along the beachfront, but it's taken years to get to this point. One of these women is Fatimah Al-Bloushi, who started cycling in the city in 2017 after deciding to take part in a week-long charity bike race in Europe. She had learned to ride as a child but stopped when she reached adulthood, as did most girls she knew, if they had learned at all. Only when she travelled abroad, to cycle-friendly cities like London and Amsterdam, would she take the opportunity to go for a ride.

To prepare for her upcoming race, which would require her to cycle up to 100 km a day for seven days, Fatimah decided she would need to train back home. At that time, she never saw any other women in Al Khobar riding. Not wanting to draw attention to herself, she opted for quiet areas early in the morning or at night. She told me that, despite there being no law against what she was doing, she was often pulled over by the police; they would reprimand her, ask her to sign something to say she wouldn't do it again, and warn her that she could face legal action if she did. Though these officers told her they were acting out of concern for her safety as a woman out on her own, the only hassle she experienced was from the police themselves. Fatimah thinks they were acting out of personal prejudice; these were men with opinions and the power to enforce them, who didn't like the fact that she was challenging Saudi cultural norms. One of them demanded accusingly, 'Where do you think you are? You are not in America. We didn't reach that level where you get to go out like that.'

Fatimah was rejected by the all-male Saudi team that was taking part in the same race, fearful they would get in trouble with the authorities for letting a woman ride with them. Instead she joined an international team of riders. When the press reported that a woman from Saudi had taken part – the first to do so – she was inundated with messages from women and girls back home. Some told her they wanted to learn to ride a bike; others hoped they could ride with her in the race next time; the majority of them were women who didn't feel confident riding on their own.

To respond to the demand, Fatimah formed the group HerRide, leading its members twice-weekly along the city's only bike path, on the corniche along the sea, which is traffic-free. The following year, four of them, including Fatimah's sister Yasa, travelled to Europe to take part in that same race, which this time started in Sweden and ended in Germany. When they returned, having competed against hundreds of cyclists from around the world, Fatimah felt that the tide was finally turning. The sight of women on bikes, at least in comparatively liberal cities like Jeddah and Al Khobar, was becoming an accepted part of life in the kingdom.

This was remarkable progress in a country where, until 2017, physical education wasn't on the school curriculum for girls. Women were not permitted to take part in the Olympics until 2012, when two made it into the delegation – much to the consternation of many hardliners – then four in 2016. Exercise too was the exclusive preserve of men; many women resorted to walking circuits around shopping malls just to stay fit. As a result, statistics show Saudi women suffer higher rates of obesity, cancer and other diseases than men. There were even prohibitions against women watching sporting events; a ban on women entering stadiums was in place until 2018.

And while there might have been a slight loosening of regulations, attitudes within this ultra-conservative society remain hostile to women taking part in sport. The claims cited by opponents are identical to the ones heard in the West during the late nineteenth century: physical activity will make women less feminine and lead to a relaxation in strict clothing rules which will in turn impact on morality. One female cyclist in Jeddah reported that when she first started going out on her bike with friends in 2015, unhappy members of the public sometimes called the police to come and stop them.

Women who want to bike in Saudi now have a powerful supporter in Princess Reema bint Bandar Al-Saud – Saudi ambassador to the US. The kingdom's first ever female envoy, she was previously president of the Saudi Federation for Community Sports, where her remit was to make sport more inclusive of women, from its administration to participation. She was largely responsible for getting physical education into schools and actively encouraged women to go out on the streets and into the public parks to exercise: 'I've been telling women they don't need permission to exercise in public, they don't need permission to activate their own sports programmes. And more and more they are doing it.' The Federation is in the process of setting up a women's cycling team.

Fatimah has benefitted from the culture change. She's been sent on courses so that she can teach other women to ride bikes, and attended training camps in the hope that she can become part of the new women's cycling team and compete in the Olympic Games.

Nadima Abu El-Einein has also benefitted from and contributed to the slight relaxation in attitudes towards women cycling in Saudi. In her home town of Jeddah on the Red Sea coast, she has become involved in encouraging and teaching women to cycle. In 2018 she organised the country's first bike race for women, its second ever women's sports race. Before this, she hadn't been immune to the negative cultural attitude to women on bikes, and had stopped when she became a teenager. When her sister and mother encouraged her to take it up again in 2015, she started sharing photos of her rides on Instagram and, like Fatimah, was soon receiving messages from other women wanting to join her. That same year, at the age of sixteen, she set up Bisklita, the country's first women-only cycling club which has grown from six to 500 members and includes a wide range of ages and abilities, not least one member who, after suffering a brain injury which left her less able to balance, joins in on a trike.

Nadima had been taught to ride by her mother, so it seems natural to her to be supporting other girls and women to do the same. She's confident that there is nothing in Islam that prohibits them from doing so. Women on bikes were a rare sight when they first started riding together, and people would shout and sometimes throw things at them. But they continued regardless and have become increasingly accepted – like the cyclists in Bamiyan – by people in the city.

The change has yet to filter through to the rest of the country; in many cities and rural areas women on bikes continue to be harassed. Though it's not a legal requirement to carry proof of SA Cycling Federation membership, Fatima has found that police back off when she shows her card. Nadima, tired of her group being stopped by the police, has written to Princess Reema to ask for the Cycling Federation to issue them with permits. In the interim, the princess arranged for them to use a local stadium so Nadima could teach her students to ride in peace.

It's difficult to say how long it will take for the situation to improve. An initiative known as Saudi Vision 2030 lists among its aims the inclusion of more women in the work-force and improved access to sporting activities for all members of society. Critics have dismissed this as 'window-dressing'; there is no mention of equality or full social and political enfranchisement for women. Women's rights activists pay a high price for trying to bring about change to the system, for the Saudi regime does not tolerate dis-sent. Women who fought to overturn the driving ban were imprisoned and, according to rights groups, some were tor-tured. Many of them remain in prison now, though the ban ended in 2018.

A repressive guardianship system requires each female citizen of Saudi Arabia to obtain permission from an as-signed male relative before they can be permitted to marry, obtain a passport, travel abroad, be released from prison or state care, apply for a life-saving abortion, or enter a shel-ter for victims of domestic abuse. And if a woman suffers abuse at the hands of her guardian, the state will do little to protect her. Which explains why Saudi Arabia occupies fifth place in the poll ranking the worst places in the world to be a woman.

Though they risk imprisonment, torture or sometimes death if they are caught, there have been a number of cases of women fleeing the country to escape this oppres-sive system. In 2019, eighteen-year-old Rahaf Mohammed al-Qunun absconded to Thailand to escape her allegedly abusive family. She locked herself in a hotel room and refused to leave until, eventually, she was offered asylum in Canada. Another woman who fled Saudi repression for freedom abroad described the joy of no longer having to ask permission to leave the house, of being able to dress as she pleases, and countless other things many of us take for granted. She is now learning to ride a bike, as well as swim and ice skate – activities that her guardian would not have permitted.

At the time of writing, it has been rumoured the kingdom is planning to relax some of its guardianship rules, suggesting that women will soon be able to obtain passports and travel abroad without the consent of a guardian. There is no commitment to dismantling the guardianship system completely, so it's unclear what impact this will have on women's rights and freedom of movement.

Meanwhile, at a grass-roots level, women like Fatimah and Nadima are at least able to enjoy an activity that would have been out of bounds less than a decade ago. They are inspiring other women to take up something which is so much about freedom, movement and physicality, with Fatimah telling me how she wants to 'empower Saudi women' and getting them on bikes is part of that.

'It fills my heart with joy,' says Nadima when asked what it means to her to teach women to ride, so that they too can 'break free from the fear of social boundaries'. She is convinced there has been a positive change in attitude in the country over the last few years, and that cycling has played a crucial part in that shift.

CHAPTER 6

Rise Up, Women!

Pedal-powering a Revolution

As Parliament prepares to open on 13 February for the formal start of the 1907 parliamentary year, over 400 women gather at 3 p.m. in London's Caxton Hall for a 'Women's Parliament'. All are members of the Women's Social and Political Union (WSPU) – suffragettes. They are here to protest the omission, yet again, of women's suffrage from the king's speech of the previous day.

When the WSPU leader, Emmeline Pankhurst, commands, 'Rise up, Women!', the hall erupts with cries of 'Now!' as the delegation divides into groups to cover the half-mile along Victoria Street to the Houses of Parliament, where they will deliver a petition to the prime minister demanding that the issue be debated. The rational dress advocate and cyclist, Lady Harberton, leads one of the groups, along with other high-profile WSPU activists.

On reaching Westminster Abbey, a line of policemen blocks their way. Instead of turning back, the marchers try to force their way through to Parliament. Police on foot and horseback respond violently, trying to disperse the crowd by laying into them with their batons; many women are injured in the brutal fray. One newspaper would later describe the scene as akin to a 'football scrummage', with women pushing against the police cordon for hour after hour.

Some women defiantly shout, 'We will not go away, we will see the prime minister!' Fifteen manage to break through the line and reach the entrance, only to be arrested. Fifty-one women are taken to Scotland Yard – including WSPU leaders Emmeline, Sylvia and Christabel Pankhurst. The women finally give up the struggle to gain entrance at 10 p.m.

Most of those arrested were sentenced the following day to two weeks in Holloway Prison. Passing sentence, the judge declared his determination to put an end to their 'disorderly and disgusting proceedings'.

Among those arrested was Alice Hawkins, a factory worker from Leicester. Alice was a machinist for the Equity Boot and Shoe factory, a co-operative that nurtured her deep-seated concerns for social justice. She had long believed that women should receive the same pay as men for doing the same work and that they should be granted the most fundamental of democratic rights – the right to vote.

Along with her husband Fred, Alice was an active campaigner, believing that women of all social classes needed a stake in the political system. The Equity was encouraging about its workers being politically engaged and supported her trip to London for the march – quite a contrast to most factories, where workers would have been fired for taking time off to attend a protest, let alone to serve time inside. Far from putting an end to her activism, the prison sentence strengthened Alice's commitment to the cause. In her account of her time in Holloway, true to her compassionate nature and commitment to social justice, she decried how badly the non-suffragette women prisoners were treated, particularly those sentenced to hard labour. She would be arrested and imprisoned a further four times over the next seven years.

On returning to Leicester after her first Holloway incarceration, even more fired up about the injustices of the political system, Alice established the Leicester branch of the WSPU and campaigned hard to recruit fellow working women from the many factories in the city. Their first meeting was held at the Boot and Shoe Hall; Sylvia Pankhurst spoke about the suffrage cause and Alice shared her experience of her time in Holloway. Soon her Leicester WSPU had opened a Votes for Women shop, which sold their newspaper and other WSPU literature to raise money for the cause, as well as a providing a meeting point for members.

Though its windows were often broken by local men who opposed their campaign, the shop remained the beating heart of Leicester's suffrage movement – thanks to Alice.

What has all this got to do with a book about women and cycling? Alice's campaign was built on pedal power. Her bike allowed her to travel around, staging rallies at factory gates and promoting upcoming WSPU meetings, in a way that she could never have done on foot. She was able to spread the word not just within the city but to villages and towns within a thirty-mile radius of Leicester. These were places where news reports of protests and arrests in London might have felt remote, irrelevant or alienating (as might the speeches of the largely middle- and upper-class WSPU), but Alice's first-hand account of the struggle struck a chord with working-class women who recognised her as one of their own.

Every Sunday, Alice – alongside fellow Leicester WSPU organiser Dorothy Pethick – would take her message about votes for women to nearby village greens and market squares, holding talks and rallies and distributing campaign literature such as the *Votes for Women* newspaper. They often met resistance from the authorities and local men, but they continued undeterred. As a direct result of their cycling campaigning, Loughborough, fourteen miles from Leicester, soon established its own branch of the WSPU.

Clarionettes to Cycling Scouts

Alice was far from the only cycling suffragette: bicycling was in the DNA of the WSPU and many of its members were keen cyclists. Fittingly, the architects of the suffragette movement, the Pankhursts, led the way.

Christabel, daughter of Emmeline and sister to Sylvia, was the keenest cyclist. From the age of thirteen, she had petitioned her barrister father for a bicycle. At first, he was apprehensive about the busy roads of their home town of Manchester, but he finally gave in to her relentless badgering in 1896, when she was sixteen. Although the family was experiencing financial pressures, she was bought a top-of-the-range Rudge-Whitworth bicycle. Sylvia, perhaps because her pleas for a bicycle were lukewarm compared to her sister's, and possibly because she was two years younger, was given a distinctly inferior bike that a 'comrade' in the local Independent Labour Party had made from bits of gas piping. This may explain why Sylvia didn't fall in love with cycling to the extent her sister did; it seems her pipe contraption proved 'a considerable handicap' when it came to keeping up with her older and fitter sister. Despite this, and testament to Sylvia's remarkable comradeship and commitment to sisterhood, every available day was spent cycling.

Christabel didn't seem so understanding of her sister's handicap and would regularly sprint off without looking back. According to Sylvia, 'she would disappear from me, climbing some hill, and arrive home sometimes an hour before me. I remember being thrown over the handlebars and rising up so shaken that I had to walk for some distance before I could re-mount.' Sylvia describes riding with her sister as a 'veritable torture'; she would struggle, red-faced and gasping – until 'it seemed my heart would burst' – while Christabel impatiently urged her to 'Come on!'

To Sylvia's relief, when they joined a local Manchester cycling club, the Clarion CC, she found herself in the company of riders who wouldn't abandon her at the bottom of a hill: 'There were usually some slow women riders among the company, and the men were kind in helping to push one up the steepest hills.' Fittingly, the club motto was 'Fellowship is life'. Soon they were joining their fellow members,

Clarionettes, every week for their Sunday runs into the countryside, away from the grime of industrial Manchester. Sylvia, the youngest member of the club, was won over by the camaraderie of these weekly jaunts and the number of willing hands to help mend her constant punctures.

Always a politically active family, in these pre-WSPU days the Pankhursts were involved with the Independent Labour Party. Their club, Clarion CC, was a cycling offshoot of a socialist weekly newspaper of the same name, founded by Robert Blatchford. Blatchford had been fired from his previous paper for writing uncompromising features about the terrible living conditions endured by Manchester's factory workers. He started the *Clarion* in 1891 to report on political injustices and the realities of life for impoverished workers.

This being the height of the bike craze, the *Clarion* established its first cycle club in Birmingham in 1894. By 1897 there were seventy clubs around the UK. Unlike many clubs, it admitted women members almost from the start, and supported rational dress. In addition to social rides each Sunday, Clarion CC's activities included picnics, cycle tours and camping trips.

The summer camps were so popular that hundreds of Clarionettes would attend. A horse-drawn caravan would transport equipment to the campsite, including a large marquee which doubled as a dining and entertainment hall. The Labour leader, Keir Hardie, stayed a night at the 1896 camp and helped with the washing-up (a welcome gesture, for the Clarion's gender equality didn't extend to all areas of club life; women were largely responsible for the catering side of things). According to Sylvia's account of her time there, fresh air, exercise and socialism weren't the only things on offer; the camp gave younger members a chance to indulge in holiday romances and flirtations.

In 1897, a year after Sylvia and Christabel joined, an 'experimental, co-operative cottage' was leased in Bucklow Hill in the Cheshire countryside to serve as a clubhouse for nearby members. Emmeline Pankhurst was one of those who supported the cottage financially. Sixty people could be accommodated in its dormitories and others could camp in the grounds.

The Manchester Cycle Club also organised camping holidays for its members, many of whom were workers in the textile mills. With holidays otherwise beyond the means of low-paid workers, these camping trips provided a much-needed respite from the grind and grime of factory labour. Alice Foley, a weaver's assistant in a Bolton cotton mill (and later influential trade unionist), was a member of the Manchester CC, saving some of her wages each week so she could purchase a bicycle and ride with the club. Children from inner-city slums were also welcomed at the cycle club camps. Sylvia Pankhurst mourned the loss of one such child, whom she described as the most beautiful and popular girl in the club; she blamed her death on 'the common tragedy of pinching scarcity in a working-class home where wages are small and life hard, as it was in those days'.

When Sylvia's father, Richard Pankhurst, died suddenly in 1898, Manchester CC members joined the funeral procession on their bikes. For the Pankhurst girls, the Sunday rides and summer camps soon became a thing of the past. All their energies now turned to women's emancipation and in 1903 they founded the WSPU. After their move to London, Christabel and Sylvia would regularly write features for the *Clarion* about the suffragette cause, helping it become one of the most widely read newspapers covering the issue. The sisters' time as Clarionettes, spreading the socialist message on their bikes by distributing copies of the newspaper and holding talks in the villages and towns they passed through, laid the foundations for the WSPU's two-wheeled efforts to spread the word. As we have seen, Alice Hawkins, a member of the Leicester branch of the Clarion CC, put those tactics to good use in her East Midlands campaign of 1909.

Many WSPU members were already keen cyclists, listing bike-riding as one of their favourite leisure activities. It seemed a natural progression to take part in processions on bicycles emblazoned with suffragette slogans to raise awareness of the cause. But it was a Scottish suffragette, Flora Drummond, who in 1907 made bicycling a key part of the organisation's national campaign drive.

As the person responsible for orchestrating the WSPU's marches and processionals, Flora understood the importance of visual impact. Known as 'The General', for her habit of attending marches on horseback dressed in a military-style uniform, she recognised that bikes would prove more practical than horses in delivering the suffragettes' message to women in rural areas. In 1907 she assembled a brigade that became known as the WSPU Cycling Scouts. With Flora as their 'captain', they would assemble every Saturday outside the Court Theatre in London's Sloane Square, then set off in procession to spread the word. They must have made quite an impression in the towns and villages they visited, all dressed in the purple, white and green livery of the suffragette movement, their bikes decorated with WSPU flags. After 1909, some would no doubt have ridden bikes specially produced for the WSPU by the Elswick Cycle Manufacturing Company in collaboration with the Women's Press. Painted in the suffragette colours, the bicycle sported a badge designed by Sylvia and featuring the union's motif: the angel of freedom, a winged female figure sounding a trumpet. The suffragettes' steed, which went on sale at the 1909 Women's Exhibition, had a drop-frame to accommodate long skirts and came with a cushioned, sprung seat, a wheel-guard to prevent skirts getting caught, and elegant curved handlebars.

Like the Clarionettes, the cycling scouts would hold impromptu meetings in the communities they passed through. Having drawn a crowd by ringing their bells as they cycled through the streets, they would come to a halt and one member of the group would stand on a box to give a speech. The scouts would then distribute copies of *Votes for Women* and other pamphlets, before cycling on to the next stop on their itinerary – singing suffragette songs all the way.

WSPU branches around the country were encouraged to start their own bicycle brigades. One member in the Lake District, a mountainous region with many isolated villages, offered an all-expenses-paid cycling holiday in the region to suffragettes who were willing to combine a cycle tour with campaigning. It provided a perfect opportunity for activists to advance the cause while exploring a beautiful part of the country with their girlfriends.

As the suffragettes' campaigning became increasingly militant in the face of the government's persistent rejection of their demands, the bicycle continued to prove useful – most notably as a getaway vehicle. In the so-called 'pillar-box outrages' of 1913, suffragettes poured ink or flammable liquids – sometimes using an inner tube – into Royal Mail post boxes, before cycling off leaving the mail within damaged or ablaze.

On 19 March 1913 two women were spotted by a policeman at one in the morning, cycling fast through the dark lanes of Egham, Surrey. A few miles further on, as they crossed Staines railway bridge, another policeman called them to a halt and issued one of them with a reprimand for travelling without a light. The offender gave her name as Phyllis Brady; once the lamp was lit, the two women were allowed to continue on their way.

Phyllis was in fact Olive Beamish, and she would later be arrested and sent to prison for having done much more than failing to keep her bicycle lamp lit. The reason Olive and her friend, Elsie Duval, were cycling fast through Surrey under cover of darkness was because they had just set fire to Trevethan, a mansion belonging to Lady White, the widow of a decorated British Army officer. The house had been empty for three years, ensuring no one would get hurt – a prerequisite for all suffragette arson attacks. In their front baskets they had carried the petrol used to set alight Trevethan's grand staircase. The fire spread rapidly through the building, the two women having first opened all the windows to ensure maximum damage. In the garden they had left handwritten signs: 'Votes for Women' and 'Stop torturing our comrades in prison'.

Less than a month later, Elsie and Olive were arrested in Croydon. Again it was one in the morning, and they were in possession of leather cases filled with flammable material. Like many suffragette prisoners, while in Holloway Prison they went on hunger strike;[*] when force-feeding didn't work, they were the first two prisoners to be given temporary release under the 'Cat and Mouse Act'. This allowed prisoners at risk of dying to be let out, with police tailing them for information and rearresting them to complete their sentence once they had recovered their strength. Both women absconded while on release; Elsie fled the country and didn't return until after the outbreak of war, while Olive carried on her militant activities, evading capture until the following year.

Edith Rigby, sentenced to nine months' hard labour in Walton Gaol after planting a bomb in the basement of the

---

[*] For which Elsie, like many others imprisoned for their activism, received a Hunger Strike Medal from the WSPU engraved with the same phrase as the Victoria Cross: 'For Valour'.

Liverpool Cotton Exchange and later setting fire to Lord Leverhulme's country residence in July 1913, was another 'Cat and Mouse' escapee. She also had the distinction of being the first woman to ride a bicycle in her home town of Preston in the 1890s, wearing bloomers – and was pelted with eggs and rotten vegetables for doing so – so it's fitting she absconded on a bicycle. Dressed in workman's clothes to avoid detection, she cycled to the Liverpool docks to board a ferry to Ireland and got as far as Galway. Even her husband had no idea where she'd gone. It is believed she spent many months on the run from the police, most likely until the First World War broke out in July 1914 and the government announced an amnesty on all imprisoned suffragettes. After this Edith was nearly always dressed in men's clothes, which she understandably found far more practical.

In April 1914, a few months before the outbreak of war, two young women on bicycles arrived at a seaside boarding house to begin a touring holiday of Suffolk. Their fortnight sojourn coincided with a string of arson attacks in the vicinity that bore all the hallmarks of the WSPU, including notes left in the wreckage proclaiming, 'There can be no peace until women get the vote'.

At 4 a.m. on the morning of Saturday, 17 April, an explosion rocked one of the pavilions on Great Yarmouth's Britannia Pier. The pier was soon engulfed in flames, destroying everything but the iron girders. The two lady cyclists were staying at a guest house in Lowestoft by this time, though they had told the owner they would be spending the night with friends instead of returning to their room. Though their accommodation was booked under the name Hilda Byron, the two women were in fact WSPU members Hilda Burkitt and Florence Tunks.

They cycled on, selecting lodgings within reach of their targets and setting fire to farmers' haystacks along the way.

Their dramatic finale was the torching of the Bath Hotel in Felixstowe on 28 April, which was closed for refurbishment at the time. The cycling arsonists were arrested the following day. Hilda was sentenced to two years and the younger Florence was given nine months. Both were released in the amnesty granted to imprisoned suffragettes when war broke out at the end of July that year.

With the start of the First World War, the WSPU suspended all militant activities in order to focus on getting women to join the war effort. By taking on men's work, they would strike a blow for equality and make it more difficult to justify denying women's suffrage. When the war ended, the 1918 Representation of the People Act granted the vote to women over the age of thirty who met the property qualifications (about 40 per cent of women in the UK). Universal suffrage followed a decade later.

Vive la Résistance

The bicycle's role in women's active resistance to oppression did not end with enfranchisement. In the Second World War it would continue to be a useful tool for those fighting for freedom.

It will come as no surprise that the Dutch resistance made use of bikes during the Nazi occupation. Which is both ironic and fitting, since Hitler wasn't a fan – his experience as a bicycle messenger in the First World War had left him with a hatred of cycling. He had already banned bikes from most German roads, and under Nazi rule a raft of anti-cycling laws were introduced in the Netherlands. Many citizens deliberately flouted the new rules, including a requirement to give way to any passing German vehicles, as part of their own small daily resistance. Despite Hitler's distaste for bikes, when fuel grew scarce he passed an official order confiscating bicycles from the Dutch (and the Danes) so they could be used by the German military. This followed a 1942 decree requiring Jewish people to hand over their bicycles to the authorities. The Dutch did their best to hang on to their bikes, hiding them anywhere they could – even burying them in their gardens – and some ended up being shot for this small act of defiance.

It's estimated that occupying forces seized half of the 4 million bicycles in use. With food in short supply due to rationing, people relied on whatever supplies they could forage in the countryside; since there was no fuel for public transport or private cars, bicycles provided their only hope of avoiding starvation. In the winter of 1944–45, when the Germans blockaded food supplies to Dutch cities, the result was a devastating famine that claimed 18,000 lives.

When the Allies liberated the Netherlands in 1945, rather than be taken prisoner many German soldiers stole bicycles to escape back to Germany. The confiscations and thefts were so controversial that for decades the Dutch chanted, 'Give us back our bicycles' whenever their team played Germany at football. In 2009 one former German soldier tried to locate the Dutch owners of the bike he had stolen so he could repay them.

Two Dutch sisters, who somehow managed to keep possession of their bikes against the odds, put them to good use in fighting the Nazi occupation – and not just in flagrantly disregarding the new anti-cycling laws.

Freddie and Truus Oversteegen were fourteen and sixteen respectively when Germany invaded their country in 1940. Raised in Haarlem, 20 km west of Amsterdam, they had been brought up by their communist mother to 'stand up for the oppressed and fight injustice'. They helped the local Communist Party distribute anti-Nazi leaflets, storing the contraband literature in their bicycle baskets, as well as defacing Nazi propaganda posters before quickly pedalling away. The family's small apartment offered a sanctuary to Dutch and German Jewish families, though the refugees couldn't stay long because the family's left-wing sympathies made their home too obvious a hiding place. In 1941, the commander of Haarlem's underground resistance cell asked their mother if he could involve the girls in their covert and highly dangerous work. Only once the Oversteegen sisters' training got under way did they find out the shocking nature of the missions he had in mind for them.

There were other women involved in resistance work at this time, most of them operating as couriers or circulating anti-Nazi propaganda. It's said the young Audrey Hepburn was one of these, using her bike to deliver resistance leaflets in her home town of Arnhem. Many were killed, including Annick Van Hardeveld, who was shot in Amsterdam in May 1945. She had been on her way to deliver a message to four resistance fighters. There is now a memorial on the spot where she died.*

For the commander of the Haarlem resistance, the sisters' youth and gender was their greatest asset. What could seem more innocuous than two schoolgirls riding their bicycles around the streets of Haarlem? No one would guess that they were carrying firearms in their front baskets, destined for resistance fighters. They graduated from arms-running to sabotaging railway lines and bridges with dynamite,

---

* The British record-breaking competitive cyclist Evelyn Hamilton claimed that she had delivered messages for the resistance in Paris during the occupation, much as Giro d'Italia and Tour de France winner Gino Bartali had famously used his training rides as a cover to carry messages that would help many Jews escape Italy. There were many women – as well as men – in the resistance pedalling all over France transporting forbidden documents, with some tragically sent to Auschwitz for their activities.

again transporting their equipment in their baskets before speeding away from the scene. Somehow their innocent appearance continued to protect them, even when the resistance tasked them with carrying out assassinations of Nazis and their Dutch collaborators. After receiving training in how to fire a gun, they would shoot their targets as they cycled past, Truus pedalling while Freddie took aim. Truus would do her share, too, seducing a Nazi officer in a bar, then suggesting a romantic walk in nearby woods – where she shot him dead.

The sisters also helped transport Jewish children to designated safe houses, carrying them on the back of their bicycles. Often they would dress in Red Cross uniforms, taking advantage of the greater freedom of movement nurses were allowed. (In occupied France, nurse Friedel Bohny-Reiter used her bike in much the same way, transporting sick Jewish babies from a prison camp to a hospital where they could receive treatment.) On one occasion the Oversteegens put on German military uniform to remove a Jewish child from a Dutch camp. Their missions weren't always successful: in 1944, Truus happened to cycle past a group of German soldiers at the moment a British plane opened fire on them, and the Jewish child seated on the back of her bike was hit by a bullet and killed. She had to continue cycling with the child until she could safely bury him at a farm.

Somehow, they managed to keep their bicycles operational. No small feat when there were no inner tubes – or other cycle parts – available for much of the war. Dutch cyclists had to resort to using items like garden hoses in lieu of tyres, or simply riding on the metal rims.

Remarkably, the two sisters survived the war, evading capture even though the Nazis placed them on their most-wanted list and offered a large reward. Their comrade in the resistance, Hannie Schaft, was not so fortunate. The roots of her famous red hair, which she had dyed black to disguise it, betrayed her identity and resulted in her capture. She was executed a few weeks before the liberation.

Freddie and Truus were awarded the Mobilisation War Cross in 2014 for their work saving lives and helping defeat the enemy.

'A Bicycle of My Own'

Meanwhile, in France, another teenage resistance fighter had taken up arms against the Nazi occupation. Eighteen-year-old Simone Segouin was from a village near Chartres, 90 km south-west of Paris. In 1944 she joined the Francs-Tireurs et Partisans, a communist resistance organisation, and was given the nomme de guerre, and all-important false identity papers, of Nicole Minet. Her first task for the group was to steal a bicycle belonging to a German military administrator – perhaps one that had been stolen from the Netherlands. After disguising it with a new paint job, it became her reconnaissance vehicle, enabling her to work as a courier for the group and conduct stakeouts. In August, Simone was part of the successful operation to capture twenty-five soldiers and liberate Chartres. She was spotted during the celebrations that followed by the war photographer Robert Capa, who took a series of iconic photographs of Simone with her Schmeisser MP-40 gun that were published in *Life* magazine the following month.

A few days after their success in Chartres, Simone went on to assist in the liberation of Paris, the city where another French woman with the same first name, the writer and philosopher Simone de Beauvoir, had been riding a stolen, repainted bicycle throughout the war as part of her own personal resistance against the Nazi occupation. She wasn't involved in any combat, but her bicycle was her personal 'freedom machine', when liberation seemed an impossibility.

Before the Nazis took control of Paris in June 1940, Simone de Beauvoir had never ridden a bicycle as her mother had deemed it unseemly for someone of her class. By the end of the war, it had become a lifeline. Simone had initially fled the city ahead of the imminent invasion as part of the great exodus of Parisians on 10 June, but had returned by the end of the month, opting to try to live a life as close as was possible to her pre-war existence of teaching, writing and socialising with the other artists and intellectuals who stayed on in the capital. Her close friend – possibly sometime lover – Natalie Sorokine gifted her a bicycle not long after her return. Natalie had become a bicycle thief to survive the privations of wartime, the money she made from her larceny enabling her to buy food – when available – on the black market.

Bicycles were valuable in occupied Paris. All the cars had been requisitioned by the Nazis and the public transport system was drastically reduced, so Parisians had no other means of transport. For those who couldn't cycle, there were 'vélo-taxis': makeshift rickshaws, with bicycles towing passengers in covered boxes on wheels. Natalie used the artist Alberto Giacometti's courtyard to repaint her purloined wheels before she sold them on and she taught Simone how to ride on one of them.

Natalie was either a good teacher or her pupil a fast learner; Simone wrote in her diary that by the end of the first lesson she could balance, mount by herself and turn corners. By her third lesson, she is boasting of taking 'real rides' to parks around Paris – though not completely without incident: 'Once I ran into a dog, and another time into two good ladies – who were very indignant about it – but for the most part it was a glorious performance.'

During this period of struggling to adapt to the grim

realities of life under occupation – and longing for the return of her lover and 'soul-partner' Jean-Paul Sartre, who had been drafted into the army before becoming a prisoner of war – Simone's accounts of her bicycling adventures in her diaries and letters sing with excitement. She writes to Jean-Paul to tell him that exploring Paris on her bicycle is 'absolutely delightful', just as reading Hegel in the library has a soothing effect at this fraught time. By August she is covering more and more miles alongside Natalie, taking in the forests and chateaux beyond the city, even going as far as Normandy: 'I pedalled on, and the sheer physical exertion kept me occupied.'

Relations between the two women were not always as blissful as their rides; Nathalie's desire to 'court scandal' wherever they went – indulging in stunts such as washing her hands in a holy font – tested Simone's customary indifference to public opinion. But the desire to ride was seemingly insatiable: 'I only wanted to eat up the kilometres on my bicycle. It's a new joy in life that I've discovered and, instead of wishing for a car, my desires will henceforth be limited to a bicycle of my own.' Thanks to Natalie's bicycle thievery, that 'bicycle of my own' was soon a reality, and Simone had no qualms about accepting it.

As the woman who would go on to write the feminist classic *The Second Sex,* in which she described femininity as a social construct, it's unsurprising that Simone so enthusiastically rebelled against the bourgeois and patriarchal childhood which had dictated that 'good' girls don't cycle. She described her cycling self as a 'lusty wench' – perhaps poking fun at the conservative beliefs of her mother's generation, who frowned on bikes as the first step on a slippery slope leading to promiscuity, though she could have meant she felt healthy and vigorous. For someone who would write about how women are not free, it's understandable she delighted in the sensations of weightlessness, physical freedom and independence as she spun through the streets of Paris. Cycling was also a personal resistance against, and temporary escape from, an oppressive occupying regime that sought to limit freedoms wherever it could.

This is not to say that the rest of her wartime experience was unendurable. Simone de Beauvoir had a much easier time of it than the likes of Truus and Freddie. Most days were spent writing at her favourite table at Café de Flore; the novels she wrote during that period made her an international literary star. She was also free to teach at the lycée and study philosophy in the library. In the evenings she would dance and drink at parties with other left-wing luminaries such as Picasso and Dora Maar, Georges Bataille and Jean Cocteau. She would watch films at the cinema, attend plays and even go on ski trips – pleasurable activities denied to most Parisians, offering a temporary escape and a means of staying sane amid wartime strictures.

Not that she was immune to the horrors of wartime Paris. Her diaries and letters are full of the terrible conditions she and her fellow Parisians had to endure, which worsened as the war progressed: near-starvation, power cuts, rat-infested accommodation, freezing temperatures, as well as the constant threat of violence and the loss of friends whose lives were cut short by war. Cycling was her escape from the horror, particularly when pedalling outside the occupied zone.

I wonder how much the experience shaped her thinking and writing. There is a long history of writers and artists who connect the activity of walking with creativity – such as Henry David Thoreau, who stated that 'the moment my legs begin to move, my thoughts begin to flow'. Scientific research into the benefits of walking supports this: a study conducted at Stanford University found that students who went for a walk came up with far more original ideas than those who stayed seated at a desk.* Some argue that cycling doesn't have the same effect because it's too fast and too physical to allow for creative thought. I disagree. I find that if I'm in the process of dealing with a knotty problem and take a break to go for a ride, new and better solutions arise without my actively looking for them. Though I'm not consciously thinking about work, ideas and connections often pop into my head that make me see things from a different angle. I sometimes have to pull up at the side of the road to note these thoughts down before I forget them. It's as if the distance from my desk allows a more expansive way of thinking; and there is something about the repetitive motion of legs turning pedals, combined with being outdoors, that enables my thoughts to percolate and order themselves – though being denied the ability to scroll dementedly through social media posts on my smartphone also helps. As Virginia Woolf said of her walks on the South Downs, 'I like to have space to spread my mind out in.' When I'm in a smooth rhythm on a quiet road, that's exactly how I feel.

The war years were an intellectually productive time for Simone, and coincidentally the time when she was doing the most cycling. I like to think the latter contributed to the former. Perhaps it was how she got to grips with Hegel's notoriously opaque *Phenomenology of the Mind*, which she started studying in 1940, around the time she started cycling. Initially she said she could 'scarcely make head nor tail of it', but after many hours in the library, and hundreds

* Four experiments carried out at Stanford in 2014 by Dr Marily Oppezzo and Professor Daniel Schwartz showed that a person's ability to produce creative ideas increased by up to 60 per cent during or just after walking. The participants didn't have to walk outside to perform better; walking on a treadmill produced the same results.

of miles covered on her bicycle, she understood 'rather better'.

In September 1940 Simone escaped to Brittany for a cycling holiday with her friend Bianca. They explored pine forests and sand dunes, gorging on lobster and pancakes. She was elated at not meeting any Germans during their two-week trip, which made them temporarily forget their wartime existence. This pedal-powered escape from life under occupation was to become a regular fixture for Simone for the rest of the war, a 'delicious form of freedom'.

The following August she took another cycling holiday, this time with Jean-Paul. This vacation was more political in its intention. Together with a number of their Parisian intellectual friends, the two had recently formed what would turn out to be a relatively short-lived and ineffectual resistance group, 'Socialism and Liberty'. They spent more time debating and discussing philosophy than engaging in active resistance work, which left members unclear about their purpose and strategies. Nor were they as clandestine as they could have been, with Natalie throwing leaflets indiscriminately from her bicycle basket as she cycled through Paris, and another member leaving a suitcase on the Métro which held sensitive documents that identified the group.

Despite the chaotic approach, Jean-Paul hoped to recruit more friends to the cause. Since the friends he had in mind were living in the so-called 'Free Zone' of the South of France under the collaborationist Vichy government, this was not a straightforward affair. To avoid attracting attention, they sent their bicycles and tents ahead before taking a train south-east out of Paris to Montceau-les-Mines in Burgundy, on the border between the occupied and free zones. There they paid a woman who worked as a *passeur* to help them across to the other side. The crossing had to be done under cover of darkness, with Simone, Jean-Paul and the *passeur* creeping through moonlit fields and woods. Once safely over, they stopped at the first inn and found it full of clandestine border crossers like themselves. This was to be the first of several covert crossings into Vichy France that the couple would take over the next few years. And each trip was an act of defiance against the German authorities that made Simone feel she had regained a little of her liberty.

Reunited with the bicycles in Roanne on the River Loire, they set out with their luggage strapped to their frames, passing through vineyards and olive groves, with views of the sparkling Mediterranean Sea to the south. When Jean-Paul's already heavily patched tyre got a puncture not long into the journey, neither of them knew how to fix it. They were saved by a passing mechanic who showed Simone how it was done; soon she became adept at fixing their worn tyres.

While Jean-Paul would often sprint ahead on the hills, she was critical of his erratic approach to cycling, accusing him of 'pedalling so indolently' on the flat, his mind wandering, that he would frequently career into a ditch at the side of the road. He would claim he was too busy thinking. Both shared a love of whizzing downhill at speed. They pedalled hundreds of miles – many mountainous – on this first trip, along the Rhône, through the forested mountains of the Cévennes and Ardèche, and down into sun-drenched Provence, 'intoxicated by the swift transformation of the landscape' compared to walking. Each evening, after a long day in the saddle, they pitched their tent, Simone feeling carefree and happy in a way that she hadn't felt since the start of the war.

Their resistance work was less rewarding. None of the friends they visited were willing to sign up to their group. The writer Colette Audry, already a member of a local resistance group in Grenoble, suggested wisely that they should 'leave espionage to those who know how to do it'. On the return journey north, passing over the steep climbs of the Maritime Alps to stay with Colette, Simone had an accident so disastrous it might have deterred a less devoted cyclist from getting into the saddle again.

Their route over the Alps to Grenoble, which included the 2,250-metre-high Col d'Allos, a Tour de France staple, would be a challenge to most cyclists, even with the advantages of today's lightweight bikes. Simone and Jean-Paul had much heavier bicycles, not to mention their luggage, and far fewer gears. The ascent wasn't the problem for Simone – it was the descent. After stopping for some lunch and a few glasses of wine, they began an exhilarating freewheel down towards Grenoble. However, the alcohol had gone to Simone's head and on encountering two cyclists coming the other way, she swerved in the wrong direction; thanks to her deficient brakes, she then found herself skidding on gravel and heading towards the precipice. When she eventually came to, she discovered that she had somehow managed to avoid flying over the edge, but she felt more than a little bruised and shaken. Once the effects of her concussion had worn off, she insisted they take a train for the rest of the way down. When Simone was finally able to survey the damage in a mirror, she could see why Colette had not recognised her when they had arrived: 'I had lost a tooth, one of my eyes was closed, my face had swollen up to twice its normal size, and the skin was all scraped raw. I couldn't get so much as a grape between my lips.' It also explained why her fellow train passengers had appeared so startled. What's unclear is why Jean-Paul hadn't mentioned any of this to her. The missing tooth made a 'miraculous' reappearance a few weeks later, back in Paris, when it emerged from a boil she squeezed on her chin.

Such a terrifying brush with mortality, and by her own

admission looking 'hideous', wasn't enough to put her off getting back in the saddle the next day to complete the last few hundred miles before re-crossing the border. She describes the final days of their journey in tones as rapturous as those before her accident, particularly the view of the Burgundy vineyards in their autumn colours. The sight of the sun breaking through the autumn mists filled her with 'a childish sense of well-being'. Even running out of money, and therefore food, couldn't dampen her enthusiasm. The traumatic experience had failed to diminish her appetite for touring by bike; the annual trip to the South of France became a treasured and longed-for wartime break for the writer.

After the return crossing over the border in the company of twenty other cyclists led by another *passeur*, the couple returned to Paris. The city had grown more tense and repressive in their absence. The Germans had violently crushed a series of communist uprisings, and those responsible had been sent to concentration camps. Simone felt as if she'd been 'reduced to a condition of total impotence'; she no longer allowed herself to dream that defeat of Hitler's Reich might be possible. It would have been a stark contrast to those sunny days of relatively carefree pedal-powered exhilaration. Understandably, by the following summer they were itching to get back to those long days in the saddle, as far away from German soldiers as was possible in the middle of wartime. They were also keen to celebrate the news that a French publisher, Gallimard, wanted to publish the novel Simone had been working on.

This time their starting point was the Basque region of the Pyrenees, and they crossed the border into the free zone at a point that was renowned for being more permeable. The inn on the other side was heaving, this time largely with Jews who were hoping to escape into Spain, out of necessity rather than choice. Like the Alps, the Pyrenees aren't without their challenges for the cyclist. Simone admitted that this trip, from the mountains of the eastern Pyrenees all the way to Marseille (around 650 km if you are going a direct route, and they weren't), and then part of the way back again, was 'pretty tiring'. Even more so if you are half-starved. She recounts in her diaries that lunch most days consisted of no more than fruit and tomatoes, with dinner usually a clear soup and unappetising vegetables. Less than ideal fuel for powering over mountains and cols. Most cyclists today wouldn't dream of attempting even part of a journey like this without saddlebags stuffed with energy gels and protein bars, and the assurance of a large meal at the end of each day.

En route to Marseille they pedalled through the departments of Ariège and neighbouring Aude, a region I've lived in. Simone and Jean-Paul had fallen in love with the place on the eve of war; in the walled city of Carcassonne – already filling with French troops – they had wandered the medieval streets and drunk wine under arbours. They delayed their return to Paris, partly to put off what lay ahead but also to explore the Cathar castles and beautiful villages nestled in the foothills of the Pyrenees, all the while trying to reassure each other that this bucolic region would remain untouched by the war. They promised themselves that they would return after the war, and throughout the dark times ahead they clung to the hope it would be there waiting for them when the occupation was over.

I've cycled through those same quiet towns and villages, which I doubt have changed much since they were there. I can imagine them, pulled up at the side of the road, grabbing handfuls of grapes from the vineyards which Simone says 'saved us from literally starving'; bunking up in hay barns for the night; or Simone bent over by the roadside, fixing yet another puncture in their well-worn inner tubes. Despite their hunger, which she describes as becoming, understandably, an 'obsession', there was no question of cutting the ride short. So single-minded was she about continuing the journey that Jean-Paul raised no objections, which she put down to not wanting to 'deprive me of my pleasure'.

The situation got properly sticky when they ran out of money a few days before re-crossing the border and weren't able to purchase the meagre rations they had been surviving on until this point. When they finally reached the house of a friend, emaciated and exhausted, Jean-Paul fainted after eating three spoonfuls of soup and was confined to bed for three days. Simone had lost 16 lb over the course of the trip. So they stayed on for another month to recover their strength.

The winter of 1942–43 was particularly bleak: when they returned from their rehabilitation in the country, they discovered that all their possessions had been thrown away by the hotel where they had been staying. With fuel for heating scarce, the temperature dropped to a record low, and Simone was left with no choice but to live in the most unimaginably squalid hotel. Food was thin on the ground, and often infested with maggots and weevils. Despite this, she writes that she could endure any austerity apart from having to give up her travels. The following summer, after being suspended from her job teaching at the lycée for her allegedly inappropriate relationship with Natalie Sorokine, she was off again with her tent and bicycle, this time alone.

In *The Second Sex*, de Beauvoir writes of T. E. Lawrence's tour through France by bicycle as a teenager, and how a young girl wouldn't have been allowed to go on such an adventure. She describes his trip as one defined by the 'headiness of freedom and discovery', one in which he 'learns to look at the entire world as his fief'.* In 1943, at the age of thirty-five, she was determined to experience the feeling for herself. De Beauvoir returned to Roanne, where she and Jean-Paul had begun their first summer cycling adventure. Each day she was on the road by 6 a.m., making her way over mountains, plagued as ever by a constantly failing inner tube. Food was a lot easier to come by on this trip, and her letters and diary are crammed with details of the delicious, non-rationed food she consumes.

Much as she enjoyed this solo adventure, she missed Jean-Paul, who had promised to join her en route. In a letter to him she writes that the thought of once more seeing his 'back on the road in front' makes her heart 'burst with joy'. Three weeks later, and several hundred miles from her start, they are reunited in Uzerche. Descriptions of them seeking cover from thunderstorms in their matching yellow rain capes, with Jean-Paul wiping water off his spectacles, are particularly enjoyable. In one torrential downpour the pages of his manuscript for *The Reprieve* escape from his bicycle bag, floating off in muddy puddles, ink running, before they are recaptured. For the most part the trip is sunny and filled with good food and scenery, a stark contrast to the previous winter.

Their return to Paris was a lot less painful than the last time. The autumn of 1943 had seen the publication of her novel, *She Came to Stay*, which was a critical and commercial success, but being a celebrated novelist hadn't been enough to put food on the table in wartime. In early 1944, when the Allies were carrying out sustained bombardments on occupied Paris, food in the city was scarcer than ever. Simone often resorted to cycling around the countryside to forage and barter for provisions. This was not without risks, even

---

* In 1908, the nineteen-year-old student Thomas Edward Lawrence cycled around 2,000 miles through France with the objective of visiting as many important medieval sites as he could manage.

with much of the area surrounding Paris now out of Nazi control. She frequently heard explosions as she cycled along the rural roads, and in one instance, on hearing the air-raid siren as she passed through the bombed-out remains of Creil, north of Paris, she was so spooked that she 'pedalled across the railway bridge at breakneck speed: the silence and solitude of the place was terrifying'. The Normandy landings in June 1944 indicated that the German occupation was finally coming to an end and by 25 August the Germans had surrendered Paris, but not without a bloody fight in which random civilians, including housewives doing their shopping, were shot dead in the streets. Finally, Simone and her fellow Parisians had their beloved city back.

The following summer, a few months after VE day, Simone was setting off on a new bicycle given to her by Jean-Paul 'on a little journey all alone', this time in the direction of the Cévennes hills, full of the same 'headiness of freedom and discovery' as Lawrence before her and with the horrors of war ebbing away. This was also the year in which women in France were given the right to vote, over twenty-five years after the UK and US.

I don't know if Simone did much cycling after this; I have found no mention of it, and it was around this time that her literary stardom took her to the US on a long lecture tour. What I do know is that during some very dark times, when freedom often felt like a distant memory, it was a way for her to experience a sense of release and liberation, whether it was during the hundreds of miles she cycled across the country or on her brief rides around Paris between the library or lycée and her table at her favourite café. As her legs turned the pedals it may have helped spark ideas which contributed to her writings on feminism and existentialism, which have made her one of the greatest thinkers of the twentieth century.

Part III

THE OPEN ROAD

CHAPTER 7

The Great Escape

Wanderlust

'What would become of us, if we walked only in a garden or a mall?' asked the outdoor enthusiast and writer Thoreau in his 1862 essay, 'Walking'. Decades later, inspired by the same sentiment – and the nineteenth-century boom in travel and tourism that swept the affluent West – cyclists began using their bikes to explore far-flung destinations.

Cycling holidays abroad became so popular that the travel company Thomas Cook started offering bike tours, though more intrepid cyclists still preferred to go it alone. In the 1890s, the *Cyclists' Touring Club Gazette* was packed with illustrated accounts of members' travels at home and abroad. As membership of the club quadrupled in the UK, many others were inspired to follow suit.

The editor of the ladies' page of the *Gazette*, Lillias Campbell Davidson, knew from personal experience that women who learned to ride would 'thirst for longer flights; for the pleasure of going on and on, and never turning back'. She encouraged her readers to sample the joys of 'an explorer venturing for the first time into a new country and discovering a world for herself'. Those who could spare the time and money followed her advice and spent weeks or even months pedalling through landscapes and countries hitherto unknown to them except through books and paintings. Some individuals blazed a trail as the first woman to cycle through a region, and one undertook a solo round-the-world pedal in 1894. The majority, however, didn't feel they needed to venture quite so far to feel like adventurers.

Today the relative cheapness and availability of mass and private transport has made the world more accessible, but a long journey by bike remains an adventure. On a bicycle it's possible to explore new terrain in a manner that can't be replicated in a vehicle. While cycling around one's city is often about getting from A to B by the most efficient and safest route, on a longer trip it is all about the journey.

Long cycle trips across continents or around the world have become a popular antidote to the pressures of our technology-driven modern lives. Stripping things down to the basics – just turning the pedals, seeing how far and where the road will take you – is a great way to feel more alive and in the moment. While some are simply looking for escape or hoping to find themselves, others crave the challenge of setting a record or testing their limits.

Juliana Buhring was the first woman to hold the record for fastest circumnavigation of the world by bike. You might think she wouldn't have had much time to take things in, but her account of that record-breaking run described the experience as being '*inside* the movie, an essential part of it. Completely reliant on your environment, you observe and absorb every sensation around you.'

When I travel by bike, I might not take in absolutely everything, but I do need to be alert and responsive in ways I'm not required to be on public transport, which gives me a heightened awareness of my surroundings. Even on routes I know well, like the one I sometimes take from London to see my family in Somerset, through the quiet lanes of Berkshire and Wiltshire, where I know every turn and anticipate the landmarks along the way, including the Bronze Age white horse carved into a hill, there is always something new to observe. Sometimes it's just about taking in the changing seasons: bluebells spiking the woodlands in April, hawthorn blossom and cowslips bursting from the hedgerows in May. These are things I would miss if – were I able to drive – I had taken the M4 motorway instead. I am moving through the landscape in a way that feels more intimate and responsive, even if it sometimes means having to endure the worst that the weather throws at me or mechanical faults. Though if the weather does happen to be foul then a hot bath, enormous meal or reviving drink at the end is more delicious and earned than it would have been otherwise.

Had I lived in France in the 1890s and wanted to join the French equivalent of the Cyclists' Touring Club, I would have needed my husband's permission. Though this wasn't a requirement in the UK, women seldom did anything unchaperoned; any that might be tempted would be warned of the dangers lurking around every corner. One Victorian writer and cyclist, Mrs Harcourt Williamson, felt that women cycling alone were in 'some considerable peril', particularly from 'tramps' – the bogeyman of the day – who might be 'desperate with hunger or naturally vicious'. Seeking strength in numbers, some hired a cyclist chaperone. These female cycling guides handled all aspects of the trip from route-planning to accommodation, as well as basic mechanics, leaving their charges free to take in the picturesque scenery and historic sites. The more intrepid joined the Lady Cyclists' Association to connect with other enthusiasts to join them on cycling adventures. The LCA handbook listed accommodation en route where women who arrived a-wheel would be welcomed.

A handbook might have come in handy for an American cyclist called Martha who set out with four girlfriends in 1892 for a touring holiday in Germany. When they disembarked in Hamburg they were met by incredulous customs officers who took some persuading that they were really the owners of the bicycles that had emerged from the ship's hold. After a few days reassembling their steel steeds in their hotel, they started out on the road to Leipzig, carrying their luggage in canvas rolls attached to their handlebars. Their packing was light – a change of underwear, combs, cosmetics, German-English dictionary and map. They must have read Maria Ward's *Bicycling for Ladies*, since they were unflustered mending punctures and broken chains.

Martha described how they became 'the observed of all observers' when 'business men, errand boys, bakers, butchers, fruit women and all sizes of children gazed at us with open-eyed, and, in many cases, often open-mouthed, astonishment'. Another member of the party wondered whether 'they think I am going to fly over their heads', but it turned out that the onlookers weren't planning a witch-hunt and eventually the crowd parted to let the women on their way.

During their journey they did not see a single other woman riding a bicycle. When they told one innkeeper that they were American, 'all seemed explained – Americans dare anything'. The Germans they met were welcoming, providing them with shelter from the rain, offering them beds for the night, and plying them with food and drink. The group made the most of the country's beer halls and inns, refuelling with wine and wurst before pedalling on to Leipzig.

Not all women felt they needed to travel with companions. Lillias Campbell Davidson in her 1896 *Handbook for Lady Cyclists* was confident that in the UK and much of Europe it was 'quite safe for a lady to ride alone without any fear of molestation or annoyance', a statement that many would have found difficult to believe, having been told the exact opposite for so long. Lillias had been encouraging women to travel solo, to take trains and even scale mountains, since she published *Hints to Lady Travellers* in 1889, a book aimed at women whose lives up to that point had been 'unnaturally cramped and contracted within doors'. Though she admitted that, earlier in the decade, women pioneers of cycling such as herself had encountered 'annoyance, unpleasant comment, and rudeness' when they travelled the country by bicycle, things had improved. By the mid 1890s, women solo tourers would 'probably receive nothing but kindness and courtesy from one end of their journey to the other . . . even if they are attired in rational dress'. Though she too warned that tramps on the big roads into cities might cause problems.

For Lillias, the main danger for women cyclists in rural areas was not people but animals; even hens were 'a great affliction to the lady cyclist'. To combat the problem of dogs running after cyclists, she recommended her readers pack a long whip to scare them off. As someone who is frequently chased by dogs when cycling through the countryside, and once a flock of angry geese, I can understand why she felt this was such a pressing issue. But since I can usually outpace a dog or goose, I haven't resorted to carrying a whip.

Where there was a possibility of encounters with more fearsome animals like bears and wolves, some cycle tourers armed themselves with deadlier weapons. In 1897 Margaret Valentine Le Long packed a borrowed pistol for her solo cycle from Chicago to San Francisco. An unwilling firearms user, she packed it in her tool bag to make it hard to get at.

Margaret's friends and family had tried to dissuade her from attempting such a journey, and hoped to scare her out of it with 'prophecies of broken limbs, starvation, death from thirst, abduction by cowboys and scalping by Indians'. Her account of her journey, published in *Outing* magazine, tells how, undeterred, she set off westward from Chicago in May. After battling the strong winds of Midwestern Illinois and Iowa, she passed through the mountains of Colorado and Wyoming and the deserts of Nevada and Utah, visiting places with such evocative names as Medicine Bow Crossing, Rattlesnake Pass, Devil's Gate and Dirty Woman's Ranch, as well as the eerie ghost towns left behind by emigrant settlers. She begged food and a bed for the night at remote farms and sometimes had to drag her bicycle over rocks and through rivers. In the desert she avoided dehydration by drinking from barrels of water buried by railway workers.

Elsewhere she dined on trout with fisherman, and antelope steak with hunters. She also went the wrong way – a lot.

The gun did get some use when a herd of cattle gathered on the path in front of her, pawing the ground and bellowing, before putting their heads down and charging. She fired five shots with her eyes shut. She opened them to discover that, thankfully, they had turned heel and dispersed.

While she may have had a uniquely adventurous journey, Margaret was less open-minded when it came to her clothes, opting for a slightly shortened skirt instead of bloomers. She credited this outfit with eliciting courtesy and kindness from those she met along the way. Though she admits that by the time she reached San Francisco she was in a somewhat dishevelled state and looked not unlike the tramps of whom she was so fearful.

Lillias would have sympathised; she was only too aware of the emphasis and expectations placed on women's appearance. Given the lack of space in a handlebar bag for anything beyond toiletries and a few essentials, she recommended that they post spare clothes ahead of them. She described how one female traveller of her acquaintance 'has two spare frocks and dispatches them alternately, so that every evening, when she halts at a new place, she is able to shed her riding costume'. Essential items included a needle and thread – including glove silk – and a supply of buttons, hooks and eyes for any repairs.

Thankfully, we no longer need to post long dresses around the country in order to look 'civilised'. Most women opt for modern cycling wear, which is lightweight and low-maintenance. I find there is a certain satisfaction in carrying everything I need with me, packing only the essentials into my bike bags. It's a salutary exercise in the benefits of minimalism – useful for someone whose wardrobe is probably more expansive than it should be and whose standard approach to packing a suitcase is to always fill it to bursting. Although sometimes I do wish I had room for just one more pair of shoes.

The Grand Bicycle Tour

Elizabeth Robins Pennell, the American biographer and art critic, didn't bother to send spare dresses ahead of her during long cycle tours in the 1880s and '90s. Instead she opted for an adjustable skirt, hooking it up when she rode and letting it down again when she dismounted, to avoid 'being stared at as a "Freak" escaped from the sideshow'. In fact, it was her husband's cycling outfit of stockings and knee-length breeches that attracted attention wherever they went.

Elizabeth considered cycle tours a liberating travel experience, particularly for women: 'hers is all the joy of motion, not to be underestimated, and of long days in the open air; all the joy of adventure and change. Hers is the delightful sense of independence and power, the charm of seeing the country in the only way in which it can be seen; instead of being carried at lightning speed from one town to another.' Liberated from a stifling life indoors, the female cycle tourer experiences 'a perfect state of physical well-being'.

Very much a 'New Woman', this former convent schoolgirl had no desire to play homemaker. Despite declaring herself unable even to boil an egg, she went on to become a celebrated food writer. Her books about her travels were illustrated with charming pen-and-ink drawings by her husband, the artist Joseph Pennell. The two of them had bid adieu to the US as soon as they were married, preferring to live in Europe. For the next three decades they divided their time between France and London, travelling whenever and wherever they could.

A Canterbury Pilgrimage, an account of the Pennells' first bicycle tour, was published in 1885. Unlike Chaucer's travellers, who walked the ancient pilgrim route from London to Canterbury Cathedral, the Pennells made the journey on a tandem tricycle. The couple had acquired their first tricycle in Philadelphia in the 1870s, but this was the longest and most arduous trip they'd undertaken to date. Elizabeth was intoxicated by wanderlust, and the bicycle was the perfect mode of transport to satisfy it: 'The world is our great book of beauty and romance, and on your cycle you can gradually master it, chapter by chapter, volume by volume.' She would later dedicate one of her travelogues to the Alpine Club, hoping to convince its mountaineer members that cycling was a superior way to see the world.

The Pennells' second tandem tricycle trip was also inspired by literature. This time they followed the route taken by the author Laurence Sterne in the 1770s (in his case, by horse and carriage) and fictionalised in his final novel, *A Sentimental Journey through France and Italy*. Like Sterne's book, their account ends before they reach Italy.

In the tradition of the Grand Tours of the seventeenth and eighteenth centuries, they planned their routes with a view to taking in important architectural sights and works of art along the way. The original Grand Tours were a far cry from a humble tricycle made for two: sons, and occasionally daughters, of the aristocracy would spend months or even years completing their education in classical art by seeing the exulted emblems of European culture in situ. Travel in those days was by private carriage or public stagecoach, over poor roads. Distances that might be covered in a ten-minute car journey today would have been much more arduous and time-consuming when relying on horsepower. Back then, the average person travelled no more than fifteen miles from their home – in their lifetime.

The arrival of mass transport in the nineteenth century, with the railways and passenger steamships, as well as smoother roads, made foreign travel possible for the wealthy middle classes. (For the working classes, foreign travel remained out of reach; with no spare income or paid holiday, they had to make do with the occasional excursion on a Sunday or Bank Holiday.) Like Elizabeth, the new breed of well-to-do travellers were clamouring to see sights that previously they could only have read and dreamed about. Publishers began producing guidebooks with suggested routes and must-see sights along the way.

Freelance and independently wealthy, the Pennells were able to spend months at a time pedalling around Europe. Their privileged backgrounds sometimes show through in Elizabeth's travelogues when destinations don't live up to expectations or their sense of entitlement leads to criticism of the locals. It didn't help that they felt they were treated as lower-class citizens on account of their chosen form of transport. In one hotel they were given a bowl of water in their room to wash with, whereas a carriage party at the same venue were allocated a private dressing room. Their dinner that evening was an omelette in the kitchen while the others feasted in the dining room.

There's a bit of national stereotyping too, as they continually suspect the French of overcharging them. They found the curiosity their tricycle generated, with crowds gathering wherever they went, more of an irritation than a compliment. It's notable that they show far less interest in the people they encounter during their *Sentimental Journey through France and Italy* than Laurence Sterne had done in his account.

A few years ago, I spent a week cycling along part of the route they took on their way to Italy – the section following the Seine from Paris, through the forests of Sénart and

Fontainebleau and down through the Loire Valley towards Lyon. Just as Elizabeth and Joseph followed the carriage tracks of Sterne, I was following their 130-year-old tricycle grooves. Unlike them, I had to share the way with motor traffic, though thankfully the road surfaces had improved. In fact a lot of my journey was on bike paths that followed the same rivers and canals the Pennells had.

The pace of our journeys was different, though. Thanks to the advantages of twenty-first-century bike design, and not being weighed down by Victorian skirts, I covered in a single day distances that had taken them several days.

We did, however, both have issues with our luggage. When the bag the Pennells had strapped to their tricycle came apart, the only option was to fix it on a blacksmith's forge. When a bolt snapped on my partner's bag rack, I had to cycle to the nearest village to find the modern equivalent to make the repair. This turned out to be an old Peugeot garage where, after much confusion due to language difficulties – and it being a workshop for cars – I was eventually able to procure a replacement to get us on the road again.

Further along the route, Elizabeth exclaims over the beauty of Nemours, though in typically haughty fashion she was far less complimentary about its inhabitants: 'the less, I think, we say of them the better . . . the people were disagreeable, that was all'. She was scathing about local restaurants that inexplicably refused to serve them; given the notoriously strict restaurant hours in France, it's probable they just arrived too late. In contrast, when we went through the town, a stallholder refused to let us pay for our drinks after hearing how far we were cycling that day. Unlike theirs, our journey didn't end with Roman police arresting us for 'furious riding' and refusing to stop; the Pennells had to sell their tricycle to pay the fine.

By the early 1890s the Pennells had moved on from

tricycles to two-wheeled safety bicycles – a relief for Joseph, who had accused Elizabeth of not pulling her weight. Their first journey on their new wheels was to Hungary, which they would later publish as *To Gypsyland*. This time their purpose wasn't to take in the highlights of Western culture, but to go in search of the 'true Romany gypsy'. With their bicycles they were able to access all the 'remote, unknown, unpronounceable villages far from railways' and travel high up into the mountains of Transylvania, 'over the wild passes where we met no one but the shepherd with his black-faced sheep'. Despite their exhaustive search, they returned disappointed; their much-fetishised travelling gypsy proved elusive. The only gypsies they found had abandoned the nomadic life for towns and villages, taking work as farm labourers. Which led the Pennells to wonder, in their overly romanticised and unreflective way, whether they, pedalling free on their bicycles, were now the only ones truly 'free as the deer in the forest/ As the fish where the river flows/ Free as the bird in the air!'

Their next trip was to be even more energy-intensive: a five-week tour crossing nine Swiss Alpine peaks. Elizabeth thought she might have been the first woman to have done such a thing: 'I am told I made a record. I think I have, and one to be proud of. I went over nine passes – six in less than a week. I worked at times as hard as a dock labourer . . . any woman who rides – and knows how to ride . . . and who is not afraid of work, may learn what pleasure there is in the exploit.' Whether she did break a record I'm not able to verify, though, according to her account, she didn't see any other women cyclists when slogging up the various mountain passes.

The only women cyclists Elizabeth encountered were on a boat crossing Lake Como in Italy, and she was quick to judge that they were no match for her athleticism. The first she described as 'a big German frau in knickerbockers and many bangles', expressing doubt that the woman was capable of cycling at all. Elizabeth, who cycled in a skirt, seems to have made up her mind that the German woman had no substance as a cyclist purely on the basis of her appearance and 'swagger'. The other tourers were two Americans who told her, possibly to Elizabeth's relief, that they had put their bikes on a train up the passes. They weren't going to be challenging her record. Instead they flattered her ego when they said they recognised her from her previous book. While Elizabeth encountered numerous male cyclists, including Americans, she noted that none were English, something she found amusingly ironic since she thought they were always crowing about their athletic prowess.

She was certainly no shrinking violet about her own athleticism, boasting that on one day they ascended two passes before lunch, declaring that she was willing to die in the attempt rather than give up: 'People may object that I rode too fast. But I had not come out to play the enthusiast and record my emotions on postcards; I had come to ride over the Alps on a bicycle.' Personality and prejudices aside, her desire to 'immortalise the name and adventures of the first woman' to climb the Alps by bicycle – i.e. herself – is to be applauded. Adventuring, and publishing accounts of foreign travels, was a male occupation for the most part.

Elizabeth's achievement is all the more impressive considering the sort of bike she was riding. Her ladies' drop-frame bicycle weighed even more than Joseph's, and neither of them had gears to assist with the ascents. She had to push her bike up the steeper climbs, making for very long days on the endlessly zigzagging roads into the clouds. It's no wonder some of the other cyclists hired carriages to get their bikes up the mountains.

The descents were no less problematic, with a deficient

braking system in which a leather strap was used to pull a brake to the tyre (rather than the wheel rim, like many of today's bikes). Often they were forced to rely on back-pedalling. And Elizabeth did all this in her long skirts. She admits her temper was prone to fray due to the physical exertion, but nothing was going to deter her from achieving her goal. Snow and wind, icy precipices and hairpin bends – with wooden crosses marking the sites where previous travellers had perished – didn't put her off her pedal strokes, even if her heart was in her mouth on the downhill runs. On St Gotthard, a 2,100-metre peak they tackled in the worst weather, where Joseph admitted he was never so close to giving up, she refused a lift from a passing cart – 'I was doing this thing myself; I had not come to have it done for me.' So much for the old adage that women were the 'weaker sex'.

Though she disapproved of bicycle racing, Elizabeth wasn't keen on other cyclists passing her. To her ill-concealed delight, one Swiss cyclist fell off after overtaking her on a descent. When he called out for help, she cycled straight past him. Similarly, when they met a Parisian who was responsible for gifting the Statue of Liberty to the USA on behalf of the French, having spent over an hour talking to the man, they left him floundering in the mud after a fall without a backward glance.

Switzerland, thanks to steam trains and Thomas Cook's tours, was one of the most visited places in Europe at this time, with the moneyed middle class making a beeline to see the Alpine peaks celebrated in the writings of Jean-Jacques Rousseau and William Wordsworth. Elizabeth huffed at the way in which tourists had turned the place into the 'playground of Europe', as they 'swarmed' over its majestic mountains and formed a 'constant procession' on horseback, in carriages, on foot and bike.

Much to her annoyance, these tourists were constantly

ambling in their way. The Pennells did their best to avoid fraternising with the masses; Elizabeth said she would rather have a modest meal with the monks on the Simplon Pass than 'dine with the fifty of sixty tourists that you find any summer evening at the St Bernard, all eating and drinking like pigs'. In her opinion, German tourists were a 'public nuisance'. She didn't care much for the Swiss either, bemoaning the 'petty persecutions' of their customs officials and feeling exploited by their rapacious tourism industry.

While she may be a bit of a snob, she's often witty and acerbic. I dread to think what she'd have made of our 'selfie culture', having read her observation that tour groups who had once 'wept over the sublimities of nature which they could not see for their tears', now barely glanced at the landscape, preferring to 'let their feelings loose upon illustrated postcards'.

This would be Elizabeth's last cycling travelogue. Perhaps she'd achieved the goal she'd set herself, or perhaps her publisher felt that a decline in the craze for cycle touring meant they were no longer commercially viable in the early twentieth century. I do know that the Pennells continued to enjoy cycling, even if they weren't writing about it.

Off the Beaten Track

While most nineteenth-century tourists flocked to European destinations, some intrepid travellers chose to go further afield. And some of those travellers were society women, mostly from the UK and America, with the resources to spend months or even years touring Africa, Asia and the Middle East. Some were driven by a desire for adventure, or an urge to show what women were capable of. Others wanted to contribute to our understanding of the world, studying the archaeology, social customs or the flora and fauna of the places they visited, though some of them were more colonial in their approach than others.

Isabella Lucy Bird, the British naturalist, photographer and writer, was one such intrepid explorer. Despite frequent ill health, she travelled unchaperoned to the USA, Hawaii and Australia, before moving on to Asia, the Middle East and North Africa. She practised medicine as a missionary, refused to ride side-saddle and was the first woman member of the Royal Geographical Society in 1892. She was also very put out when *The Times* wrongly claimed she wore trousers during her 800-mile journey across Colorado's Rockies in 1873.

Mary Kingsley, the British explorer and ethnographer, travelled unaccompanied to Africa, living with locals to gain an insight into how to survive in the remote and wild places she would then explore. She collected wildlife specimens and wrote about the practices of the local tribes in the many books she published. Mary did not consider herself a 'New Woman', deeming the question of women's suffrage of minor importance. She made her way through the jungle in traditional nineteenth-century English attire of long dress, hat and umbrella.

By contrast, the Swiss traveller Isabelle Eberhardt adopted the clothing of a male Berber in order to move around more freely and avoid unwanted attention in 1890s Islamic Algeria.

Fanny Bullock Workman was another who wanted to make history as an adventurer, to be acknowledged for her important discoveries, and to contribute to the growing literature about less-travelled parts of the globe.

Born into one of the richest families in Massachusetts in 1859, she was educated at an elite US school before attending finishing schools in Europe. The stories she penned as a teen about girls running away to become mountaineers and explorers were a precursor to the life she would eventually lead. Playing the Victorian domestic goddess had never been her idea of a fulfilling life. By her twenties she was climbing the highest peaks of the north-eastern US, where she benefitted from the progressive attitude of American mountaineering clubs which, unlike their European counterparts, allowed women members. But this wasn't enough to satisfy her restless desire to explore.

Many women with similar ambitions lacked the money to achieve them, but Fanny and her husband, Dr William Hunter Workman, were both beneficiaries of substantial family inheritances. They could afford to devote their lives to travelling the globe, leaving their children in the care of governesses. In the process, they became world-famous for their exploits as mountaineers and cyclists. Eventually, like Isabella Bird before her, Fanny was welcomed into the hallowed and overwhelmingly male ranks of the Royal Geographical Society.

In his dedication to Fanny in one of their bicycle travelogues, William praised her 'courage, endurance and enthusiasm, often under circumstances of hardship and sometimes of danger' which 'have never failed'. Since she was the prime instigator, there is no question that she was his equal as an adventurer. Despite this, she never exchanged her long skirts in favour of something more suited to the wild places they visited and the arduous journeys they undertook.

The Workmans' enthusiasm for cycle touring began with the purchase of two Rover Safety bicycles. The couple, now living in Germany, used their bikes to explore the neighbouring countries of France, Italy and Switzerland before moving further off the beaten track. After their four-year-old son died of pneumonia, they left their daughter in the care of nursemaids and governesses and set off in 1895 on the first of their lengthy bicycle tours – a year they would spend almost entirely on the road, biking 2,800 miles across Spain and 1,500 miles around Algeria. They would later publish accounts of these trips, largely written by Fanny.

Like Elizabeth Robins Pennell before her, Fanny laid claim to a title – in her case, that of the first woman to cycle around Spain, and presumably Algeria. It was allegedly the most extensive bike tour anyone had undertaken in either country. (Fanny had already become the first woman to climb Mont Blanc by this point – competition wasn't something she ever shied away from.)

On their tour around Spain, their 'Don Quixotian days on the turnpike', they averaged forty-five miles a day, sometimes racking up as many as eighty miles in their quest to find a bed for the night. The terrain was mountainous, which would have been no mean feat on heavy Safety bikes weighed down with luggage. Despite the effort involved – and the almost daily punctures – they felt the bicycle was the ideal mode of transport, 'enabling us an entire independence of the usual hindrances of the traveller, to pass through the country at leisure, stopping where and when we pleased'. They weren't just trying to get from A to B, they wanted to experience the landscape and history, its people and culture, up close, even if they were inclined to be rather judgemental and less open to the locals than they perhaps realised.

Spain enabled them to live up to their image of themselves as adventurers, for they perceived it to be 'not so far advanced in civilisation' – a comment which speaks volumes about their waspish American privilege and the prevailing attitudes of the day. The tone of their accounts is quite different to the Pennells' – there are less capers and literary references and more detailed accounts of what they encounter, from archaeological sites to the customs of the locals. Evidence of Fanny wanting to be accepted into the ranks of serious travellers and geographers.

There was so much interest in their Spanish trip that the country's newspapers frequently reported on their progress, though the couple, for reasons unclear, held their cards close to their chests in the interviews they gave, despite claiming to speak the language well. Consequently, journalists resorted to speculation. The Spanish were intrigued by this American couple on their bicycles, and the Workmans felt they were observed 'with much the same awe-inspired expression as might have been called forth had we been inhabitants of one of the heavenly bodies', though it's possible they enjoyed this more than they were willing to let on.

While they did meet some Spaniards who cycled, the couple found the activity to be popular exclusively among 'the better classes' – rich people like themselves, in other words, since it's likely they were the only ones who could afford a bicycle. Members of local cycling clubs would ride out to meet them en route and escort them into their city. They would take them into their homes, refuse to let them pay for anything and ride with them for a time the following day. No wonder they were more willing to share details of their itinerary with these clubs than with the press.

Not everyone was pleased to see them. They complained of being chased out of villages by children who threw stones. And as they travelled further south it became apparent that bicycles were not a common sight on the roads. While the locals tended to be intrigued rather than hostile, the animals were terrified. Cart-pulling mules would go into meltdown at the sight of them, and on one occasion a mule bolted, throwing his passenger into the road. The furious rider picked himself up, grabbed a long-bladed farm tool and charged the Workmans. They quickly pulled out their revolvers, stopping him in his tracks so they could make their getaway.

During their travels through Valencia, another mule fracas led to the beast's owner threatening them with a twelve-inch knife: 'there seemed to be no chance of escape. The stab of the gleaming blade could almost be felt.' Fortunately the man's companion pulled him back, allowing them to get away. They were so shaken they considered giving up the journey, but this close shave proved the last of its kind; they concluded that the people of Valencia were 'the most ill-disposed and revengeful of any in Spain'. They weren't, however, the last Spaniards to be judged so harshly: elsewhere the cyclists accused the locals of 'backwardness', in Aragon 'the women stared like cattle' while 'the men and boys could not keep their hands off our bicycles, ringing the bells, feeling the tyres, and pressing the saddles as if these vehicles were on exhibition for their particular entertainment and instruction'.

Their fellow foreign tourists also came in for criticism: in Granada's Alhambra they encountered 'philistines'. Presumably the Workmans judged them insufficiently cultured to appreciate this architectural wonder of Moorish Spain.

In Barcelona, Fanny found herself subjected to unwanted attention, despite her modest long dress. After being hassled by men on the street, she warned her readers that it is 'not a pleasant place for a woman to visit with a bicycle'. In Algeria, it was once again the animals who reacted unfavourably; Fanny believed the local horses and mules took particular offence to the presence of a woman on a bike, and packs of dogs – 'gaunt, wolfish-looking beasts' – were more liable to chase her than William: 'it may be that dogs, which seem to regard themselves as a sort of special police, consider women out of place on a wheel, and in need of correction'.

As befitted a woman who would be photographed in 1912 in the Himalayas holding a copy of the WSPU's *Votes for Women* newspaper, the condition of women in the countries they cycled through attracted Fanny's attention. When French colonialists told them the Kabylie women in northern Algeria were relatively free, Fanny questioned their judgement: 'one must look deeper than this and see how man regards woman, and how woman regards herself in Kabylie land'. She drew a very different conclusion to the French, based in part on the discovery that Kabylie law permits men to murder their wives if 'necessary'. In addition, she reported that Kabylie women were often denied education and routinely sold into marriage and 'a life of continued drudgery' from the age of twelve. This would have been unfathomable to the highly educated Fanny, who had the means to reject domesticity or manual labour in favour of a life of adventuring and learning. She concluded that the women of Algeria look upon European women with a combination of 'envy and hopelessness'.

She might not have been qualified to cast judgement on the circumstances of these women's lives, but there is no question that Fanny was committed to women's rights and education. The photograph of her, complete with suffragette newspaper in hand, featured on the cover of a book about her climbing feats. She also became the first woman to lecture at Paris's Sorbonne University and left money in her will to four US women's colleges.

In November 1897, the couple set off on their most epic journey yet. Over the next two and a half years they cycled 14,000 miles across South East Asia, through Myanmar, Sri Lanka, Java and India, travelling by steamship from one country to the next and resorting to trains when the roads became impassable. Along the way they visited the region's famed, and at that time little-explored, archaeological sites and temples.

The book they wrote about this trip focused exclusively on the Indian leg of the journey. Again, Fanny contemplated the lives of women, such as those she spent time with in Hyderabad, wives of local rulers who spent their days in purdah, confined to women-only quarters. Their lack of physical, economic or social freedom was anathema to Fanny's Western feminist ideology, defined by movement and independence. She viewed their condition as a product of the general inequality between men and women and hoped that 'light may fall upon the souls of the men, that they may realise the great injustice practised on the weaker sex, and that a day of awakening may come, when the latter may be free to develop as their nature demands'.

For the most part the Workmans seemed unfazed by the hardships they had to endure, like having to sleep on wooden benches in railway stations for want of any other bed for the night. The assistance of a servant, who travelled by train to meet them every few days, literally lightened the load by allowing them to carry just the essentials. They took their food rations in tiffin tins, dining under the watchful gaze of monkeys, while flocks of wild parakeets soared overhead. On the days they met up with their servant he was required to cook their meals and find their accommodation, much like a valet. When he failed in his duties, and the couple arrived to find no meal or bed waiting for them, they dealt with their servant in a very high-handed manner.

In addition to long days in the saddle in hot and humid conditions, with little food and water, they had to contend with a plague of punctures – as many as forty a day. On routes through remote regions off the railway network, where their servant wasn't able to meet up with them for many days, they had to carry everything they would need: 45 kg of supplies between them strapped to their bikes. Time and again they were warned by officials to steer clear of areas afflicted by famine, for fear the starving people might attack them. But they took no heed. Similarly, they didn't worry about rumours of elephants on the road ahead, despite their previous history with bikes and animals. The rifles in their saddlebags remained unused.

The end of this journey in northern India was the start of a new phase in Fanny's career as an explorer. To escape the heat of summer, they left their bikes and headed up to the high passes of the Himalayas, an area they were so taken with that they returned eight times over the next fourteen years. Here Fanny revived her first love, mountaineering, making increasingly challenging and dangerous ascents and breaking several female altitude records. As a climber, Fanny showed the same grit and determination that had powered her through her long cycle tours. She wasn't only the first woman to climb many of these mountains; the Workmans were the first Westerners to make an attempt on several of them. They named one of the mountains they conquered, a peak over 5,900 metres high in the Karakoram, Mount Bullock Workman. Another they christened Siegfriedhorn after their son who had died, though both mountains have long since been renamed. One sour note was that, for all their remarkable records and their reputation as accomplished mountaineers, the couple seem to have treated the local porters with a disappointing lack of empathy.

Fanny led the way on their two-month-long trek, entirely above 4,500 metres in altitude, to the Rose and Siachen glaciers in the Karakoram, the most inaccessible and unexplored in the world at that time. The trip made them miss their daughter's wedding and resulted in the death of one of their guides, who was killed by falling into a crevasse – an accident that Fanny narrowly survived.

It was during this expedition that William photographed Fanny holding her *Votes for Women* newspaper on top of a 6,400-metre peak, wearing her favoured outfit of hobnailed boots and long skirt. Her passionate support of women's rights didn't extend to her applauding the feats of other female mountaineers though. When, in 1909, her fellow American Annie Smith Peck claimed to have climbed 7,000 metres in Peru, Fanny hired a team of French surveyors, at a cost of $13,000, to confirm that the Peruvian peak wasn't that high. It took them four months to reach this conclusion, leaving Fanny's own altitude record of 6,930 metres untouched until 1934.

Competitiveness aside, she was undoubtedly one of the most intrepid and indefatigable explorers of her time. Someone who trampled and cycled over any prevailing prejudices about what women were or were not capable of achieving.

CHAPTER 8

Going the Distance

The Great Outdoors

Marylou Jackson, Velma Jackson, Ethyl Miller, Leolya Nelson and Constance White were met by reporters when they wheeled into Washington DC on Easter Sunday 1928, dressed in bloomers and caps. The five African American cyclists from New York City had spent the last three days pedalling from their home city to the capital, covering 250 miles via Philadelphia and Wilmington, Delaware. Each night of the trip they had stayed at a YWCA hostel before arriving in DC, where they found time to fit in a bit of sight-seeing despite having cycled 100 miles.

Two of the women worked in sports – one was the physical education director of the Harlem YWCA – and it's likely that they were members of cycling clubs in the city. They told a reporter their 'love of the great out-of-doors' had motivated them to set out on this journey and they hoped other women would try to better their distance record. The following day, Easter Monday, they boarded the train home to their lives and work in NYC. Constance White, filled with wanderlust, would soon leave Harlem for travels in Russia, and then through Europe, where she stayed for some time after falling in love with a woman there, before they settled together in the US.

I don't know how many other women back then followed their lead, but over eighty years later their ride continues to inspire people to get on their bikes. In 2013 a black cyclists' collective completed the women's route in reverse as part of their ambition to diversify the image of cyclists in the US and encourage others to join them.

By the early twentieth century cycle touring had fallen out of fashion among the wealthy middle and upper classes, who had moved on to the car instead.* This trend was reflected by the cycling section of *Outing* magazine, which had once been crammed with accounts of incredible worldwide journeys on two wheels; by the turn of the century it had disappeared. A motoring section took its place.

Constance and her friends proved that there were still people – including many women – who were continuing to clock up the miles under their own steam. They were part of a new generation eager to explore the world. And now that tourism and leisure time were no longer the preserve of the rich, it was the turn of a new class of traveller. In Europe the pastime enjoyed such a surge in popularity that the period from the 1920s to the late 1950s is now seen as the golden age of bicycle touring.

In the 1890s the average working week in Europe had been over sixty hours, by 1910 in the UK it was around fifty-three hours and by the 1930s it had gone down to forty-three hours. Many of these workers were women; in the UK, they made up a third of the workforce by the mid-1930s. While there was a stark gender pay gap and many lingering inequalities, they had the vote and more freedoms than previous generations. It would take another world war for trousers to become accepted attire, but attitudes to women's clothing were much more relaxed than they had been the previous century.

The global economic downturn that followed the Wall Street Crash in 1929 meant that cars were beyond the reach of most people; in the UK, only one family in ten owned a car in 1931. Many could stretch to a bicycle, though, and for some it was more than a cheap way of getting to work. Mrs Cattaneo, who worked in a factory in York in

* Cars were increasingly affordable by this point: whereas the average price of a Ford Model-T was $850 in 1909, it was $260 by the early 1920s.

the 1930s, described the weekend rides with her cycle club as the highlight of her life: 'I had never known holidays or been anywhere until we got this bike and went all over . . . I didn't want money then 'cos I had this bike. We would pack up on a Sunday and we would call anywhere at these cafes, and they would give you as much tea as you wanted to drink for fourpence . . . I loved that cycle and I loved every Sunday.'

There were countless others with increasing leisure time and a limited budget who shared Constance's love of the outdoors. Jumping into the saddle offered an escape from the grind of daily life, especially for city dwellers. Some would cover astonishing – even record-breaking – distances on their machines, going far off the beaten track. The renewed interest in touring the countryside on a bike in Europe, and to a lesser extent the US, became part of a general outdoors movement in the interwar period. Youth hostels began opening across Europe and North America, offering cheap accommodation in scenic locations for walkers and cyclists. The countryside became hip again for a time, just as it had when the Romantic poets were writing about it at the end of the eighteenth century and as it is again today, with the Instagram generation posing for selfies in scenic spots. Indeed, weekend touring became so popular in the UK that in 1937 a reader wrote to *Cycling* magazine to complain that it was *too* popular, with 'hordes' of cyclists ruining every good view.

It helped that bikes were more affordable and that this new generation of long-distance cyclists could benefit from lightweight bikes designed specifically for touring. They also had a range of gears to tackle hills and even mountains, a welcome evolution after those heavy Safety bicycles on which the Pennells and Workmans had valiantly slogged through their epic journeys. Perversely, in the US bicycles were getting heavier and slower, with a trend for new cruiser styles that looked more like motorcycles, complete with balloon tyres. Many models weighed over 20 kg, more than double that of European bikes, which might explain why cycle touring didn't take off again there to the same extent.

The membership of the UK's Cyclists' Touring Club began to swell once more, as did that of its European counterparts. The CTC organised train excursions for cyclists so they could travel with their bikes to enjoy a day of cycling in the countryside. Illustrations of an idealised English landscape, the work of artists such as Frank Patterson, filled the pages of cycling magazines. These scenes were a long way from modernity and war, and suggestive of more innocent times – something people were understandably nostalgic for, even if it had never existed.

As social codes became more relaxed, unmarried couples were able to go out unchaperoned. Bike adverts reflected this, featuring white, heterosexual young couples having fun on their touring cycles. An advert for a Hercules bike in 1934 depicts a teenage couple in a passionate embrace above a picture of a bicycle, the accompanying text suggesting that a day out on a Hercules with your love interest, followed by 'that glorious moonlight ride home', inevitably ends the same way: buy this bike and you will get the girl. Though, laughably, 'Joan' is still expected to pour the tea when they stop for lunch. In other ads they cycle along lanes holding hands or sit on beaches looking at their maps with their bicycles beside them.

The 1949 British romantic comedy film *A Boy, a Girl and a Bike* features a Yorkshire cycling club whose social lives revolve around their weekly rides in the Yorkshire Dales and summer camps on the moors, starring the glamorous

Honor Blackman and a teenage Diana Dors, the UK's
Marilyn Monroe.*

Bicycles made for two were surging in popularity, with
one magazine promoting a tandem race from Birmingham
to Gretna Green, the UK's premiere elopement destination,
to be the first to arrive and get married. The cycling press
regularly included photographs of cycling-themed weddings, with guests holding bicycles aloft over the bride and
groom as they exit the church, couples who had presumably
met through their cycling club.

If the newly married cyclists went on to have children,
it didn't necessarily mean an end to those carefree days in
the saddle – families would simply bring their kids along
for the ride. Cycle-mad parents got inventive, with couples
on tandems pulling trailers or sidecars loaded with toddlers
and babies too young to cycle, much like the cargo bikes
used today to do the school run in cities like Amsterdam
and Copenhagen, and increasingly in London. I've even
seen a picture of a pram mounted to a bicycle – not a trend
that stood the test of time, and probably for a good reason.
Those with older children could opt for a triplet bike so
the family could ride on one machine. There were bikes for
larger families and there is a British Pathé film from 1961
which features the Fosters, a family of ten from Lincoln-
shire, who ride a quad tandem pulling a trailer filled with
two of the youngest children and camping equipment. Their
other children bring up the rear on tandems and regular
bikes.

---

* When a wealthy young man falls in love with Honor Blackman's
character and joins the club to be close to her, his family are horrified that he's taking up what they see as a working-class activity
– an indication of how much the upper classes had fallen out of love
with cycling by this point.

Keep Fit, Girls

In 1938, twenty-four-year-old Billie Fleming (then Dovey), a secretary and typist, was a keen cyclist who wanted to inspire more women to take up the sport, and in so doing became a household name for her long-distance achievements. Billie had been taught to ride by a boyfriend when she was eighteen and quickly became 'besotted'. So much so that she decided she would cycle around the UK every day for a year, so she didn't have to stop. She wrote to Rudge-Whitworth asking for sponsorship and they promptly agreed, appointing her their 'Keep-Fit Girl' and giving her a bicycle and the necessary financial backing to stay on the road for 365 days straight. That year she racked up 29,603.4 miles (more than the circumference of the earth) on a bike with just three gears – and set a world record for women's long-distance cycling – an achievement Billie put down to being 'young and fit and ready to take on anything'. Amazingly, she only had one puncture.

Her routine was to ride every day of the year, regardless of weather. Her evenings were spent giving talks to promote the health benefits of cycling. She carried only a change of clothes and some tools in a small saddlebag. Cadbury sent her chocolate every month and in return she appeared in some adverts. Her distances were confirmed through a system of checking cards signed by witnesses which were then verified by *Cycling* magazine. The cards show she averaged 81 miles a day and the furthest she cycled in one day was 186 miles, when she decided she wanted to spend the night in her own bed. The magazine regularly checked her cyclometer to ensure nothing was amiss.

Billie lived to be 100, so she was clearly right about the health benefits. She has remained an inspiration, with many attempting to beat her record. In 1942 Australia's

Pat Hawkins claimed to have cycled over 54,000 miles. The cycling authorities threw the claim out when they scrutinised her records and found they didn't add up. Remarkably, it took until 2016 for Billie's record to be beaten, when Swedish-born Kajsa Tylen took on the challenge and clocked up 32,326 miles between New Year's Day and the following New Year's Eve.

Had the Second World War not broken out, Billie would have cycled across the United States as her next challenge. She might have seen more women on bikes there than a decade before, even if they weren't quite matching her miles. The Great Depression had boosted bicycle sales as many opted to bike to work – or look for a job – during this time of extreme austerity, and soon the industry decided it would specifically target women by encouraging them to take up cycling for fitness.

Hollywood lent a hand when in 1934 the actor Joan Crawford was snapped for the cover of a magazine in trousers and a sweater riding a men's bicycle on rollers – the indoor trainer of the 1930s. She told the magazine that she and her then husband, Douglas Fairbanks, Jr, had started cycling to keep in shape. Twelve years later she was photographed with a US-made Schwinn bike, again eulogising about the health benefits of the activity, 'I recommend bicycling on a Schwinn to anyone who seeks exercise for good health, a good figure and good fun.'

Other actresses were photographed throughout the 1930s and '40s on bikes, including Katharine Hepburn. She had been riding a bicycle since she was three and a half, so didn't need a sponsorship deal to encourage her to ride around the Warner Brothers lot or when taking a break from filming on location, something she would continue to do for decades. With this stamp of Hollywood approval, women were soon keen to be seen on two wheels, and as a result they went from 10 per cent to 33 per cent of the market in the 1930s. Department stores in cities across the US began stocking the latest cycling fashions. At coastal resorts they could hire bikes to ride up and down the boardwalks, like Joan in Venice Beach, Los Angeles. As a trend, it was short-lived. Before long, most bikes manufactured in the country were made for children.

Cycling remained popular during the war, often out of necessity since petrol was so scarce. Post-war austerity made cycle touring popular in Europe again as people looked for an economical holiday. However, its days as a mass activity were numbered; by the mid 1950s there were three times more cars on the road in Europe than there had been the previous decade. In 1960 in the US there was one car for every three people; by 1970 it was one for every two.

Cycle touring and cycling in general – apart from racing – was falling out of favour, something reflected in the CTC's membership figures, which halved between 1939 and 1969. Soon it became seen as something you did because you couldn't afford a car, a stigma that would stick for decades, except in countries like the Netherlands and Denmark where cycling remains to this day an essential component of daily life as a result of an infrastructure that makes it as easy as walking. Elsewhere, those who continued to ride had to battle a lot more traffic than they had a decade before, something not everyone was willing to face.

While most Western countries fell out of love with cycling, by the 1960s a cycling boom was happening in other parts of the world, most significantly in Asia. There were so many bikes on the streets in China that it became known as the 'Bicycle Kingdom'. Between 1948 and 1958 the number of bikes in the country doubled to 1 million. By the 1990s it peaked at around 670 million, before nose-diving as cars became more affordable for its population – a boom and bust that the West had already experienced.

Dunkirk to Delhi

In 1963, as cycle touring was falling out of fashion, a thirty-one-year-old woman from rural Ireland set out to cycle alone from Dunkirk to Delhi, a six-month journey of around 3,000 miles through Europe, Iran, Afghanistan, Pakistan and India. Dervla Murphy decided on this specific destination, and the general route she would follow, shortly after being gifted an atlas and second-hand bicycle for her tenth birthday. She had homed in on India after a penfriend in the Punjab had awakened her interest in this 'wondrous land'.

The idea of travelling independently appealed to Dervla. She was already climbing mountains, swimming in the River Blackwater, and cycling long distances in her home county of Waterford, all unaccompanied. She would go on to spend her life exploring the world on foot and cycle, mostly solo. As she looked down at her feet powering the pedals of her new bike, the thought came to her: 'If I went on doing this for long enough, I could get to India.' Her plan had to be put on hold for over two decades, but she never lost sight of it. Just as some people see their future marked out by events such as going to university, or getting married and having kids, for Dervla biking to India was part of her life plan.

Four years after making her decision, Dervla had to leave school to look after her mother, who had become all but paralysed by rheumatoid arthritis. The former child ad-venturer would be her main carer for over eighteen years, trapped in a 'domestic cage'. For much of that time she was unable to leave the house because her mother couldn't be left alone for any length of time. For someone who had thrived on immersing herself in the outdoors, roaming wherever she fancied, it's understandable that this drastic change in her routine, and the overwhelming weight of her new responsibilities, made her feel 'completely trapped and miserable', and that she 'just wanted to be free'.

As her mother's health continued to deteriorate, those precious moments of liberty were gradually 'whittled away', leaving her longing for the kind of freedoms taken for granted by her peers. The situation became even more of a struggle when her father died suddenly, leaving her sole carer. She survived with the support of friends – and by escaping on her bike whenever she got the chance.

Before her marriage, Dervla's mother had travelled alone, so she recognised her daughter's needed to experience the same sense of freedom. She urged her to make the most of her occasional respite breaks to explore the world. Dervla's cycle tours became lifelines during these years of diminishing personal freedom. The first trip was three weeks in the summer of 1951 which she spent cycling around Wales and the south of England, staying in youth hostels – a 'seminal' trip for someone who had spent most of her life within a 30-mile radius of the town of Lismore.

Some of the neighbours back home were 'aghast' that she was making such a trip on her own. In rural Ireland in the 1950s, this wasn't something girls did. In this predominantly conservative Catholic country, daughters were expected to be self-sacrificing, so the idea of a young woman going on a solo cycling holiday was viewed by some as more shocking than giving up an education to care for her mother. Among many things, the trip proved she could pedal 100 miles a day without undue effort, further evidence that her longed-for 3,000-mile journey was in reach.

The following year she escaped for five weeks to cycle
through Flanders, Germany and France – another restorative trip, though on the way home she narrowly escaped
kidnap by a couple in Paris who she believed were planning
to force her into sex work. Undeterred, two years later
she set off for Spain on a journey that was further off the
beaten track than any she had done before. She managed
120 miles a day on a heavy bike loaded with large panniers
over mountainous terrain. The following year she returned,
having fallen in love with the country. On her way home
she crossed the Pyrenees loaded with twelve large bottles
of brandy rolled up in her sleeping bag as a souvenir. The
weight eventually buckled a wheel beyond repair, but it was
a useful lesson in packing economically.

Dervla's trips served further to fan the flames of her desire
to get to India. And lacking that one essential component –
the freedom to do so – was to torment her for the remaining
years as her mother's carer. Confined by the 'suffocating
monotony' of her routine – some days even being outdoors
in daylight was an impossibility – she spiralled into periods
of depression. Her mother's health deteriorated to the point
where Dervla had to sleep in her room so as to be on hand
at all times.

When her mother died in 1962, thirty-year-old Dervla
mourned her loss but was understandably 'exalted by the
realisation of freedom'. She describes currents of liberty
running through her like 'mild electric shocks'. If her confinement had continued, she felt it would eventually have
destroyed her.

Finally, in January 1963, one of the coldest winters in
living memory, Dervla set off east on her bicycle, on an icy
road out of Dunkirk – at last realising the plan she had
made as a ten-year-old on a hilltop in Lismore. Her bicycle
was a men's Armstrong Cadet she had bought a few years

before and named Roz, after Don Quixote's long-suffering horse, Rocinante. *Rocín* means workhorse – apt for a bike that would diligently carry its rider through many miles and adventures. Roz would take such a hammering over bad or non-existent roads that at times he had to be held together with wire and string. Roz weighed a not insignificant 16 kg and was loaded down with another 12 kg in luggage. Dervla would feel every kilogram during the times she had no choice but to carry it – sometimes for miles – over difficult terrain.

Before she left, she spent a month studying road maps to plan the best route to Delhi, and posting spare tyres to consulates in cities she would pass through – 3,000 miles would wear through a lot of rubber. Convinced Roz's gears wouldn't survive the bad roads through Asia, she had them removed, rendering it a single speed – a startling decision, given the fact she would be going over a lot of mountains. She practised firing the .25 gun that she had decided to carry with her and which, not long after setting out, she would be extremely grateful to have packed.

After waiting twenty-one years to start her journey, she was forced to delay setting off for yet another week because Europe was going through its coldest winter in eighty years. When the thaw didn't come, she continued with her plans regardless. This was something she came close to regretting over the next weeks of arctic temperatures through France, Italy and what was then Yugoslavia. She endured frost-bitten hands and feet as she cycled through blizzards and floods, as well as gales that knocked her off Roz, while trying to follow roads hidden below drifts of snow and black ice. Her delight at finally being on her way to India was severely impeded by conditions that were so challenging that it was more about survival than the carefree days she'd hoped for, pedalling east as far as her legs would take her. But no matter how close to unendurable it felt at times, this would be a story worth telling when she was finally through it.

Even Dervla had to admit she wasn't invincible at this point, despite her winter amour of ski cap, balaclava and fur-lined mittens. She eventually resorted to taking a train over the Alps into Italy, since they were completely impassable by bike, as well as having to 'ignominiously' accept lifts on the snowbound mountain roads though large swathes of Eastern Europe, where it was too icy to cycle without the risk of skidding straight off the edge. All incredibly frustrating for someone more than capable of making her way independently in ordinary circumstances, and who now, for very different reasons from before, did not have the freedom to do so.

Not that being in a motor vehicle in this environment was any guarantee of safety. One truck she travelled in through Serbia slipped off the road and hit a tree. Though she suffered a minor head injury in the collision, Dervla left the driver to go in search of help from the nearest village. On the way there she was jumped on by three emaciated wolves, with one taking purchase on the shoulder of her jacket, another her trouser leg and the third preparing to pounce. Her time spent practising whipping her .25 from her pocket and taking aim paid off, as she swiftly shot the two that were on her while the other scarpered. All the while she was wondering if she was dreaming; hallucination would have been a real possibility due to the head injury she'd sustained. The police later told her that the 'wolves' may well have been wild dogs. Regardless, this terrifying incident in a remote snowy forest, like something out of a Grimms' fairy tale, was certainly a story worth repeating, the first of many that would make it into *Full Tilt*, her account of this remarkable ride, where it was always about the journey rather than the end point.

It's All About the Journey

I was reminded of those wolves when in late December 2018 I spent a few days cycling from the ferry in Rosslare through south-east Ireland to visit Dervla, then eighty-seven, at her home in Lismore. Not that there are any wolves in Ireland, but there are lots of dogs, particularly little yapping ones, that love to chase cyclists passing through their territory. A nuisance, but there was no danger of being mauled to death. More of a problem was my lack of preparation; I'd imagined I was in for a few days of relatively easy cycling, around 180 miles there and back.

Unlike Dervla, I had not paid due diligence to the journey ahead. Instead I had opted to take a bike I'd never done any touring on before, on the basis that its mudguards and robust tyres would be better suited to Irish rural roads in winter. The first rule of cycling anywhere of any distance, though, is to make sure your mount is in good working order. Mine had done hundreds of wet miles around London since it was last serviced and was in dire need of some TLC. It's a good job I wasn't cycling to India, because when I tried to attach my bag rack after wheeling off the ferry, it wouldn't fit on the saddle unless I moved it into a position which wasn't comfortable to ride on.

Twenty-five miles into the journey, after a second puncture, I realised that the tyres were going to be my downfall. On close inspection I saw how worn they were, and little tears were likely harbouring bits of stone or glass that were piercing each fresh inner tube. A plague of punctures on the first day made me lose so much precious mid-winter daylight that I had to complete the last twenty-five miles of my ride, thankfully along the car-free Waterford Greenway, entirely in the dark. What should have been a speedy, stress-free section was made painfully slow by not having lights designed for dark country roads, so I couldn't see more than a few feet in front of me. Needless to say, this is not cycle touring best practice. Though at least it didn't rain, which is unusual for Ireland in December. On the return journey I took a detour to a bike shop for a replacement tyre and had a blissfully puncture-free final leg.

The experience brought to mind Lillias Campbell Davidson's advice from 1896 that women should make sure they can mend a puncture before they head out on a tour. She thought that this knowledge was worth risking breaking a nail to acquire, even if she regarded it as generally 'a hideous bit of business' and couldn't imagine why anyone would do it if a willing man was available – something Dervla, despite her thousands of miles, or perhaps because of them, advocates. She joked with me that 'that's what men are for'.

In the most remote places on that first long journey, and the ones that followed, someone would usually come past to whom she could hand over the inner tube. On my journey to Lismore I let an eager local man who was walking his dog help fix one of my punctures; by that point I was thoroughly bored of doing it myself. In extremis, though, such as the middle of the desert in Afghanistan, Dervla was able to get back on the road herself; she just chose not to if she didn't absolutely have to. A surprising insight into someone whose life has been defined by independence and self-sufficiency.

Involving someone in fixing a puncture is of course a good way to engage with people as you pass through their country. My puncture-mender was keen to chat, telling me about local landmarks and his own cycling. As I sat with Dervla in her study – one of a series of ancient stone buildings that had been part of the old market in Lismore – warmed by the wood burner, and with her dogs snoring at our feet, she told me that her way of travelling was entirely dependent on the locals since she was so far from the tourist trail. They would often invite her into their homes, give her a bed for the night, feed her and recommend places to visit or to avoid, which was particularly welcome so far off the beaten track.

These were the sort of experiences Dervla had dreamed of, allowing her to get to know a country through its people, something that's possible when travelling by bike and not so easy when speeding through in a car, train or coach. The writer and activist Rebecca Solnit has described how modern life is increasingly a 'series of interiors', which has made us disconnected from the world around us and other people. She is passionate about walking, which, like cycling, is about being in a public space, where the 'random, the unscreened, allows you to find what you don't know you are looking for, and you don't know a place until it surprises you'. In her view, our reliance on technology is making us miss out, and she describes how walking can be a way of being, rather than just a way to get from A to B. For Dervla too, travel – on bike or foot – is all about the journey, which, as is her way, is full of the unplanned and unexpected, free from schedules and time constraints.

With Roz she could cover good distances – she was doing around eighty miles a day on the India trip – but she was also immersed in the fabric of the countries she passed through, soaking up the environment around her and interacting with the people she encountered. Equally important for Dervla was that the journey was on her terms; as a solo traveller she could stop or detour whenever or wherever she liked, independence as well as openness to new experiences and cultures being core to Dervla's nature. When someone once asked her if she'd been to Central America, she told them she hadn't. She'd forgotten that she had passed through on the way back from Peru, but as she hadn't been on a bike or on foot, she didn't count it as travel and it may as well not have happened.

The cycle tourer and writer Anne Mustoe came to the same conclusion in 1983 when travelling by bus across India. On looking out of the window and seeing a man cycling across the Great Thar Desert, she was 'seized with sudden envy . . . I wanted to be out there myself on that road on a bicycle, alone and free, feeling the reality of India, not gazing at it through a pane of glass.' Two years later the fifty-four-year-old headmistress was still certain that this was the best way to travel, one that would allow her time to think, observe and proceed at her own pace, so she set off to cycle around the world from west to east. Like Dervla, Anne felt that the richest experiences came through her interactions with strangers. Thanks to the 'classlessness' of the bicycle, she met these strangers on 'a level of mutual trust'. After that first journey of 12,000 miles in fifteen months, Anne was such a convert to cycle touring that she devoted the rest of her life to exploring the world on two wheels, including another round-the-world trip, this time from east to west. She died aged seventy-six after falling ill in Syria in 2009 on her final bicycle trip.

For Dervla a journey is something that doesn't just happen to you – it is active, not passive. It's an idea of travel which aligns more closely with its etymological origin from the middle ages of *travailen*, which stems from *travailler*, meaning to work, toil or suffer, from a time when travelling was always an arduous undertaking. Though in Dervla's case it's less about suffering and more about effort, and the enrichment that comes with it. At times she pushed herself to the limits of her physical endurance, but even then she derived a sense of elation from the experience. Fleas, bed bugs, sand flies, mosquitoes, stings from scorpions and hornets, dehydration, sunstroke, dysentery and broken ribs were minor inconveniences in comparison. She once tried to convey this to an American engineer when she was pedalling Roz towards Afghanistan along a desert road in Iran. He had stopped his jeep to ask, 'What the hell are you doing on this goddammed road?' and insist she sling her bike in the back so she could be driven over the border. She refused, explaining that cycling was her preferred way to travel, that Roz, the sky and earth were enough for total happiness. He eventually drove off calling her a 'nutcase'.

Nevertheless, a woman cycling alone through countries like Iran, Afghanistan, Pakistan and India was not a common occurrence in the early 1960s. This was several years before it became part of the hippy trail, and even then, I don't think many – if any – were doing it on a bike. In less accessible places, such as the high mountain passes of Kashmir, the same mountains where earlier that century Fanny Bullock Workman had carried out her pioneering mountaineering expeditions, Dervla was possibly the first woman to have cycled through. Some of the more remote communities had never seen a bicycle, let alone a woman riding one, and she was repeatedly called upon to give demonstrations and let locals have a go.

So unusual was the idea of a lone woman making this kind of journey that the Afghan embassy in Iran refused to grant her the visa she needed to travel on the grounds that they deemed it unsafe. Instead they offered her free transport to Kabul, assuming she was cycling because she couldn't afford to travel any other way. They had in fact banned all solo women travellers after a Swedish woman on a motorcycle had been murdered. Dervla was undeterred, telling them that women get murdered in Europe too. She eventually persuaded a senior official at the US embassy to ask them to grant her a visa on the understanding that she was entering the country at her own risk.

Afghanistan, when she finally entered it, was the country she would fall in love with more than any other on her trip. A country that was, sadly, already in a tug of war between Russia and the USA, causing her to change her route to avoid conflict zones, and where she was constantly told about foreigners who had been murdered. She found the people welcoming and kind; though they had very little, they went out of their way to share what they did have with her. Not even the broken ribs she acquired after being accidentally hit by a rifle butt belonging to a fellow bus passenger, after a bad road destroyed Roz's tyres and forced her to take public transport, dented her enthusiasm for the country.

Women solo travellers today are constantly asked if they are afraid and told what they are doing isn't safe, the implication being that they are more vulnerable and thus reckless, alone and lonely. Men, on the other hand, are adventurous. The endurance athlete and adventurer Jenny Tough has spent a lot of time cycling and running alone in remote and inaccessible places and has been repeatedly asked if she's fearful for her safety. Running 700 km across the Bolivian Andes, she was told by people in villages that what she was doing was dangerous, that she could be killed. As more people warned her to be afraid, she felt the doubt creep in, but each day she got up and kept going, proving that fear isn't a useful response.

When she ran across the Atlas Mountains in Morocco, she was followed almost daily by police who kept telling her it wasn't safe. Just as the Afghan embassy had tried to prevent Dervla entering the country on the grounds of the perceived risk to her personal safety, the police tried to dissuade Jenny from following her route, offering her lifts and insisting she stayed each night in villages to keep her 'safe'. In the land of the Berbers, the self-described 'free people', she says she never felt less free. She was physically and mentally stressed by the constant watchful gaze she was under.

When I type 'women solo travel' into Google, 'Is solo female travel safe?' is one of the first things that comes up under the 'People also ask' section. Yet the idea of men going it alone in the wilderness has always been accepted and celebrated as a masculine rite of passage; the rugged, frozen-beard archetypes who resort to eating their dogs as they cross Antarctica or the intrepid adventurers getting lost in the Amazon and living with an undiscovered tribe. Their stories are embedded in our history, while accounts by women who've made similar journeys tend to be forgotten and overlooked. The writer Kate Harris, who has cycled the length of the Silk Road, observed that women explorers are too often typified as making such journeys as a way to 'find themselves' in response to an emotional crisis of some kind, an outlook that restricts female adventuring to an *Eat Pray Love* self-discovery narrative, and a way of feminising their experience. They aren't seen as exploring for the sake of adventure but fleeing from something.

It's also true that while men are free to be rugged, fearless and independent explorers, women who want to do the same regularly complain that they are subjected to interrogations about their plans, a list of risks they could encounter and moral judgements if they have children. Dervla has no time for that, telling me that it's 'ridiculous' that people see that first journey as a great achievement, that 'there's just nothing to getting on a bicycle and going to India'. That's not to say that she didn't find herself in difficult or threatening situations. Ironically, the only instances of threat specific to being a woman travelling alone happened before she even got to Afghanistan, the one country they tried to stop her entering because of the potential risks. The first was in Turkey, on the border with Iran, when she woke in the middle of the night in the flea-infested bed of her lodgings to find her covers removed and a six-foot Kurdish man standing over her. Once again, her lightning-fast reflexes were tested as she grabbed her gun from under her pillow and fired into the ceiling, causing the man to scarper. No one came to find out why a gun had gone off in the middle of the night.

In Azerbaijan, on the border with Iran, she was to have an even closer shave and then considered it the only place she wouldn't return to on her own. First, bandits armed with shovels had tried to steal Roz, but a few rounds from her gun fired into the air sent them running. The second was a policeman who locked her inside a compound with him while he attempted to sexually assault her. In her book she says the tactics she used to temporarily paralyse him with pain, so she could grab the keys from his discarded trousers and escape, were 'unprintable'. Despite these instances, Dervla baulks at the idea of being called courageous for choosing to travel alone, arguing that it's self-preservation rather than courage that gets her through any difficult situations. It helps that she is not a pessimist, refusing to believe in disaster until it's happening.

She has never believed anything is out of bounds to her as a female traveller, taking inspiration from those Victorian women pioneers of exploration. She told me she feels closest to Isabella Bird Bishop, who she thought travelled for the 'hell of it, to enjoy travelling'. Though when Dervla travelled through the Middle East and India, as Isabella had done nearly a hundred years before, many people in the region still found the concept of a lone woman traveller an alien one – as some do today. In Iran, people assumed that Dervla was a man and so she would be given a bed in men's dormitories. Her short haircut, utilitarian boots and shirt donated by the US army may have helped with that misconception. For Dervla this ambiguity was liberating; being seen as 'merely a human being' by the people she passed on Roz freed her from the judgements that come with the identification of gender, nationality and class. Likewise the Belgian-French explorer Alexandra David-Néel found freedom in her disguise as a beggar and Buddhist monk when in the winter of 1924 she made her extraordinary journey, crossing the Himalayas to enter the forbidden Tibetan city of Lhasa, something that would have been impossible had her sex been revealed.

For Dervla, an androgynous appearance came in handy in areas of Iran where anti-women's emancipation riots were taking place and women had been murdered, after the religious leaders rejected the then shah's plans to modernise the country. In a state where women were less free, being mistaken for a man could be an asset.

Even when she was recognised as a woman, as a foreigner she was mostly exempt from the restrictions, particularly on movement, placed on women in some of the more conservative areas she travelled through. Her position as an outsider was unique in that she could talk to men and with women, including those who were obliged to observe strict purdah customs and remain indoors. When the US writer and activist Shannon Galpin biked in Afghanistan over forty years later, she described how being a foreign woman meant she was seen as a 'hybrid gender' or 'an honorary man'. Though there were occasions when Afghan men tried to flirt, or in one instance grope her, assuming that as a Western woman she must be promiscuous, most of the time it meant she could talk to men more or less as their equal, as well as the women, giving her a deeper insight into the country.

Back in the early 1960s, many people whom Dervla met during her travels, as well as back home in Ireland, may have wondered why a woman in her early thirties wasn't at home, married with children, the spectre of the spinster looming large. Since she was in her teens she had known that she didn't want that kind of life, describing it as the 'antithesis of my ideal unplanned existence'.

When she did get pregnant in her late thirties, she travelled through Turkey up until the end of her second trimester and raised her daughter alone, which is unsurprising for someone who describes themselves as 'solitary' by nature. She didn't care what people thought and told me that motherhood didn't change her, she still wanted to spend her life travelling and writing. When her daughter, Rachel, was old enough, they travelled together: around southern India when Rachel was five; walking 1,600 miles across the high Peruvian Andes when she was nine; then around Madagascar when she was fourteen. It sent minor ripples of shock around her home town.

Once Rachel was an adult, Dervla packed up her panniers again for more long solo journeys, including a 3,000-mile ride from Kenya to Zimbabwe on a mountain bike. Yet despite being a woman in her sixties by that point, her plans were still a source of concern. A worried-looking airport official in Nairobi questioned her about her bicycle, telling her that 'old people' should be travelling in vehicles. In this instance Dervla was happy to put his misplaced solicitude down to the African custom of cherishing the elders in society.

While osteoarthritis has now put an end to Dervla's years in the saddle, she told me that she still receives letters from women – and men – telling her that *Full Tilt* has inspired them to go on their own long cycle trips. Technology has changed the way we make such journeys; while Dervla was untroubled about having no means to get in touch with people back home, today's travellers seldom go more than a few hours without being able to connect with friends and family. In fact, it's expected. And instead of the series of paper maps with which Dervla planned her routes, most of us would be lost without our GPS. She thinks that her style of travel, which relied so much on strangers welcoming her into their homes, is less possible now, though there are people who travel in a similar way, with apps like Couch-surfing connecting them with hosts around the world who are willing to put them up for the night for free. Technology makes it easy, if a lot less spontaneous, to facilitate mean-ingful interactions between relative strangers.

Travel – particularly on a bike or on foot – is still full of unexpected and meaningful encounters; my relatively short journey to Lismore provided me with some memorable ones. Before I headed back on the road towards the ferry to Wales, Dervla invited me to lunch with Rachel and her granddaughter. While she prepared the soup, she recom-mended I bike up the hill outside town to take in the view. It is indeed a good vantage point from which to look out over the green rolling hills of Waterford and the River Black-water. Sadly, I forgot to ask if it was the same hill where she had made that decision to cycle to India all those years ago.

CHAPTER 9

Around the World

A Race Against the Clock

Crowds lined the streets of Naples as a motorcade drove through the city towards Piazza del Plebiscito on 22 December 2012. People weren't gathered to see the men on their Harleys, though, they were here to see the woman on her bicycle following behind – the exhausted but elated cyclist who was about to cross the finish line to become the first woman to hold a Guinness World Record for circumnavigating the globe on a bicycle. A journey which, unlike Dervla Murphy's, is very much about getting to that end point, and within a punishing time frame. The world's press was there to capture the historic moment.

When the cyclist, Juliana Buhring, had left her home city on her record-breaking journey 152 days before, few had taken her attempt seriously. Her trainer had told her she needed at least another year of putting the miles in before undertaking such an audacious endeavour. No sponsors had been willing to fund the attempt, though men had been breaking the record for decades. They may have had reservations about a woman being able to do such a thing, but it's likely they had doubts that this particular thirty-one-year-old, who had only started cycling eight months before, could pull it off. Apart from the support of friends, Juliana was on her own when she cycled out of Naples, heading west first to Lisbon and then on to America, for over five months of life on the road.

Juliana may be the first female record holder for cycling around the world, but she wasn't the first to attempt to do so. Almost 118 years earlier, in June 1894, a twenty-four-year-old woman was being waved off by a crowd, which included suffragists and Christian Women's Temperance Society members, as she pedalled out of Boston bound for New York on the first leg of her journey. Like Juliana, she wasn't an obvious contender; Annie Kopchovsky, a Latvian Jewish immigrant, had never even been on a bicycle until a few days before she set out.

Until then, Annie had worked for local newspapers selling advertising space, while living in a tenement in Boston with her husband Max and their three children, all under five. Though she may not have been anyone's idea of a record-breaking cyclist, Annie told the press that she had been chosen by two wealthy Bostonian merchants who had made a wager about whether a woman could get around the world on a bike within fifteen months. At the time, the record of 13,500 miles in thirty-two months was held by an Englishman, Thomas Stevens, who had done the journey the previous decade on a penny-farthing. If she succeeded, they would reward her with $10,000 – a huge amount of money at a time when the average annual income was around $1,000.

The Victorian era was one of invention, exploration and adventure. It was also one of competition, with people attempting to be the first or fastest to do a dizzying range of feats, such as scaling uncharted peaks and making the highest balloon flight. The quest to circumnavigate the globe against the clock was popular in part because of the commercial success of Jules Verne's fictional creation Phileas Fogg. Most famously, Elizabeth Cochrane, a fearless investigative journalist for the *New York World* writing under the pseudonym Nellie Bly, made it around the world in 1889 in a record-breaking seventy-two days using an array of transport from steam trains and ships to horses and rickshaws. Readers back home eagerly awaited the articles published daily about her progress. It was a symbolic moment at a point in history where mass travel was making the world smaller and more accessible than many had ever thought possible.

Annie was the first woman to attempt such a thing on a bicycle, in an age when the idea of women cycling around the local park wasn't universally accepted. She wasn't the only one undertaking a solo global bicycle race at that time though. US adventurer Frank Lenz, the son of German immigrants, had already been on the road for two years when Annie pedalled out of Boston. Frank had been writing regular reports on his journey which were published in *Outing* magazine. The month before Annie set off, he had made it to Tabriz in Iran. This was the last anyone ever heard from him; a year later it was confirmed that he had been killed by Kurdish bandits in Turkey after insulting one of their chiefs.

According to Annie, she had fifteen months to get back to Boston to collect her prize. She also claimed that the wager required her to make $5,000 during her journey and not accept a single cent without having earned it – something she started working on before she even got on her bike. Knowing the power, and value, of advertising, she set about selling ad space on her bicycle and herself, in much the same way she had for her newspaper pages. The first deal was with Londonderry Lithia Spring Water; Annie agreed to hang a signboard for their product on her bike and to rename herself Annie 'Londonderry'. It seems that even Annie's personal identity had a price, and in this instance it was $100. Along the way she would make many similar deals, her bike weighed down with streamers and boards advertising a range of products and services. Annie became a global sensation, attracting attention in every country she passed through, and she worked hard to keep herself in the papers. She understood publicity and how to get it, even if it meant a little, and sometimes a lot, of exaggeration or invention.

Annie displayed remarkable nous, guts and an innate flair for self-promotion, but even then it seems quite a leap to go from a Boston tenement, caring for her children and struggling to make ends meet, to leaving home for over a year to become a worldwide phenomenon as the first round-the-world female cyclist – a scenario that sounds more like a Jules Verne creation. Which makes it even harder to understand how it was all but forgotten until the late 1990s, when her great-grandnephew, Peter Zheutlin, decided to research her story and write her biography. Peter himself, along with the rest of his immediate family, had never heard of their illustrious ancestor. It was only when a researcher who had stumbled across an archived newspaper story about Annie's journey contacted him for more information that Peter jumped on the trail to unearth her extraordinary story. What he discovered was a journey that was 'audacious and unprecedented', a 'tour de force of moxie, self-promotion *and* athleticism'.

While he describes Annie as 'the embodiment of the New Woman' for disregarding society's expectations, one of the wild woman pioneers who displayed chutzpah and determination to succeed, he believes there were a fair few inconsistencies in her account. The first was the wager itself, which he thinks never existed – possibly explaining the riddle of how the two men could have settled on Annie as their woman. The wagering merchants didn't exist and the whole race was Annie's own bombastic and incredible invention. The fact that she gives inconsistent accounts of the rules of their bet in many of her interviews seems to back this up; though in my view it serves to make the whole endeavour even more brilliant. Two men didn't make her a star, instead she invented them as part of her strategy to capture the world's attention. And it worked.

In the absence of a real wager, Annie could afford to be flexible when it came to the rules of her fifteen-month mission. The time limit appeared to be the only non-negotiable condition – a stark contrast to the terms currently laid down by Guinness World Records. When Juliana Buhring wrote to the organisation in 2012 to inform them of her intention to attempt to become the first woman to hold the record, they responded with the long list of rules she needed to comply with. The first was that she had to travel more than 24,900 miles (over the length of the equator), 18,000 of which must be completed on the bike. The route must be continuous in either an east-to-west or west-to-east direction, passing two antipodal points, and a GPS spot tracker must be attached to the bike so her progress could be followed at all times. In addition, Juliana, like Billie Fleming in her record attempt in 1938 for most miles in one year, had to get signatures from people along the way as further proof.

A few weeks before Juliana started, Guinness informed her they had changed the rules and that the clock would no longer stop when she was travelling off the bike. Now, when she took a flight, that time would be included in her final total, which meant she would need to get through airports and set off again in the shortest time possible. They had also decided to set a time limit of 150 days for both men *and* women; an oddly punishing decision when no man had yet made that time, despite multiple record attempts. The time frame required her to cycle around 125 miles a day – more than she had been doing during her training – and allowed for no rest days. When she queried why they had settled on this particular number, they didn't seem able to explain. However, five days before she was due to depart, they contacted her again to say they had decided to change the women's maximum time to 175 days. Juliana decided to go for the men's record anyway.

At this point Juliana took the decision to swap her comfortable touring bike for a nippy carbon road bike weighing under 7 kg, which she named Pegasus after the mythical winged horse that the Greek hero Bellerophon rode to defeat the monstrous Chimera. She stripped her luggage down to the minimum, with just a change of cycle clothing and some other essentials.

Annie wasn't travelling so light and free. Her Columbia ladies' bicycle, most likely given to her as a promotional exercise by the Boston-based Pope Company, weighed a hefty 20 kg. Its drop-frame meant she could wear her regular outfit of long skirts and corsets, but the combined weight of the bike and clothing made long days in the saddle rather more arduous than they might have been. Apart from her pearl-handled revolver, she packed light, sending trunks with spare clothes on ahead of her. Her first destination was New York City where, seemingly unfazed by the clock ticking, she stayed for an entire month, giving interviews to raise further awareness of her endeavour.

In late September 1894, 1,000 miles and three months in, she arrived in Chicago. Annie wasn't feeling so gung-ho about her plans as she wheeled into the Windy City. The immensity of the remaining journey, and the utter of exhaustion of life on the road on her heavy bike, resulted in her announcing she was abandoning her endeavour. Instead she would settle for setting a new record cycling back to NYC. That was until another company, Sterling Bicycles, stepped into the breach to help resuscitate her ambitious plans. They offered her a men's bicycle that weighed half that of her Columbia in exchange for promoting their brand. Like Juliana's upgrade, it would make the miles go that bit faster and easier. She also abandoned skirts and corsets in favour of bloomers. She became such a convert that she eulogised to the press about the benefits of rational dress.

Annie had another problem that wasn't quite so easy to fix. It dawned on her that her planned route west was flawed: she wouldn't make it across the mountains to reach

San Francisco before the winter snows. The only option was to head back east, retracing her route 1,000 miles, to NYC to catch a boat to Europe, abandoning the plan to head for the west coast and then on to Asia. One consolation was that her Sterling meant that the return journey wouldn't be quite so tiring.

For any cyclist, weather can be a challenging adversary. When you are on a strict schedule, it can send best-laid plans into disarray. In Annie's case, the enemy was poor planning, not unexpected weather. Of the riders hoping to achieve a record for around-the-world cycling, the majority head east since this is viewed as a better direction for prevailing winds. Juliana, departing in mid-summer in Europe, calculated that if she headed east she would hit the monsoons in Asia, so opted to battle the headwinds and pedal westwards. She rode from southern Italy into France, through 40-degree heat and the devastation wreaked by forest fires in Spain, and on to Lisbon, to catch her flight to America. Once there, leaving her home city of Boston, she felt the full force of the winds she'd been warned about, along with rain, hills and countless punctures.

As she crossed America people told her she was heading the wrong way – not helpful advice since a change of direction was out of the question. She describes riding constantly into wind as something that 'drains your morale, saps your energy and makes you want to scream, weep and beat the handlebars in frustration'. I know this feeling well and I've never tried to cycle around the world: I have lived in the windiest *département* in France and there were days when it felt like pedalling on a spin bike on the high setting. When the wind's in the right direction, though, it can feel closer to flying. By the time Juliana reached the flat Midwest the wind had become so unbearable that she opted to reroute, adding more miles to her journey by zigzagging in an effort to avoid the continual full-frontal assault.

All this and she still didn't escape the rain in Asia; a typhoon landed right in the middle of her route through India. She spent days cycling in wind and rain on roads that had turned into a mudbath mixed with rubbish and – more unpleasantly – excrement, which covered her and Pegasus from head to pedal. Again she was forced into an urgent reroute to avoid becoming seriously unwell.

Annie's change of route didn't avoid inclement weather either. When she reached France, it was early December; she left Paris in freezing rain, which had turned to snow by the time she hit the Loire. She didn't have to brave the elements alone, though: she had a relay team of fans to cycle with her all the way from Paris to Marseille. She had spent several weeks in Paris, giving interviews and lectures, attending a bicycle exhibition to help promote various products, and generally building hype. By the time she left it's likely there wasn't a single person in the country who didn't know about the American woman making her way south on her Sterling, and many cyclists were keen to accompany her for part of the way. She arrived in Marseille to a hero's welcome; crowds lined the streets, eager to greet the woman they had read so much about. Annie was a cycling celebrity.

In France, where women riding bikes in bloomers raised fewer eyebrows than in most countries at that time, they couldn't get enough of this globe-circling cyclist. However elated she might have felt, by this point she must have been looking and feeling like she'd gone through quite an ordeal. As she wheeled into the city flanked by riders from a local cycling club, she was pedalling one-legged, the other leg bandaged and propped up on her handlebars. She told the press it had been damaged when highwaymen tried to rob her near Avignon. Peter, her great-grandnephew, concluded that this was an unlikely story. The injury probably resulted from a far more mundane accident near Lyon.

Annie basked in the attention; it must have felt a million miles from her anonymous life in Boston. With her new name she had created a new persona, and the stories she spun were an important part of that. The fiction was financially rewarding too. Her celebrity status meant she could sell autographed photos and promote products, from perfume to tyres, appearing in adverts and adding more banners to her bike. People paid to hear her talk about her travels, and to keep the crowd's attention she was inclined to let her storytelling run away with her.

Juliana's challenge, unlike Annie's, didn't require her to earn $5,000 while cycling around the world. Before setting off, she had tried to find a brand sponsor to cover some of the costs, but none came forward. She hoped that once she'd covered a bit of ground, and people saw how determined she was, someone might come on board with much-needed funds, but it didn't happen. By the time she crossed New Zealand, she was running out of money. This was a low point in the journey in other respects too: a non-functioning GPS meant she had gone miles off route and over unnecessary mountains, while being battered by cold, rain and gale-force winds.

She was on the verge of giving up and heading home, when the internet came to her rescue. Just as people had followed Annie's journey from Boston through stories and interviews in the press, in 2012 increasing numbers had been monitoring Juliana's GPS tracker online and via her messages and videos on Facebook. When they heard she might have to abandon the attempt, many dug deep to keep Juliana on the road, crowdfunding her journey. Others, many of them women, met her en route, buying her food and drinks. Friends, and friends of friends, put her up for the night and did everything they could to keep her on track. Unlike Annie, Juliana didn't have to weave fiction into her account: there was enough drama in her journey without having to invent anything.

Juliana's GPS spot tracker meant it would have been impossible to falsify the route she took and how far she cycled. All Annie had was a cyclometer which notched up her miles. On her return to Boston, she claimed she had cycled over 9,000 miles. She had of course covered a lot of ground retracing her route back to Boston, and in seven weeks between leaving Marseille on 20 January and arriving in Japan. She said the journey had taken her through North Africa and the Middle East, over the Himalayas and across China. Among other tales of adventure, she told reporters and audiences in packed lecture halls that she had been imprisoned after arriving at the front line of the Sino-Japanese war, that she'd hunted tigers in Bengal, witnessed Russian prison camps in Siberia and been shot in the shoulder during her journey east.

After examining the reams of press coverage, Peter Zheutlin concluded that much of her journey from France to Japan was pure fantasy. It would have been impossible to cycle all that way on her Sterling, while fitting in the many scrapes and adventures she claimed, in such a short space of time. No wonder her accounts tended to contradict one another, with each interviewer getting a different version.

There is no question that the steamer she boarded in Marseille was the same ship she disembarked from in Yokohoma in March 1895. Though it disproves the tall stories of her adventures en route, this did not negate the terms of the 'wager'; in all Annie's explanations of the wager, she made no mention of any rule stipulating the number of miles she had to cover on her bicycle. In France, while it's incontrovertible that she cycled hundreds of miles in the company of other cyclists who could bear witness, she jumped on a few trains too. It's possible she got off the steamship and cycled around the ports where it docked along the way. But by the time she disembarked in San Francisco to complete the final leg of her journey, her entertaining but conflicting stories had begun to catch up with her. The press were no longer ready to believe everything she threw at them.

As she made her way back to Boston, increasingly cynical reporters cast doubt on her accounts of adventures along the way. She had chosen a challenging and indirect route that took her south down the California coast, then east across Arizona and New Mexico, before heading back up north to Chicago, crossing arid deserts and mountains. She pulled in huge audiences who paid to hear this remarkable and gutsy woman. In El Paso they couldn't get enough of her wild tales, though the press reported that she arrived and departed on a train.

Though she undoubtedly hopped on some trains, she also cycled at least part of the way and had a broken wrist to show for it after a collision with some pigs, or a farmer, depending on the account you read. When she arrived back in Boston, fifteen months to the day of her departure, her arm was encased in plaster. Broken limbs aside, this young mother had made history as the first woman to get around the world on – and sometimes with – a bike, making herself a star in the process. Whether the wager existed or not, Annie was triumphant. Her journey showed that women need not be defined solely as wives and mothers.

It's notable that, when she changed her name, she created a new identity for herself. As Annie Londonderry, she never mentioned her marital status or the children she had left behind, a wise tactic to avoid castigation for abandoning her family for such a long time. Had her husband, Max, set off to cycle the world, I doubt he would have been criticised for his dereliction of fatherly duties. Men were entitled to head off in search of adventure; it's a double standard that persists to this day.

We can only guess at Annie's motivation and her feelings at being separated from her family for such a long time. There can be no doubt, however, that in late-nineteenth-century America women had fewer choices in every area of life, from freedom of movement to family planning. Annie made an active choice to have her own independent adventure that far exceeded the expectations of a working-class Jewish mother of three in Boston. It's significant that she chose to do this on a bicycle, a symbol of the great disruption of strict Victorian gender codes and the wider push towards greater freedom for women. It's just a shame her story was forgotten for so long.

Throwing Down the Gauntlet

Perhaps if Annie's journey hadn't faded from the history books, it wouldn't have taken until 2012 for someone to attempt an official women's record for circumnavigating the globe by bike.

Juliana admits that, because she had never previously shown any interest in sport, there was 'nothing to qualify me for such a huge undertaking'. It was 'willpower and the determination to finish, no matter what' that kept her on the road, as well as the desire to prove that 'anything is possible'. A bereavement had initially pushed her to attempt such a seemingly impossible feat, but in the process it changed her. She had grown up in a repressive religious cult until she escaped at twenty-three, having been separated from her parents for many of those years and enduring a difficult childhood and adolescence. An experience like that would have put the gruelling hours in the saddle into perspective. She thinks her eight-year-old self would never have believed she would one day take on such a challenge, let alone succeed.

Juliana's childhood traumas made her tough, able to endure high levels of physical and mental pain, and more equipped to deal with the worst the trip threw at her. Her traits of independence, self-reliance and adaptability came to the forefront during the long, lonely days on the road when the rough conditions would otherwise have defeated her.

Arguably one of the greatest female endurance athletes in the world, she puts her success down to stubbornness rather than strength. She was the only woman to take part in the 2013 inaugural Transcontinental race, the toughest unsupported race across Europe, starting in Belgium and ending in Istanbul, where she finished ninth overall. Her extraordinary achievements also include the 4,200 mile Trans Am bike race, where she was the first woman over the line and fourth competitor to finish. Where other people might give up and go home, she refuses to quit. On her bike, she says she becomes 'another being, I just lose all sense of identity and even of sex – as in being feminine – I just become an animal, and I just go, it's like a horse smelling that finish line'. Though her achievements are exceptional, she sees herself as entirely ordinary, believing that many people possess untapped potential.

There is something undeniably epic about a lone biker battling against the clock, the weather, the environment and countless other obstacles. Another hero who overcame the odds is Jenny Graham, who in 2018, aged thirty-eight, became the fastest woman to circumnavigate the globe on a bike. She was the third to do so, the second being the Italian

Paola Gianotti in 2014, whose record attempt of 144 days was upheld by Guinness despite her having had to stop the clock for four months after she fractured some vertebrae in a road accident. Jenny covered 18,428 miles in 124 days. Going east from Berlin, she had followed a similar route to Mark Beaumont, who in 2017 set a new men's record of 79 days, smashing his previous 2008 record of 194 days. Clearly it was a good route.

I met Jenny in a café in north London five months after she claimed the world record. Like Juliana, she believes that we can achieve much more than we think, her own journey to world record-breaker being a case in point. Back when she was an eighteen-year-old new mother, the achievements of athletes like Mark Beaumont seemed entirely remote and out of reach.

She admits that she had never been into sports at school, skipping lessons whenever she could. But as her son grew older, she started getting into mountain biking in the hills around her home town of Inverness. This in itself makes her remarkable. For parents – or those responsible for some-one's care – free time is a luxury in scarce supply. And in our society, the role of caregiver tends to fall to women. Research shows that women who parent are less likely to spend any free time they have doing something for them-selves, like physical activity. They report feeling guilty and self-indulgent if they do. It might explain why there are lots of men in my cycling club who have young kids but still manage to get out on a Sunday morning, while hardly any mothers of small children join us on the club run. Jenny believes the lack of time made her feel motivated to use the few hours she did manage to snatch here and there in a more focused way. When her son started going to after-school clubs, she would grab the opportunity to jump on her bike and go. As her son got older and she had more free time, she began cycling longer distances and competing in increasingly tough challenges.

Jenny didn't start out thinking of herself as an adventurer; she turned herself into one a step at a time, pushing herself further and further just to see how far she could go. Men had been setting round-the-world cycling records for decades before Juliana made her attempt. The fact that there were no women doing the same suggests they lacked the belief they could do it, a legacy of being told women weren't physically capable of such things.

Even in the run-up to her departure, Jenny says she felt like an 'imposter'. She tells me that it was the 'hardest part of the whole thing, getting to the start line and working through all those doubts', particularly the thought of 'failing spectacularly' with so many eyes on her.

Whatever her own doubts, she had a strong support network who believed she could do it, including the members of the Adventure Syndicate, a global collective of women endurance bike riders. Through their first-hand accounts and organised group rides, the Syndicate aim to change the narrative about what is possible for women and girls, and inspire them go out on their own cycle adventures. As an aspiring endurance cyclist, Jenny had borrowed money from her son, by this time an adult, to get to one of their camps. It was worth it: the camp's coach offered to train her for free for a year. She recognised this as a 'life-changing' opportunity, though it wasn't until a few months later, having read about Juliana's round-the-world ride, that Jenny decided what her next challenge would be.

Having secured sponsorship, and plotted a route from Berlin, heading east through Poland, Latvia, Lithuania, Russia, Mongolia and to Beijing, before hopping on a flight to Australia, Jenny arrived at the start line filled with a sense of purpose. She banished doubts by telling herself: 'I was born to be here, this is what I was made for, this is what I should be doing right here, right now.' About to embark on a race against the clock, spending an average of sixteen hours a day on the bike to cover around 180 miles daily, she was living in the moment in a way that is hard to do in our normal lives. Juliana, too, described her ride as 'a kind of meditation. A complete stillness.' It shows that, even on a journey of this nature, it's possible to be immersed in the here and now, rather than the next food or sleep stop, or indeed the finish line.

Unlike Dervla Murphy on her leisurely travels, Jenny didn't have the luxury of stopping and spending time in places that took her fancy. Nevertheless she experienced 'gorgeous interactions with people' along the way, which felt all the more meaningful knowing that she would never see them again. There were challenges en route, but she saw these as fleeting moments and didn't allow them to disturb the general sense of contentment she felt.

In person, Jenny is brimming with energy and positivity, which I'm sure went a long way to push her through the tough times – lack of sleep and exhaustion, freezing-cold temperatures, or having to ride at night to avoid getting mown down by trucks on the roads through Russia. She makes sleeping in drainage ditches under the road sound as comfortable as a night in a well-appointed hotel. Listening to her, I wonder whether I would have persevered or been defeated by such obstacles.

To fill the lonely hours, she would sing along to playlists friends had compiled for her. She also listened to audio-books, including Apsley Cherry-Garrard's *The Worst Journey in the World*. This gripping account of the disastrous 1910–13 Terra Nova Antarctic expedition, in which Robert Falcon Scott and several others froze to death on the way back from the South Pole, helped keep Jenny from falling asleep on the road and put her own trials into perspective. Women were excluded from Scott's party because they weren't deemed capable of taking on such a challenge – an erroneous assumption, as it has since been proved that women are better able to cope in the harsh polar environment. In 1937 over a thousand women applied to be part of another Antarctic expedition but not one was accepted. For decades the US enforced a ban on women going to the area. It's a recent development that women have been accepted – as scientists and explorers – in this exclusively male, Western and white territory.

While women are now gaining ground in Antarctica and elsewhere, they remain less likely to attempt endurance challenges, particularly solo ones. As we have seen, this is in part due to a lack of representation. With the likes of Jenny and Juliana showing that women are capable of such feats, hopefully that will change. But there are other factors standing in the way of female participation. A recent Gallup survey revealed that 34 per cent of American women worry about being sexually assaulted, compared to only 5 per cent of men. Many are afraid to walk in their own neighbourhoods after dark, let alone cycle around the world. Just as Victorian clothing made women immobile, the perceived or real threat of sexual violence or harassment stops many women from moving freely.

Jenny tells me that she didn't feel vulnerable as a solo female traveller, though she researched women's rights in the countries she would be travelling through to prepare herself for the reception she would receive as a female cyclist. She occasionally took precautions, adapting her behaviour to dodge threatening situations, steering well clear of Russian truck stops to avoid alerting the men there to the fact that there was a woman cycling through the night alone. Her tactic was to make herself 'an invisible person, so not a male or a female, non-threatening, just a silhouette, just passing through not drawing attention to yourself'. I doubt Mark Beamount gave much thought to remaining invisible on his round-the-world rides.

She describes a handful of incidents which seemed to her 'inappropriate': instances where truckers followed or waited for her on the road and she had to keep cycling to shake them off. She never felt it was something she couldn't handle, and the uncomfortable moments were outweighed by the positive interactions she had with strangers. Her biggest concern was making sure she wouldn't be run over by those same truckers where there was no room for them to pass her safely, which was why she had switched to cycling through the night in the first place.

A 2018 Thomson Reuters poll of experts listed India as the most dangerous country for women, due to the high incidence of sexual violence and slave labour. The statistics are appalling, with an estimated four rapes taking place every hour. Perpetrators are seldom convicted, and there are multiple barriers to women reporting the crime or being taken seriously if they do. India was the place where Julianna felt most uncomfortable as a lone female cyclist; she had to abandon cycling after dark because it seemed too risky. In addition to dealing with severe stomach problems and sickness, dodgy roads and dangerous traffic, she frequently drew crowds of 'circus freak show proportions'. She describes how, particularly on the eastern coast, she would be surrounded by 'hordes of silent, staring men'. On one occasion the police had to disperse the crowd with their batons. In other instances, she was followed for miles by men on scooters, something she understandably found threatening. She developed a technique of shouting aggressively and waving her fist to disperse them – a 'highly effective weapon in a lone female's arsenal'.

While developing countries make up most of the Thomson Reuters top ten list of the most dangerous countries for women, it's a misconception that sexual violence is less of an issue in Western countries. In the same poll, the USA was listed jointly with Syria as the third most dangerous country for women. Cindy Southworth, executive vice-president of the Washington-based National Network to End Domestic Violence, commented: 'People want to think income means you're protected from misogyny, and sadly that's not the case.'

It may come as a shock that Sweden is cited as having one of the highest incidences of rape in the world. The statistics may be skewed by the fact that, in some countries, women are too fearful or ashamed to report that they have been sexually assaulted, especially when they know the authorities are unlikely to take action. It's also the case that, worldwide, women are more likely to be assaulted by someone they know; a 2018 study of rape and sexual assault victims by Glasgow University found that 90 per cent knew their attacker.

That's not to say terrible things don't happen. But they occur less often than we are led to believe by stories that exploit women's fear of violent assault by a stranger and disproportionately represent the risks they face. During her ride across the Australian Outback, Juliana was repeatedly warned of the risk she was taking. *Wolf Creek* was frequently cited in these warnings. In the movie, two female backpackers are kidnapped, tortured and killed. The marketing for the film was purposely ambiguous, trying to convince viewers it was based on real-life events when in fact it had been heavily fictionalised, and so adding to a mythology about the dangers lurking in the Australian Outback for lone women travellers.

Juliana hadn't seen the film, but she decided to heed

the advice of numerous Australian women – as I'm sure I would too – who told her never to ride at night through the remoter parts of the country, one of whom advised her to avoid the sparsely populated coast road and take a busier inland route instead.

Despite the cautions, she experienced nothing but generosity and kindness, much as Dervla Murphy had in Afghanistan. As women, whether travelling alone or going about our daily lives at home, we're constantly adapting our behaviour to avoid hazardous situations. Due to a combination of negative personal experience and narratives that purposely inflate risk, not drawing attention to ourselves becomes automatic and deep-rooted behaviour. So much so, that sometimes we don't realise we're doing it.

The biggest threat Jenny faced in Australia was nature. First the rain and freezing winter temperatures and then the animals, specifically kangaroos. Cycling through the dark she would see these huge mammals, sometimes as tall as six feet, looming at the side of the road. Though they seldom attack humans unless provoked – unlike the magpies that tormented Juliana by dive-bombing her – they are a terrifying sight when you're alone on the road at night.

In Alaska, locals were horrified to discover that Jenny was unarmed. Especially since she was cycling through the wilderness, sleeping in a bivvy bag at the side of the road most nights, at a time of year when bears stockpile food to prepare for winter hibernation. Jenny thinks that sheer exhaustion escalated the potential threat in her head. Rather than carrying a gun to ward off bear attack, she took the precaution of purchasing a deterrent spray and attaching a bell to her handlebars to warn unsuspecting bears that she was approaching. She would also sing loudly when she was on the road in the dark so there was no possibility of her startling them.

Down through the Yukon, she added bison to the list of slightly terrifying animals. The huge herds she passed in the dark did not detract from the wonder of the Northern Lights or the daytime beauty of the landscape.

Jenny tells me that the hardest part of the journey was the last leg through Europe, when the immensity of what she was doing finally caught up with her. She experienced of number of mini emotional breakdowns at the side of the road as a result of feeling 'so overwhelmed, it all came crashing down on me'. The nearer she got to the finish line, the more people became involved, until she felt she was no longer in control. It was a culture shock after thousands of miles pedalling away on her own, making all the decisions. For Jenny had chosen to do her trip the same way Juliana had: entirely self-supported. Unlike some round-the-world cyclists, including Mark Beaumont, she had no one following her in a van and providing food, a place to sleep, emotional support, massages; there was no logistical support booking flights and arranging border crossings. Strangely, Guinness make no distinction between supported and unsupported record attempts.

Jenny carried everything she needed with her and was entirely self-reliant, cycling in the way she has always done and enjoys the most. When Lee Craigie from the Adventure Syndicate joined her for part of the final leg through Spain and France, Jenny insisted on strict rules to ensure that the ride would remain solo. Lee could only ride with her for a few hours here and there, but she broke the rules on the last day, when she gave an exhausted Jenny a hug at 3 a.m. in a McDonald's. In Jenny's rulebook, cuddles were out. Unless she definitely needed one – and in this instance, she did.

After 124 days on the road, she found herself craving home and normality. But instead of resuming her old life, Jenny decided to give up her job and join Lee as a co-director of the Adventure Syndicate. During her record attempt she had received messages from women who had been inspired by her example to go on their own adventures; her new role would allow her to continue that work – reaching out to schoolgirls who hate sport and young mums who would never previously have thought themselves capable. When we met she had just arrived back in the UK after guiding a group of female cyclists – perhaps some who might go on to challenge Jenny's own record – for a week through the Sierra Nevada Mountains in Spain. Her bike, parked outside the café, was loaded down with all her kit.

We now know that such a thing is entirely possible, thanks to Juliana, Jenny and Paola, as well as the intrepid and indefatigable Annie Kopchovsky, even if her miles fall a long way short of the record holders. They have all played their part in rewriting the rules for what women can do, helping open up a world that many may have been wrongly led to believe was a boys-only club.

Part IV

QUEENS OF TRACK, ROAD AND MOUNTAIN

CHAPTER 10

To Race Is Life

Interlopers

It's September 1941 and seventy-five men have gathered in the clubhouse of a golf course on the shores of Lake Michigan to reminisce about their sporting glory days. Their triumphs had occurred at the tail end of the previous century, and these men were winners not of golf tournaments but of bicycle races. Several had competed on high wheels, others had been champions on Safety bicycles in the 1890s. A number had taken part in six-day races; a popular format considered to be the ultimate test of endurance and stamina, these events involved cycling laps around a track for up to twenty hours a day, grabbing a few hours' sleep when they could no longer turn the pedals or began hallucinating from exhaustion. The winner was the one who racked up the greatest distance before the clock stopped.

They might have relied on drugs supplied by their soigneur to do so; strychnine, trimethyl, heroin, cocaine and morphine were all legal and permissible on the track. Sometimes they competed against horses, in cowboy vs bicycle races. While the horsemen – including Buffalo Bill Cody, no less – were allowed to change their mounts when they tired, the cyclists had to carry on regardless. Thousands turned out to watch and there was a lot of money to be won. The men had been national, in some cases international, stars, when bike racing was the most popular spectator sport of the era. They had pushed their bodies to the limits and broken records previously thought impossible. Here was an opportunity to bask in the memories of those golden years when they had been at the peak of physical fitness and life was all about the bike. What they hadn't expected from this nostalgia-fest was that there would be an interloper who would disrupt proceedings and crush the idea that the world of nineteenth-century racing was a boys' club.

As the afternoon progressed and the men each took to the stand to reminisce about the good old days, a woman in her sixties crossed the pristine lawn and made straight for the party. When she introduced herself, they knew why she had come – it was Tillie Anderson, one of the greatest women bicycle racers of the 1890s. She had records to match most – and even surpass some – of those gathered, from her time spent spinning around tracks across the US in front of huge crowds. Despite this, Tillie hadn't been invited to this 'stars of the nineteenth century' event because women's cycle racing wasn't considered part of the official story of the sport. Tillie's achievements, along with those of her female contemporaries and many who came after, had been pushed to the margins, forgotten and overlooked.

Female bicycle racers had once brought in huge crowds – and their money – and helped sell newspapers, but once their novelty had run its course they were no longer of value to the sport and the overwhelmingly male image it wanted to present. It seems Tillie was warmly received by her male contemporaries gathered at the golf course, but she had to force her way into the men's party to take up her rightful place. She was one in a long line of women throughout the history of cycle racing who had to fight to be recognised in what the former Olympic and all-round superstar cyclist, Nicole Cooke, described in 2017 as 'a sport run by men, for men'.

Women's racing is now officially recognised by the Union Cycliste Internationale (UCI), the sport's global governing body, but there remains some way to go before we achieve parity with men. Ever since Tillie's day, women have been fighting for recognition, equal pay, opportunities and to be taken seriously. Progress has been slow. Women's track racing became part of the Olympic Games in 1988, though women had been racing on the track for over a hundred years by that point. In fact, there was no women's cycling whatsoever at the Olympics until 1984, while men have competed since 1896. Only since 2012 have there been an equal number of men's and women's cycling events.

Cycling has a long history of sidelining female participants. Flick through Olympian and Tour de France winner Bradley Wiggins's 2018 book *Icons*, in which he writes about twenty-one of his cycling heroes, and you'll see that not one of them is a woman.

Adamant that she was as worthy as any man of being acknowledged a 'star' in the sport, Tillie Anderson attended every subsequent annual gathering of champions until her death, aged ninety.

Strong Women and High Wheels

My great-grandfather, Samuel Moss, won many medals at London's Herne Hill Velodrome in the 1890s and 1900s. Built in 1891, it is one of the oldest and most famous remaining outdoor tracks, one of the few to survive the end of the cycling boom. During the era when Samuel was pedalling around the track, its legendary Good Friday races would attract upwards of 10,000 spectators. When Frank Shorland, one of the era's most successful cyclists in the UK, took to the track in 1894 for a twenty-four-hour race, 20,000 turned out to watch him, many of whom had broken through the barricades to see his triumphant ride. Police served as bodyguards to avoid him being mobbed when he left the stadium.

The huge popularity of these events made me wonder if there were women's races too, but a book on Herne Hill's history makes no mention of any during this period. I initially assumed that, given the resistance to women sedately getting around on a bicycle, they might have been banned from participating in races until well into the twentieth century. It turns out this wasn't the case. While they struggled to be recognised by the cycling authorities, that didn't stop them. In fact, cycling was one of the first competitive sports that women participated in – which makes the decades of marginalisation bitterly ironic.

It is generally agreed that the first women's cycle race took place in November 1868 at the Parc Bordelais in Bordeaux, a few months after the first recorded men's race. Watched by thousands of spectators, four women competed on velocipedes. The winner, Mlle Julie, narrowly beat Mlle Louise, who had led the pack for most of the race. In an illustration of the event, the 'vélocipèdiennes' are shown dressed in mid-length skirts that flow out behind; their stockinged, or possibly bare, legs are thrust out in front, turning the pedals attached to their front wheels. In the US the image was censored for inclusion in *Harper's* magazine, with decency preserved by the addition of billowy bloomers to cover the women's legs.

The following year, at another French event, it was reported that three women competed among a field of 120 men in the first long-distance road race. Only thirty-three entrants managed to finish the 76-mile course from Paris to Rouen; twenty-ninth across the line was a woman from Lyon riding under the name 'Miss America'. Her husband apparently came thirtieth. She soon became a fixture in races around France throughout the velocipede craze.

When the high wheel won people's hearts in the 1880s, a handful of women, mostly in North America, were determined to make their mark in the racing world. They would challenge other women, men and even horses to see who was fastest. In 1881, Elsa von Blumen, born Caroline Wilhelmina Kiner in 1859 to German immigrant parents in Kansas, took on a horse named 'Hattie R' on her high wheel in front of 2,500 spectators at Driving Park in Rochester, New York. As a teen, Elsa had been diagnosed with consumption and had taken up walking to regain her health. She quickly discovered she had remarkable endurance and by 1879 she was a champion competitive walker, the 'Queen of Lady Pedestriennes'.

At that time walking races were as popular a spectator sport as baseball, though it's hard to fathom the appeal of watching someone walk round and round a small track for hours, sometimes days, with only short breaks for food. Elsa regularly took part in 100-mile events on specially built indoor tracks or sawdust loops on music-hall stages, completing the distance in twenty-seven hours. By 1880 she had moved on to the high wheel, which was a lot faster and decidedly more dangerous. After her contest with the horse, she pedalled 1,000 miles in six days on a course in Pittsburgh. One picture shows Elsa wearing buttoned-up leather ankle boots, peaked hat, neatly fitting bloomers and jacket, with a little fringed skirt over the top; no female high wheel would have risked a long skirt.

Elsa often competed against men, but her main female rival was the French-Canadian Louise Armaindo, who had also come to cycling through the competitive walking route. The daughter of a circus strongwoman, Louise had started out as a trapeze artist and strongwoman in a Chicago circus. She boasted that, in her prime, her mother could lift 400 kg, so notions of female frailty were utter nonsense in her experience. In 1882 Louise and Elsa raced each other in one of the first recorded women-only high-wheel races, consisting of five-mile heats over six days. Louise won and held the crown of women's champion high wheel for most of the decade.

Like Elsa, Louise didn't shy away from competing against men. In 1883 she took on US champions William

M. Woodside and William J. Morgan in a six-day race on a
makeshift cinder track in the Armory near the waterfront in
Chicago. The three flew around the track for twelve hours
a day in front of an audience of 2,000, with adjudicators
carefully counting the laps of each rider. Taking a break
would have allowed the other riders to gain ground, so
they avoided stopping as much as possible. By the end of
the first day there wasn't much between the three, but by
the fourth Louise had started to overtake the men. She increased her lead still further over the final two days, ending
the seventy-second hour triumphant, with 843 miles compared to Morgan's 820 and Woodside's meagre 723. She
told a journalist that 'no one can have any idea how I had
to punish myself to hold to the end; but I had determined to
beat those two men, and I did it'.

Unhappy about being surpassed by a girl, William
Woodside challenged her to a 120-mile race spread across
three evenings the following week in Wisconsin. Morgan
also took part, and again Louise beat the two men.
William didn't leave it there: the three came together again
in Milwaukee for a three-hour-a-night six-day race. He was
so confident he would win this time that he gave Louise
a thirty-mile advantage and William Morgan twelve miles.
Once again Louise won, with 294 miles to Morgan and
Woodside's 285 and 277 respectively. By the end of the
year she is alleged to have earned the equivalent of around
$100,000 in today's money for her remarkable racing
prowess.

Queen Louise continued to see off all contenders for her
crown until the end of the decade. A new crop of young
riders in their teens and early twenties had entered the
scene – perhaps inspired by Louise – and were testing their
mettle on cinder tracks all over the US, bringing her reign
to an end. Before she retired from her life on the road,

taking on whoever would challenge her at track after track, Louise joined a touring troupe of female high-wheelers who travelled the country racing each other, sometimes for eight hours a day, six days a week in front of packed stadiums like Madison Square Gardens in New York. From September 1889 to January 1890, Louise and her fellow cyclists toured the UK, competing against each other in towns such as Grimsby, North Shields, Long Eaton, Sheffield and Northampton. Thousands came to watch, most of whom would never have seen a woman race a bike before. The women worked hard, competing in everything from a twenty-hour race over six days to 100-mile competitions, as well as taking on male challengers.

Louise never managed to claw her way back to the top against her stronger new rivals. One of these was Lottie Stanley, who stayed on in the UK to continue to race against men, such was the novelty of a woman cycle racer. One of her events, at Wolverhampton Wanderers Football Club, attracted 17,000 spectators.

Tillie the Terrible and Mlle Lisette

While Louise's star had waned, she had been a remarkable rider in her prime and, like Tillie Anderson, had earned as much right as any male cyclist to be included in an event celebrating the sport's champions. Tragically, a hotel fire in 1896 left her with such severe injuries that she could never race again and in 1900 she died in obscurity.

In her final decade she would have seen great changes in the world of cycling, not least the meteoric rise of the new queen of bike racing, Tillie Anderson. The high wheel's domination had given way to the new, more practical Safety bicycles, and bicycle racing had become an official sport. In the US it was regulated by the League of American

Wheelman (LAW), which acted as an advocate for cyclists in general, ran races and kept records. High-wheel racing had been a relative sporting Wild West, where anyone could take on anyone or anything, but those days were gone. As we saw in Chapter 5, with the introduction of a ban on non-white members in 1894, the LAW was not an inclusive organisation. It objected to women's participation in cycle racing, and refused to grant Tillie and her contemporaries official recognition. None of their races were included in the LAW's records, and velodromes that ran women's cycling events were liable to be blacklisted.

Despite the fact that riders like Louise had been proving that they were strong and fearless and could take on, and even beat, men, it's likely the LAW had a similar view to many at that time; women sweating it out on the track was both unacceptable and too controversial to get involved with. At a time when women were still having to prove they had as much right to ride a bike as men, even many of those who strongly supported them in doing so felt that racing was a pedal stroke too far.

Magazines and much of the cycling press at this time were full of warnings of the 'scorcher' – someone riding fast and furiously – and for women to 'scorch' was so far from the ideals of femininity that the LAW wanted no part in it. For many conservatives it was the most extreme example of the damage that could be done to a woman from riding a bike. Many in the UK shared these views, including *Cycling* magazine, which declared in 1894 that the sport 'is not, nor can it ever be, a fit thing for ladies to indulge in. The feminine constitution was never intended to withstand the strain of such competition' and 'it should be derogatory to any woman's sense of modesty'. Elizabeth Robins Pennell concurred that, for women, 'if carried to excess, cycling becomes a positive evil'.

In France, home of the first races to feature female riders, women continued to compete without attracting controversy. In 1893 Mlle de Saint-Sauveur became the first woman to claim the 'hour record' – for the longest distance covered in sixty minutes – at the Buffalo Velodrome in Paris, inspiring others to have a go at beating her time. There were regular women's races on road and track, as well as women competing against men. Some of these riders became international stars, like Lisette and Belgium's Hélène Dutrieu, who was awarded a medal for her cycling achievements by King Leopold II.

In the UK and America, women had few opportunities to participate in public sporting competitions of any kind. Tennis was an exception, with women taking part in Wimbledon as early as 1884, but participants would have demonstrated little of the physicality of the Williams sisters today, not least because they were required to wear their regulation long skirts. Maud Watson, winner of the first Wimbledon Ladies' Singles title, did so wearing an all-white ensemble of woollen ankle-length skirt complete with small bustle, long-sleeved silk blouse and sailor hat. Not exactly an outfit designed to help you fly around the court returning tricky serves. Twenty-year-old Blanche Bingley competed at that same event wearing a whalebone corset that pierced her skin as she played, resulting in her bleeding through her white blouse. Another competitor fainted, perhaps because her outfit was unsuited to the heat. When women were permitted to compete at tennis in the 1900 Olympics – as well as in the upper-class sports of sailing, croquet, equestrianism and golf – their clothing remained as impractical as ever.

Whereas tennis could just about be managed in Victorian womenswear, the same could not be said of cycle racing. As the 1890s progressed and competition on the track intensified, Louise and Elsa's bloomer costumes gave way to aero short-shorts and tights. Some male spectators may have been drawn to the races by the rare spectacle of female legs. Perhaps the LAW felt this prurient interest would taint the serious image they hoped to project of the new sport. The fact that some of the female riders were former circus or music-hall performers may have contributed to the perception of women's racing as a risqué sideshow spectacle rather than a serious competition between true athletes.

It's true that the sight of women on a racetrack using their bodies in such a physical way would have been a novelty, but contemporary accounts show that spectators recognised that these women had an objective other than titillation. In 1889, a Sheffield newspaper reporting on a race staged by Louise and her high-wheel gang acknowledged that 'instead of a demonstration of limbs', the women 'rode with speed and skill worthy of the best male bicycle riders'.

Not that Tillie and other female racers of the 1890s, and most particularly their agents and managers, weren't unaware of the impact of their bodies. The press was fixated on their outfits, looks and body shapes. Then as now, sex sells, and some riders exploited this to raise their profile. One of Tillie's rivals, Dottie Farnsworth, wore a costume of eye-catching scarlet satin shorts and top which earned her the nickname the Red Bird. She had previously worked in the theatre and understood the value of making an entrance and would walk onto the track wearing a long white robe which she would then remove to reveal her sensational outfit. The press and spectators loved it.

The top riders were celebrities, interviewed in the media and photographed in glamorous poses with their bikes, like Hollywood stars the following century. Aside from boosting profits, they were under pressure to prove that, while they might be demons on the track, cycling had not turned them into men. Before one race, Tillie's legs were examined by a doctor in the presence of a journalist to determine whether they had been made manly in the process of her training. It was reported that they had a 'beautiful' shape, but that her veins, which they felt were too prominent, did detract rather.

Tillie's career was based on a lot more than her image. She had arrived in Chicago from Sweden in 1891 and worked in laundries and as a seamstress. Seeing women riding about the city on their bicycles, she began to desire her own. By 1894 she had not only managed to obtain one but had discovered that she possessed a natural talent. She took to training each day before work, and the following year she set a century (100-mile) record on the Elgin Aurora course in Chicago, where she was spotted by a sponsor and given a better bike.

Her next challenge was a six-day race which consisted of three hours' racing a day, with Tillie easily beating her more established rivals to scoop the $200 prize. Though women's racing was not recognised by the LAW, she realised it offered far better financial prospects than life as a seamstress, not to mention fame and adulation. Such was her talent and determination, in 1895 it's estimated she earned the equivalent of $150,000 in today's money – an astonishing figure for someone who had been living with her parents above a meat market, struggling to make ends meet. She was a formidable athlete, training full-time and winning 123 out of 130 races between 1895 and 1902. 'Tillie the Terrible', as she was dubbed in the press, was determined to test her strength against the men, but the LAW ban meant she could not do so in an officially sanctioned race. When she was finally given a chance at an informal race in Chicago, she duly wiped the floor with her male opponent.

Despite its outsider status, from the mid to late 1890s women's bike racing in the US was big business, with audiences in their thousands flocking to see Tillie and others battle it out on the track. The sport thrived, to such an extent that it could not be put down to spectators wanting to catch a glimpse of women's legs. Part of the appeal might have been that men's races involved competitors slogging around a track for up to twenty hours a day, six days straight, guaranteed to result in fatigue for spectators as well as participants. The women's version was limited to three or four hours a day, which made for a faster and more gripping competition and involved far less commitment from the audience.

The ban on women competing in the same venues as the men had been overcome by canny organisers who built temporary velodromes that consisted of steep-sided wooden oval tracks, on theatre and music-hall stages or wherever else would accommodate them. It was quite a skill to manoeuvre safely around these petite courses with their sides sloping to as much as 45 degrees. Accidents – including broken bones and severe concussion – weren't uncommon. Those that raced deemed it worth the risk to earn a good living; some managed to earn more than the men, making today's huge gender pay gap in professional cycling look like a backward step. No doubt the women's managers and agents were also making a lot of money in fees, leaving riders with only a small proportion of their earnings.

A day at the cycle races, pre-cinema, was one of the most popular attractions across Europe, North America, Australia and elsewhere, and organisers worked hard to pull in the crowds. Orchestras were hired to accompany the racing, upping the anticipation and excitement levels. Unlike the rarefied and hushed atmosphere of Wimbledon, cycle racing would have been loud and raucous, with drinking and betting. Not least at the Royal Aquarium in London, which regularly put on women's six-day races and attracted star riders from France and Belgium to compete against UK talent.

Organisers found the inclusion of a programme of women's cycling alongside the men's – in the UK there was no ban on women racing in the same venues as men – a highly lucrative endeavour. During lulls in the action on the track, the audience would be entertained by acrobats, clowns, strong men and women, Japanese jugglers, synchronised swimmers, human cannonballs and morally questionable acts such as performing elephants, minstrels and a 'human horse'.

In November 1895, all eyes were on the track for the women's international six-day race, described by the London *Standard* as the 'talk of the world'. Cheered on by an audience of thousands, the UK's Monica Harwood came from complete obscurity to win. A few months previously Monica had answered an advert looking for women to race across England and Scotland. Like Tillie, she wiped the floor with the established competition, including the celebrated Clara Grace (or Mrs Grace, as she was called by the press), who came ninth after a fall on the fifth day, and who it turns out had helped train her new rival.

The cyclist who came second, with 368 miles and six laps to Monica's 371 and two laps, was France's Lisette, touted as the greatest female rider in the world despite there being no official way to verify this claim. That was far from the end of the track for Lisette; the following May she competed against Clara Grace on home turf, at the Vélodrome d'Hiver in Paris, beating her over a distance of 100 km. That same year she broke a new women's hour paced record (where riders in front set the speed and give the competitor the advantage of drafting behind them) with 43.461 km, which was unbeaten for many years. She also took on, and was beaten by, the star Welsh racer Jimmy Michael in a 50 km race in Paris. Then she returned once more to London's Royal Aquarium, emerging triumphant this time, pushing her rival Monica into second place in another six-day race.

Lisette was a global cycling star who worked hard to create a mythology around her origins, no doubt to keep the media and public interested. In one version she claimed to have been a shepherdess in Brittany; a passing cyclist, on learning of her desire to take up cycling, gifted her a bike, whereupon she discovered a natural talent for the sport. In another she was an orphan in Paris, working long hours in a factory which made her sickly, and so took up cycling for the sake of her health before going on to race.

Whatever her true origins, her real name was Amélie le Gall and she was a formidable talent – though perhaps not the greatest in the world, as became apparent in 1898 when she set her sights on conquering America. Over the following years she took part in a series of races against the 'big five', which included Tillie and Dottie, the 'Red Bird'. Lisette didn't win a single race, but the crowd still went wild about this French legend who didn't wear shorts, just tights. She may have been handicapped by the steep-sided tracks that Tillie and the other American women had adapted to, which were a far cry from the full-sized velodromes she was used to at home. This may have contributed to the bad fall she took on the second day of her first six-day race, which was witnessed by a crowd of 4,000. Unwilling to admit defeat, she got back on, but a few days later another crash left her with concussion. Dottie, who had fallen in front of Lisette's path and caused the collision, claimed to have suffered a broken rib. Despite the severity of their injuries, they were both back on their bikes for the third night. In the end it was Tillie who finished triumphant, with Lisette in second place and Dottie pushed into fourth. Rather than return to France, Lisette decided to stay on in America, perhaps because it was more lucrative to do so.

The papers and crowds loved the enigmatic French cyclist. A report published in Chicago's *Inter Ocean* newspaper, ahead of her racing in the city, showed the extent to which so many had bought into Lisette's mythology. Disregarding her inability to beat Tillie, they referred to her as the 'speediest of all cyclists', and erroneously claimed she had beaten Jimmy Michael. Most of all, they adored her Frenchness, which they described as a 'winning "chic" that brands the real Parisian' and praised her for following a training schedule 'much less severe' than that of her US and UK counterparts, by which I assume they meant it seemed more appropriately feminine.

No matter how 'chic', Lisette couldn't prevent the decline of women's racing in the US. Men's racing was also hit, with audiences moving on to other sports like baseball. Star female riders began wheeling off the track to earn a living elsewhere. One of the first was Dottie, who joined a circus troupe to perform stunts on a tiny, even steeper-sided track known as the Cycle-Dazzle. Then one fateful night Dottie went right over the edge of the Cycle-Dazzle, sustaining injuries so serious she died a few hours later. Her fellow racers moved on to safer pursuits: Tillie became a masseuse, and Lisette moved into the restaurant business, opening establishments in New Orleans and then Miami with her husband.

With the dawn of the new century, enthusiasm for women's track racing evaporated in the UK and France too. London's once-famous Aquarium, where the champion Lisette unexpectedly lost out to a British newcomer, was demolished in 1903. Its former stars were soon forgotten and as that generation died out, with no official records to keep alive their achievements, most of their descendants had no idea they had a celebrated, fearless, indefatigable and powerful 'cyclienne' in their family tree.

Not the End of the Road

If women racing on track wasn't the draw it had been at the start of the twentieth century, it didn't mean they had stopped being competitive about their cycling. Women the world over were intent on breaking records, though this was more often a matter of notching up road miles rather than laps in a stadium.

German-born Margaret Gast had previously competed in six-day races in the US and in 1901, aged eighteen (having told the organisers she was twenty-one so she could take part), cycled 2,000 miles in 9 days 8 hours and 5.5 minutes by riding a 25-mile road circuit on Long Island built by the Vanderbilts for their new motor cars. She beat the previous men's record by three hours and one minute. Margaret had originally set out to better the 1,500-mile women's record but felt so full of energy when she reached that milestone that she decided to carry on for another 500. When she got to 2,000, with only a few hours' sleep snatched here and there – having fallen off several times from sheer exhaustion, and endured thunderstorms and torrential rain that turned the road to mud – she still wasn't done. It wasn't until she had racked up 2,600 miles, breaking a new distance record for men and women, that she stopped pedalling. Had it been up to her, she would have continued until she'd made 3,000, but the residents living on the road had her stopped.

They shared the view of a newspaper article which condemned Margaret as a 'disgraceful exhibition' and told a journalist they feared for the effect the 'spectacle' would have on the minds of the children. I assume they meant they wouldn't want their own daughters thinking this was an appropriate activity, and so duly made sure it couldn't happen again on their rarefied patch. Other papers, while admitting that this was a remarkable achievement, were keen to point out the physical toll it had taken, with one declaring that she was 'far from a pleasant picture to look upon'. Prioritising her femininity over her achievements is something Margaret would have profoundly disagreed with. She would later donate a valuable puppy to an auction in New York to raise money for women's suffrage.

After her Vanderbilt record, she may have felt she had achieved what she wanted as a cyclist. Like Dottie, she moved on to performing stunts on stage. In Margaret's case she dropped the bicycle altogether for another invention, the motorcycle, continuing to defy expectations for her gender as the 'mile a minute girl' riding a 'wall of death', as well as competing with men in races. Despite several close shaves, unlike poor Dottie she survived her stunt years and excelled as a competitor. She was once asked by a journalist if she felt women needed a different type of motorbike and she responded, true to form, that women who race want a 'machine that is just as hard to handle as the man's'.

Devil in a Dress

Italy had its own cycling pioneer in Alfonsina Strada (née Morini). Born in 1891, she learned to ride at the age of ten on her father's bike, tearing around the roads in her village near Modena. She was reportedly nicknamed the 'Devil in a Dress', and won her first race age thirteen, for which she was awarded a pig. Like Lisette before her, Alfonsina didn't discourage the press from mythologising her rural peasant roots, but it's likely the family were grateful for the animal even if it seems they would rather she had taken up sewing as a profession.

Alfonsina was nothing if not determined, and having won many of her early races, against both girls and boys, she acquired a reputation as a formidable competitor. At eighteen she travelled to St Petersburg to compete in a Grand Prix and was awarded a medal by Tsar Nicholas II, which must have been quite an experience for the teenager when few, if any, members of her family had travelled beyond Modena.

In 1911, she broke the women's (unofficial) hour record at a velodrome in Turin, with 37.192 km, a record that would hold for twenty-six years. Hopefully this would have convinced any remaining doubters in her family that she'd made the right career choice. And if it didn't, at least she had the full support of her future husband, Luigi Strada. A metalworker who raced in his spare time, Luigi was so convinced of his wife's capabilities that he put his own racing career on the back-burner to focus on her training. When they married in 1915, his wedding gift to Alfonsina was a new racing bicycle. Over the following decades she would pedal her way to becoming the Regina della Pedivella, the 'Queen of the Cranks', a true legend in cycling history.

Frustrated by the lack of racing opportunities available to women, Alfonsina leaped at the chance to take part in the Giro di Lombardia in 1917 as the first female competitor. The race had never specifically omitted women, but Italy in those days was such a conservative country that it's possible Italians assumed that no woman would entertain the thought of entering. The organiser of the race, Armando Cougnet, was editor of the *Gazzetta dello Sport* and understood the power of a good story. With many of the star riders off fighting the war, he was looking to inject some interest into the competition and invited her to take part. The only woman in the 204 km race, the 'Queen of the Cranks' finished last, an hour and thirty-four minutes behind the winner, though with only a few seconds between her and the previous two finishers. Twenty-three riders failed to complete the course.

The following year she took her place once more, again amid a field of exclusively male competitors. This time she finished second to last, a mere twenty-three minutes behind the winner and only a fraction behind the five riders ahead of her. Fourteen riders failed to finish. This was to be her final Lombardia. The organisers now had their big-name riders back from the war and no longer needed the extra publicity that came with pitting a woman against the men. Armando, like those managers and race organisers before him who had enthusiastically promoted women's racing in the 1890s, had lost interest as soon as the financial motivation ceased to be compelling. I don't doubt he thought Alfonsina was a formidable and impressive rider, but he had no real interest in changing the status quo and opening up cycling to women. In fact, the race rules were tightened up, and women were no longer permitted to enter. To this day, Il Lombardia, as it's now known, is open only to men. There is no women's version. Alfonsina remains the only female entrant of this classic one-day race.

I imagine she was somewhat surprised when six years later Armando came cap in hand to ask the thirty-three-year-old to compete in another of his men-only races: the Giro d'Italia. Also known as the *Corsa Rosa* on account of the pink jersey worn by stage winners, this multi-stage event is one of the most famous and demanding races in the world. Armando was once again faced with the problem of maintaining public interest in the race, with a number of his star male riders missing. This time it wasn't military service keeping them away but a dispute over fees; when the organisers refused to meet the riders' demands, the two sides reached an impasse. Armando needed the greatest Italian woman cyclist of the day to provide drama and excitement. Alfonsina couldn't pass up this opportunity to show the world what she – and by extension her gender – was capable of in her country's legendary 'Grand Départ', an iconic race on a level with the Tour de France.

In 1924 the route was a punishing 3,613 km long, with stages ranging from 250 to 415 km, many of which involved long mountain climbs. The 2019 edition was marginally shorter, with no stage longer than 232 km. And there is a huge disparity in the quality of road surfaces now compared to then, as well as the weight of bikes. Alfonsina and her contemporaries rode steel machines that had no gearing and weighed almost twice as much as the carbon frames of today's peloton.

Armando entered his secret publicity weapon under the name Alfonsin Strada, though it's unlikely he was fooling anybody, since she was a household name by then. When the riders crossed the start line in Milan on 10 May for the 300 km first stage to Genoa, anyone who might have doubted that Alfonsin was Alfonsina now had incontrovertible evidence that *he* was indeed *she* in her signature black shorts and sweater emblazoned with her name.

On most of the early stages she finished between forty-five minutes and a few hours behind the lead rider, but she wasn't always last over the line, and hung on in there in the face of much adversity while two-thirds of her competitors dropped out. The ecstatic crowds who lined the streets to watch her pass, showering her with flowers and gifts, lifting her from her bicycle to hold her aloft when she'd completed another stage, must have helped keep her going. A crash in terrible weather during the seventh stage on unpaved and icy mountain roads in the south left her with a painfully damaged knee, but she pushed on to finish that day's 304 km route.

The following day Alfonsina came close to abandoning the Giro altogether: still in pain and inflicted with multiple punctures, her handlebars gave way and she resorted to fixing them with a broomstick to get her to that day's finish line. The accident resulted in her official expulsion from the race, since she had arrived at the day's end point in Perugia long past the cut-off. However, with her participation the talk of Italy and beyond, she was too valuable an asset for Armando to let it end there. Although she wouldn't be officially recorded as having finished the race, he paid her to complete the remaining stages regardless. It wasn't her last crash, but her grit and determination saw her through to the very end. On the final day she rode back into Milan thirty-three hours behind the winner, Giuseppe Enrici, but a hero to the people waiting to see her finish. Even the King of Italy sent his congratulations to the 'Queen of the Cranks'.

When it came to registering her place for the 1925 Giro, she was surprised – and doubtless angered – to find her application was blocked by the very people who had called on her the previous year to help deliver precious column inches. Alfonsina had served her purpose and now they had all the star male riders they needed to ensure the public stayed interested, she was surplus to requirements. They never had any plans to change the rules and let women compete long-term, or to launch a women's version (that wouldn't happen until 1988, too late for Alfonsina). It was, and would remain, a men-only competition with no further exceptions.

It wasn't the end for Alfonsina. She continued to compete for more than a decade in races where she was welcome. In 1938 she broke another women's hour record with 32.58 km, which would hold for seventeen years. Eventually she retired to run a bike shop in Milan with her second husband, another former racing cyclist, and with the passing years her achievements began to fall into obscurity, like those of Tillie, Louise and countless other female racing cyclists before her. Her new husband had hoped to write a book about her incredible career, but he died without being able to secure a publisher.

Alfonsina died of a heart attack in 1959 and the remarkable story of the only woman to have competed in her country's world-famous Giro was all but forgotten. That is until the first decade of the following century, when she finally got the biography, and consequently the acclaim and acknowledgement, she had earned. Were she alive today, she would be pleased I'm sure that women can finally race the Giro, albeit in a women-only version, but she might wonder why the women aren't racing as far or receiving anywhere near the amount of money or media coverage as the men.

CHAPTER 11

Cycling Like a Girl

'In the Rosslyn They Were All Lesbians . . .'

In 2005 the art critic and cyclist Tim Hilton received a letter
in which the correspondent told him she'd like to 'gouge his
eyes out'. He had just published a well-reviewed book about
cycling and possibly hadn't expected to provoke this violent
reaction. The would-be eye-gouger was – perhaps even more
surprisingly– a woman in her nineties. She had taken offence
at comments he'd included about the cycling club she'd belonged to for decades, the Rosslyn Ladies CC. It wasn't the
only critical letter he received from disgruntled members,
but it was the only one threatening physical violence.

His reference to the club is brief, little more than a page,
but what his critics were vehemently objecting to was the
inclusion of the following unverified hearsay:

> In the Rosslyn they were all lesbians, it was said. Or they
> were all so voracious that no man was safe in their company.
> Warn your son against them. None of them was married.
> Or, said another story, they kept their club membership
> secret from their husbands. They kept a list of hated male
> riders. When someone was on that list the Rosslyn Ladies
> would gather on a hill to jeer and taunt him. They did a lot
> of knitting.

These were remarks Tim had heard over the years, from
sources who were unlikely to have met any Rosslyn members. To them, the club was a mythical group on whom to
project various contradictory prejudices about women who
cycle competitively. Apart from the unfounded gossip, Tim
hadn't managed to uncover anything much that was based
on fact – undoubtedly another point of contention for the
women, although Tim did not set out to convey the remarks
as anything more than hearsay.

The Rosslyn Ladies' achievements weren't the stuff of myth – they were genuinely legendary. Most of the members are now in their seventies, eighties and nineties and they no longer race. But in their heyday they were a formidable force on the road and track, women who rode steel and were as strong as steel. Founded in 1922, it was the longest-running women's cycling club in the UK.

Pat Seeger first joined the Rosslyn in 1946, at the age of twenty. Now ninety-two, she was one of the club's most successful road racers. When I visited her at her home in rural Essex, we talked in her sitting room surrounded by her many medals and trophies. She grew up in the borough of Haringey in north London – only a few streets away from where I live now – and was taught by a boyfriend to ride a bike when she was fifteen. He persuaded her to join his mixed club, which then had only a handful of women members.

After she married (another cycling boyfriend), she decided to join the all-women Rosslyn, which still had some of its founders as active members. One of these was Nellie, who told Pat that in the early years they often had stones thrown at them, as well as insults like 'fast hussies', when they rode out together from Hackney. It's possible that the writer of Tim Hilton's incensed poison pen letter had been on those rides with Nellie and had endured such abuse.

Pat tells me that she joined the Rosslyn because the club was always in the cycling press on account of winning (as well as organising) so many races. That their results were recorded at all was thanks to Evelyn Parkes, who had founded the UK's Women's Road Record Association in 1934. The fact that decades of women's cycling had not been given official recognition made her realise that if women's records were ever going to be formalised, she'd have to do it herself, even if the official cycling organisations wouldn't accept them.

For despite the achievements of Tillie, Lisette and other stars who came before, the suitability of women racing was still being hotly debated well into the twentieth century. In 1937, the British cyclist Albert Lusty declared that women doing so was not just 'injurious to the game itself', but also to 'the interests of the nation'. In the decades before the second wave of feminism of the 1960s, despite women having joined the workforce en masse during two world wars, it was still widely accepted that women's place was in the home, that they should leave the sweaty stuff to the men and stick to the housework and child-rearing, tasks Albert saw as in the national interest.

Albert would have been happier in the Netherlands, where women's racing was banned in the 1930s and '40s, and anyone wanting to compete had to do so outside the country. After moving to Belgium, Mien Van Bree won many big races, only for the Dutch newspapers to declare that she should have 'stayed home, in her kitchen'. Times have indeed changed; the Netherlands has more than embraced women's competitive cycling, with the likes of Marianne Vos, Annemiek van Vleuten and Anna van der Breggen dominating the sport internationally in road, track, cyclo-cross and mountain bike. It's a shame the turnaround came too late for Mien.

The mother of the American cyclist Nancy Neiman Baranet, the four-time US National champion who in 1956 competed in a short-lived precursor to the women's Tour de France, subscribed to the view that a woman's place was in the home and refused to watch her daughter compete. When Nancy joined a cycle club in Detroit her mother was appalled, protesting: 'What will the neighbours think?' Nancy's father had only agreed to her riding a bike in the first place because he was more opposed to the idea of women driving cars.

Cycling wasn't alone in this; sportswomen across the board were meeting resistance if they wanted to participate in longer or harder events. In running, they could take part in the Olympics (unlike women's cycling prior to 1984), but the longest race before 1960 was 200 metres. There had been an 800-metre event in the 1928 Games, but it was dropped after it was inaccurately reported that those who finished collapsed or fainted after crossing the line. Women were not allowed to enter marathons until 1972, though a number had attempted to unofficially run in them. In football the women's game had thrived in the UK during the First World War and after, but in 1921 the UK's Football Association banned them from playing at club grounds after they declared it an unsuitable sport for women, a ruling that wasn't lifted until 1971.

The Blonde Bombshell and the Mighty Atom

Coventry-born Eileen Sheridan, now in her nineties, often raced against Pat and other Rosslyn Ladies in the 1940s and became one of the greatest competitive cyclists of the twentieth century, earning her the nickname the 'Mighty Atom' because of her immense power, speed and diminutive stature of just under five feet. In her memoir she describes how, when she started getting into competitions, she wasn't exactly welcomed with open arms. At her first audax, a long-distance ride of 140 miles to be completed in twelve hours, she was the only female entrant. The organisers, believing that a woman would hold everyone else back, tried to persuade her husband to take her home before it started. Eileen refused to drop out. Fifty miles into the ride they stopped asking if she was surviving, and after 100 miles, having proved she could more than keep up, she says she was finally accepted as 'one of the gang, initiated and admitted to the inner circle'.

When she joined her mixed local club, the Coventry CC, she says she was again made to feel that she and her bike had 'strayed into a world where they were sadly out of place'. On her first ride, the leaders kept upping the pace to try to drop Eileen, who they assumed wouldn't be able to keep up. She more than held her own. She was often the only woman out on rides with the club, so she was the one required to pour the tea when they stopped for a break, but she could easily outpace most of her fellow members. In the words of one magazine at the time, she 'rocked the racing world, setting up completely new standards for women's records', some of which would remain unbeaten for decades.

Marguerite Wilson, the UK's first professional female cyclist, dubbed the 'Blonde Bombshell' and whose records Eileen would go on to beat, had met similar resistance and scepticism in the 1930s. Before cycling, she had tried athletics, attempting to set up a women's club in her home town of Bournemouth. She gave up and switched to cycling after it became clear that men at other athletics clubs 'resented the intrusion of women into their pastime'. She didn't think her parents would approve of her decision, so she would creep out of the house with her home-made racing outfit hidden in her bag.

She was soon winning races and looking for greater challenges. In 1937 she entered her first twelve-hour race – organised by the Rosslyn – in which competitors endeavour to cover as much distance as possible in that time. Her male peers told her that 'it takes a man to ride a twelve', but the nineteen-year-old knew she could prove them wrong. She travelled to the race after finishing work on a Saturday afternoon, snatching a few hours' sleep in the car. The youngest entrant, she nevertheless finished with 209.25 miles. The next female rider was seven miles behind.

When Eileen entered her first twelve-hour in 1949, people again underestimated her. On the day, she completed the 223-mile women's course with forty minutes left on the clock, leaving the race organisers no choice but to direct her on to the men's course so she could continue until the time was up. She finished with 237.628 miles, beating the existing women's national record by seventeen miles. Taken alongside the men's results, her distance placed her fifth overall. For this and other results that year she was awarded Women's British Best-All-Rounder at a glitzy ceremony in London.

Remarkably, there were not a few who refused to believe her results, with some accusing Eileen of cutting a section of the course or suggesting there had been an error adding up her distance. She told herself she would beat, or at least equalise, her record the following year to prove the doubters wrong.

Once again, she ran out of course and had to go on to the men's. Extremely challenging weather meant she finished a mile short of her previous record, but fifteen miles ahead of the next woman. In the men's race, half the field dropped out because they couldn't handle the conditions. That year she won the Best-All-Rounder again, as well as the prestigious Bidlake Memorial Prize, an award given to one British cyclist a year for their contribution to the sport. It had only been open to women since 1939, when it was won by Marguerite, Eileen's record-breaking predecessor.

End-to-End

This should have been the proof needed to shut the doubters down; it was certainly enough to convince the Hercules Cycle Company to sign up Eileen as a professional cyclist in 1951. They wanted her to break the twenty-one long-distance place-to-place records – such as Land's End to London, Liverpool to Edinburgh and London to York – that had been set by Marguerite in the late 1930s and early '40s, again for Hercules. These events had just one rider, and they started as early as 2 a.m. to avoid traffic, the country roads being lit by the cyclist's front light and the headlights of the Hercules team car following the regulation 100 metres behind. Eileen set about bettering each of Marguerite's already extraordinary records. The most daunting of these was the End-to-End – 872 miles from Land's End, the most south-westerly point in Cornwall, to John O'Groats in the far north of Scotland.

Marguerite's End-to-End had taken place in August 1939, as the country was on the brink of war with Germany. Only one woman, Lilian Dredge, had taken on the challenge before. Thirty-two-year-old Lilian had completed the arduous ride in 1938 with a time of 3 days 20 hours and 54 minutes, but not without battling much prejudice from within the cycling world about her ability to manage such a feat of endurance. Apparently, as a result of the scrutiny she was under, Lilian opted to get some sleep each night to avoid looking too exhausted. The effortlessly glamorous Marguerite, on the other hand, decided she could better Lilian's time by seventeen hours if she only slept when absolutely necessary. She reached the hotel in John O'Groats, more than twenty hours faster, in 2 days 22 hours and 52 mins, with only three hours spent sleeping. Afterwards she said that it wasn't the lack of sleep that was the problem, it was the loneliness, since she was someone who loved to talk. Nevertheless, after a warm bath, followed by a large breakfast, she jumped back into the saddle. She wanted to try for the 1,000-mile record by pedalling 130 additional miles, as Lilian had done before her.

When she finally dismounted in Wick at the end of the

ride, she had made an incredible record of 1,000 miles –
with 11,000 metres of climbing – in 3 days 11 hours and 44
minutes (compared to Lilian's 4 days 19 hours and 14 minutes), a time only two men had previously bettered. She later
said she'd felt that she had the energy to do another 1,000.
If she hadn't already done more than enough to disprove
the theory that 'it takes a man to ride a twelve' wrong, then
she certainly had now. However, all around her the town
was in total darkness; unbeknownst to Marguerite and her
team, war had officially been declared during the record
attempt and the country was now under enforced blackout
every evening. She had achieved something remarkable, but
understandably her celebrations were marred by the terrible
news. She arrived back in London to the sound of the first
air-raid sirens.

Marguerite continued to set records during the first few
years of war, but her attempts were thwarted by wartime
measures – the removal of road signs, sudden roadblocks
and the cessation of weather forecasts, which were crucial
to planning long rides that require advantageous conditions.
In 1941 she had to put cycling aside completely to join the
war effort, volunteering as an ambulance driver in South-
ampton. She told a fellow cyclist that she would 'never be
able to forgive Hitler' for putting an end to her career.

She got back into the sport when she relocated to Canada
in 1948 with her husband, Ronnie, but found that when
she joined a Canadian cycling club, she was required to
prove herself once again. On her first rides the men did their
utmost to try to drop her as quickly as they could, much as
Eileen had experienced in her early days. The Canadians
were 'astonished' that instead of being left in their dust,
Marguerite could more than keep up. She started competing
in amateur races and the men became less hostile towards
the speedy Brit. When she eventually returned home, the

UK's National Cyclists' Union refused to grant her an amateur racing licence because she had previously raced as a professional. This, combined with a back injury, signalled the end of her days as a competitive cyclist.

Marguerite also would have seen her records tumble as Eileen set to work on bettering each and every one. On 9 June 1954 the 'Mighty Atom' set off to take on the jewel in Marguerite's crown, her End-to-End and 1,000 miles, the latter having remained unbeaten for fifteen years. Eileen had been in Cornwall for weeks, carefully preparing for this mammoth ride, but as she set off from Land's End on her steel bicycle with three gears (like Marguerite before her), it turned out to be far from the clement summer weather the team had expected. It wasn't long before Eileen was doing battle with strong crosswinds and unseasonably cold rain.

By the time she reached Exeter, 120 miles away, she was already thirty minutes down on the schedule she needed to keep to in order to improve on Marguerite's record. Nevertheless, she rode for twelve hours straight without taking her feet from the pedals, refuelling with food stored in a cannister on her handlebars. Her first break off the bike was momentary, just long enough to put on warmer clothing and some bike lights for the moonless and rainy night of riding ahead of her.

After twenty-four hours and over 450 miles, including some tough climbs in the Lake District, she came across a group of expectant journalists who hoped by this point she would stop for her first proper break and update them on her progress. She just pedalled on past. At the 470-mile mark the cold finally got to her, so she stopped to warm up in the caravan being towed behind her, changing her wet clothes and filling up on hot soup by the gas fire. She allowed herself a fifteen-minute nap which – unbelievably – she says left her feeling 'wonderfully fresh' and ready to tackle the next 800 miles. Even so, her manager insisted on carrying her onto her bicycle to preserve her energy.

On the road again, she battled with strong headwinds and torrential rain while struggling up the big hills over the Scottish border – it was a low point of the ride and Eileen suffered. Yet she wasn't about to give in and eventually the rain eased off. After Perth she was cycling into her second night, through the Grampian Mountains which loomed eerily out of the darkness, snowdrifts visible in their crevasses, the temperature plummeting. After 673 miles, frozen feet and blistered hands forced another brief stop to thaw out in the caravan. Her manager wrapped more tape round the handlebars to save her injured hands as Eileen put on a second pair of gloves before heading into the darkness.

It wasn't until she'd completed 700 miles, suffering badly from the cold, that she relented and took a nap – for thirty minutes. As dawn broke on the third morning, blue skies and sunshine helped lift her spirits during a slog over more Scottish mountains. But the break in the weather didn't last; as the day wore on she was up against the wind once more, enduring cold and intense tiredness. She persevered and finally reached her destination, the John O'Groats hotel, that evening, in a total of 2 days 11 hours and 7 minutes. She had beaten Marguerite's record by 11 hours and 45 minutes.

After a bath and snooze of just under two hours in total, she was back in the saddle for another 130 miles in the hope of adding the 1,000-mile record to her wins. This last push was gruelling, with prolonged lack of sleep and physical exhaustion so acute that she began to hallucinate. First, she started seeing people who were directing her the wrong way, then, in the hedges in the darkness on either side of her, large and brightly coloured animals, including polar bears, appeared. Before long she was dodging imaginary obstacles on the road ahead. After sixty miles it was too dangerous to continue so she slept for an hour, but of course it wasn't anywhere near enough, and when she set off again she was falling asleep while turning the pedals. After another thirty miles she had to stop and sleep for an hour to minimise the very real possibility of a crash. Her manager forked food into her mouth because her hands were too sore to hold the cutlery.

Once on the road again she was buoyed by the re-emergence of the sun and the appearance of Lilian Dredge, that first female 1,000-mile record holder, cheering her on as she approached the last twenty miles. It put a spring in her pedal stroke and by the time Eileen neared the John O'Groats hotel for the second time, her pace had quickened to an average of eighteen to twenty miles an hour. She arrived back at the hotel's front door with three days and one hour on the clock, a mammoth 10 hours 44 minutes ahead of Marguerite's own 1,000. Only one man at that point had recorded a faster time, and it was forty-eight years before Eileen's record was broken, when Lynne Biddulph did the same route in 2 days 16 hours and 38 minutes.

Housewives and Hardmen

Cycling culture celebrates those who suffer. This is why the big multi-stage races like the Giro d'Italia and Tour de France are so long and, to mere mortals, seem impossibly challenging.

The sport's icons are given the godlike status of 'hardmen' on account of the epic amounts of pain they overcome to win. Men like Andy Hampsten and Bernard Hinault have gone down in history for races in which they have perse-vered and triumphed through dangerous amounts of snow, ice and sub-zero temperatures, conditions which forced many others to abandon the race; and riders like Fausto Coppi, who was compared by some to crucified Christ when he was close to complete physical and mental break-down during the 1951 Tour de France; or Louison Bobet, winner of the Tour for three consecutive years in the early 1950s, but at the expense of saddle sores that resulted in such serious tissue damage that large amounts of his flesh had to be surgically removed.

By contrast, Eileen was described by one writer as a 'dainty lady'. And in a 1956 British Pathé short film, where she is shown feeding her baby daughter and putting her to bed before starting her training, cycling on rollers and lifting weights in the garage, the commentator lists her incredible records and ends by saying, 'No wonder she wins races, she has to in order to get back to catch up with the housework.' It's hard to imagine them saying the same about Louison Bobet, who won the Tour de France less than two months after Eileen was on the road to John O'Groats, and who held himself in such high regard that he often referred to himself in the third person – although I doubt he did that much hoovering when he was off the bike.

Eileen wouldn't have been offended by the film – she was as proud of being a wife and mother as she was of her achievements on the bike – but throughout her career she continually came up against the idea that women should leave the cycling, and all the pain, suffering and glory that comes with it, to the men. One audience member at an event in 1953 told her it was 'wrong' for women to com-pete in sport and she should stay in the kitchen. Yet what she, Marguerite and Lilian before her went through during their record attempts involved an epic amount of endurance and suffering – although thankfully no surgery. They could more than handle the pain; like the bikes they rode, they were made of steel. They were unbeatable, and having to fit their training and racing around a packed schedule of work, child-rearing and housework wasn't about to stop them riding to victory.

Before Eileen turned professional and could give up her job to focus on her training, she would carefully manage her schedule to make sure she always had time to train. This would involve rising early to get her household chores done, sometimes even baking a cake, leaving just enough time to cycle to the office, pedalling at breakneck speed through the streets, straight through the car showroom where she worked, and dismounting at her desk. She had the evenings free to cover as many miles as she could. While doing chores like the washing-up, she would be working on the strategy for her next race.

When Eileen was pregnant with her first child, Clive, in 1946, she admits to having felt a slight sense of trepidation, writing in her memoir that she had worried that the 'happy and longed-for event' might 'put an end to my racing career'. After the birth, a friend asked Eileen if she had put racing behind her for good. Six months later the friend had her answer when Eileen was back on her bike and winning races, showing that motherhood was no barrier. Her doctor had told her to refrain from cycling for a year after giving birth, but within seven weeks she had got in the saddle again.

As her later remarkable records show, her greatest achievements were still ahead of her. It wasn't long before baby Clive was joining Eileen on her training rides, where he would sleep in a little trailer attached to her husband's bike. When Clive was bigger she placed him in a seat on the back of her bicycle, his weight providing an extra training challenge, particularly when going uphill.

Pat Seeger of the Rosslyn Ladies was another mother who didn't see why the birth of her son, Tony, meant the end of her racing days. She tells me that during her pregnancy she continued going out on her bike until she could no longer fit comfortably behind the handlebars. After he was born, she too put him in a sidecar trailer so she could join the others on the weekend club run. In those days there was less traffic on the road, so many members with small children did the same.

The Yorkshire Housewife

By the time Eileen took the decision to retire – after breaking and still holding by 1955 all twenty-one existing records held by the Women's Road Records Association – another British cyclist, who would come to be considered one of the greatest athletes of all time and who embodied the 'hard-man' ideal, was also putting in the miles with her baby in a sidecar.

Beryl Burton was nineteen when she gave birth to Denise in 1956, and her astonishing decades-long international career was very much ahead of her. Denise accompanied Beryl to all her races from when she was a tiny baby, along with her dad, Charlie. Before Beryl met Charlie, she had barely been on a bike. They had met at the clothing factory in Leeds where they both worked and soon started dating, with Charlie, a keen cyclist and amateur racer, lending Beryl a bike so they could ride together.

There was little to indicate then that Beryl would go on to have the stellar career on the bike that she eventually did. As a child, she had been struck down with rheumatic fever shortly after failing her 11+ school exam. The illness left her temporarily paralysed and with limited speech, keeping her in hospital for nine months, then off school recovering for over a year, resulting in her leaving school at fifteen. She was warned by her doctor to avoid strenuous exercise, as he believed the illness had weakened her heart. But when she fell in love with cycling, she didn't give it a second thought. She had found something she enjoyed and through sheer determination – an attribute that was at the core of all she achieved – could succeed in. And so she began powering past the competition. She later described her astonishing career as 'retribution' for having endured such trauma.

In 1957, the year after Denise was born, Beryl won three national titles. Two years later she raced on the track in Liège in Belgium and won her first world title. Her career is so lengthy and outstanding that it's impossible to sum up in its entirety here – we don't even have an accurate record of how many races she won as they are so numerous, possibly close to 1,000 according to some sources. What we do know is that she achieved seven gold world titles across track and road, plus dozens of national championships, and she held the UK Road Time Trials Council's women's best all-round title (the same award Eileen won twice) for twenty-five consecutive years. She was the first woman to go under an hour for 25 miles, two hours for 50 miles, and under four hours for 100. Some of her record times remain unbeaten to this day. Yet she never turned professional. She worked out her own training programmes and her career was entirely self-funded.

Beryl was such a dominant force in the sport that for decades few could beat her, much like the Belgian Eddy Merckx, who became an unstoppable force in European cycling at that time. While the press dubbed Eddy 'the cannibal' for his determination, it's telling that Beryl was most frequently referred to as the 'Yorkshire housewife'. Unlike her predecessors, she did at least benefit from official recognition of women's records, for in 1955 the Union Cycliste Internationale had finally relented and announced it would

recognise women's world cycling records. That year Daisy
Franks achieved the first-ever 'official' women's hour record
at the Herne Hill Velodrome. This volte-face was largely
thanks to Eileen Gray, a British former track cyclist, whose
own frustration about the lack of medals or titles for women
competitors, and limited opportunities to race, led her to
set up the Women's Cycle Racing Association and campaign
for the women's side of the sport to be recognised internationally. She met a lot of opposition, particularly from the
Netherlands, a country which even in the 1950s didn't think
women should race.

Eileen eventually made many of her adversaries see sense
and in 1958 the UCI held the inaugural Women's Road
World Championship race in France – sixty-five years after
the first men's one – which was won by Elsy Jacobs from
Luxembourg. The Luxembourgians, however, had yet to
come on board with women's racing. Elsy may have been
crowned world champion, as well as holding a new hour
record that was unbroken for fourteen years, but she
couldn't compete to be a national champion in her own
country because women were not eligible at that time. Luxembourg belatedly woke up the following year, doubtless
after recognising they had some serious home-grown talent,
and Elsy was finally able to add national champion to her
growing list of palmares in 1959.

One of the British women Eileen Gray chose to represent
Britain at that first Road World Championships was Eileen
Cropper. Decades later she told a journalist about the huge
gulf between the way the women's and men's teams were
treated at the event, with a limited budget requiring the
women's team to pay for most of their equipment themselves. At eighty-four she was still outraged by the inequality,
describing their accommodation as a 'doss house', three to a
room. She recalled race adjudicators employing guesswork

to decide the order in which the riders came over the line after the winner. There was quite a difference, too, in the press coverage of the men's and women's races: 'If the men did anything it was all over the papers', while 'the women were ignored'.

The resistance to female interlopers in what was considered a man's world continued. Eileen Gray witnessed it repeatedly in her role assisting women's teams competing at home and abroad. Once, while accompanying a team of British women to a competition in Leipzig, a member of the men's team snuck off with all their spare inner tubes and tyres (equipment they'd had to pay for themselves), in an attempt to scupper their chances. It didn't work and the team triumphed, coming home with gold, silver and bronze medals. On another occasion, the celebrated British cyclist Reg Harris had women banned from one track. This understandably enraged Eileen, who said later, 'It would have been nice to have had even a little of the amount of help that he's had. But we were never going to get it.'

Discrimination only succeeded in making Eileen Gray and her team 'more determined to succeed'. She continued to push for equal opportunities in her later role as president of the British Cycling Federation, where her tireless campaigning to get women's cycling into the Olympic Games finally bore fruit in 1984.

Beryl's daughter Denise felt that her mother would let nothing stand in the way of her success either, and many now consider her one of the greatest cyclists of all time. Like Eileen Sheridan, Beryl fitted her cycling around work and family life, doing more and more miles each evening after her already strenuous day job on a Yorkshire rhubarb farm – work that involved 'carrying, lifting, bending, digging, all day long in all weathers' and left her body aching. After downing tools on the farm each evening she would get on the bike, pedalling up to 500 miles a week under the supervision of her boss, Norman 'Nim' Carline, who was a formidable time-triallist.

Although her husband was a passionate cyclist, Beryl wasn't expected to stay home with the washing-up so he could race – though she certainly managed to squeeze in her share of the housework when she wasn't training or heaving rhubarb. As Beryl began to win nearly every competition she entered, Charlie left his own racing days behind so he could support her fully. He was the reason she had taken up the sport, but he recognised she had the potential to become a true legend. Her daughter has since said that Beryl couldn't have achieved the victories she did without Charlie's support. He was her mechanic and driver (when they could afford a car and no longer had to cycle hundreds of miles to get to a race), he looked after Denise during her long hours of training, and was her rock through good and bad during four decades of competing. Eileen Sheridan's husband Ken was similarly supportive, getting her bike ready when she put Clive to bed so she could get out to do some miles, encouraging her back on the bike after the birth of both her children, and helping her work out a training regime.

When their wives progressed from winning women's races to overtaking the men, there were more than a few feathers ruffled elsewhere. The 'housewives' hadn't just entered this man's world, they were threatening to beat them at their own game. Eileen sensed how it would go down when, in a 50-mile time-trial in 1945, she passed all the other women competitors who had set off before her and started catching up with the men's field, whose last rider had started off ten minutes before the women. No one had expected the women to catch up, but Eileen was so strong that she easily made up the time. As she drew up alongside the first man, she knew his pride would take a knock and said to him sympathetically, 'Golly, isn't this tough,' as she sped ahead. Eileen Cropper was less sympathetic when a male competitor in a time-trial begged her not to pass him, responding, 'Sod off, I'm passing you!'

Beryl was such an outstanding cyclist that she became accustomed to frequently bettering men's times and distances. In 1967 Beryl entered a twelve-hour time-trial in Yorkshire, and as with Eileen's 50-mile race, the women rode the same course as the men but were staggered some distance behind them. Beryl had soon passed all the other women in the field, and started catching up with and passing the men. At this point there was a 21-mile gap between the men's and women's twelve-hour records. Many had anticipated that Beryl would rack up the most miles of all the women entered, no one expected that the 'Yorkshire housewife' was capable of bridging that gap to trouble the men's record.

After 100 miles, she was only two and a half minutes down on the men's favourite, Mike McNamara. Another 100 miles and she had gained a couple of seconds on him. After 250 miles, with over eleven hours in the saddle and the sun starting to set, she had passed all ninety-eight other male cyclists in the event and could see Mike ahead of her. She had – extraordinarily – closed the gap between the men's and women's records and was about to pass him. At that moment even Beryl, who was more than used to overtaking men, was overcome by the immensity of the moment, writing in her autobiography: 'I froze, the urge in my legs to go faster and faster vanished as though with the click of a switch. Goose pimples broke out all over me, and for some seconds I just stared at his heaving shoulders, the sweat-stained jersey. I could hardly accept after all those hours and miles I had finally caught up with one of the country's great riders.'

She quickly recovered and was soon overtaking him in what has gone down as one of the most legendary moments in cycling history: as she pulled up alongside Mike – a man on course to make a new men's record, but who had no idea he was about to be overtaken by Beryl – she offered him a Liquorice Allsort. He took it, thanking her as she pushed ahead and continued on her record-breaking ride.

Even then, she felt conflicted: 'There I was, first on the road, ninety-nine men behind me, not knowing whether to feel elated or sorrowful. Mac was doing a sensational ride but his glory, richly deserved, was going to be overshadowed by a woman.' This was unusual for Beryl; in other races when she passed the men, she quite rightly had no qualms. One of her competitors recalled her shouting out, 'Eh lad, you're not trying!' as she flew past.

Mike's dented ego aside, she had much to celebrate when she was through. She had cycled 277.5 miles in twelve hours, beating the existing women's record by nearly forty miles. It was five miles more than the previous men's twelve-hour record. Mike had made a new record too, with 276.52 miles, but he hadn't managed to surpass Beryl. It was on account of this that she was awarded her third Bidlake Memorial Award, the only time in the history of the prize it's been given to the same cyclist more than twice. It took two years for another man to beat her distance. It was fifty years before another woman improved on it – despite the technical developments in the interim – when in 2017 Alice Lethbridge achieved 285.65 miles.

It seems that Mike never quite recovered from the shock of his defeat by a woman, since he refused to talk about that day. Beryl, on the other hand, was granted the opportunity to take part in the Grand Prix des Nations in Cannes the following year, the first and only time a woman was allowed in this prestigious time-trial in its seventy-two-year history.

She had to ride before the men, and her time was unofficial, but she finished so far ahead of expectations that the last few laps which took place in the velodrome occurred while another race was still going on – no one had expected her to arrive back so soon. The Grand Prix was won by 'the Phoenix', Felice Gimondi, but Beryl was only twelve minutes slower than him and one minute behind the last man, all of whom were highly decorated full-time professional cyclists.

She continued setting records into the early 1980s and was awarded her twenty-fifth and final consecutive Best All-Rounder in 1983. She never stopped cycling. Fittingly, but tragically, she died on her bike while out delivering invites to her fifty-ninth birthday in 1996. She had been scheduled to take part in a 10-mile national time-trial the following weekend. Many believe her heart gave out from being pushed so hard for decades.

Her lengthy list of achievements is unique and phenomenal in the cycling world, one in the eye for anyone who thinks women aren't up to it, though sadly we will never know what she might have achieved had women been allowed to compete in the Olympics. If she'd had the benefit of later technological advances in bikes and training, I can only guess that her records would have been even more astounding and unbeatable.

Now more women have the opportunity to take part in tougher sporting contests, we are seeing evidence that, in the world of ultra-endurance events, which would include something as arduous as Beryl's twelve-hour or Eileen and Marguerite's End-to-Ends, the gap between the sexes is starting to level out, with women now regularly beating the men – much as Beryl showed all those decades ago. In 2016 the Alaskan Lael Wilcox was the first to finish the 4,200-mile Trans Am Bike Race, which crosses the USA from the Pacific to the Atlantic coast. The previous year she had set a new women's record on the Tour Divide, a 2,745-mile mountain bike route the length of the Rockies, from Canada to the Mexican border.

Then, in 2019, Germany's Fiona Kolbinger made history as the first woman to win the punishing Transcontinental Race outright, cycling 2,485 miles from Bulgaria to France in 10 days, 2 hours and 48 minutes. She crossed the finish line over six hours ahead of the next person. In the world of ultra-endurance running that same year, the UK's Jasmin Paris won the tough 268-mile Montane Spine Race. She broke the existing record by twelve hours, sleeping for just seven hours out of over eighty-three hours on the trail. On top of this, she also managed to find time to express milk for her baby.*

Dirt Grrrls

Beryl had broken new ground for women cyclists, and by the time she retired from international contests in the mid 1980s, women's cycling was entering a new era which, although still a long way from being equal to the men's, was finally presenting them with long-overdue opportunities to prove what they were capable of. And the more they proved they could hold their own in competition, the harder it became for critics to say they would be better off sticking to the washing-up. Any doubters who required further proof needed only to look at a scene emerging on the west coast of America in the 1970s and early '80s, where a group of women cyclists were riding hard and fast over the concept of the 'dainty lady'.

---

* Remarkably, women's capabilities in sport are still doubted by some. In a revealing 2019 YouGov poll, one in eight men said they thought they would be able to score a point off Serena Williams, possibly the greatest tennis player in the world right now.

The origin of mountain biking (MTB) is contested ground, but it's generally accepted that a group of cycle-mad hippies living in Marin County in the late 1960s and '70s played a major part in inventing a new type of bike and riding style. Many were competitive road cyclists who found that scene overly conformist and rule-obsessed. After all, this was just over the bridge from San Francisco's Haight–Ashbury district, the epicentre of the counterculture movement, psychedelia and the summer of love.

To let off steam, the group took to riding around the dirt tracks of Mount Tamalpais on old balloon-tyre cruisers from the 1930s and '40s that they had scavenged from junkyards. The type of heavy (20 kg-plus) bikes that the likes of Joan Crawford had once promoted now, due to their weighty construction, proved a more robust option for off-road biking. These adapted bikes became known as Clunkers, and soon enthusiasts began to create their own bikes that were more suited for their style of fast downhill riding over rough ground.

It started out as a collaborative and anti-consumerist scene, with bikes made from salvaged parts, a pure DIY ethos, but would end up making a huge amount of money for some of the early founders when the scene exploded into the mainstream in the mid 1980s. The development of the mountain bike was a revolution in cycling and is now such a significant part of the industry that it's hard to imagine there was a time when people didn't think of venturing off-tarmac. Those who did feel the urge found there were no bikes designed to handle the terrain. It was a new frontier, one that was adrenaline-fuelled, exhilarating, brought you closer to nature, away from cars and urban areas, but could also result in some seriously nasty, even fatal, spills.

Downhill MTB racing riders descend at high speeds down steep and technical courses, like off-season ski slopes, that are covered in rocks, ruts, tree roots and other obstacles. It's fast and furious and all over in five minutes. The first down-hill event, which became known as the Repack Race and ran sporadically from 1976 to 1984, took place on a steep two-mile stretch of near-vertical fire road on Tamalpais. If you look at photographs of these early races, it's a challenge to spot a woman among the line-up of men tearing down the trail in jeans and work boots. Some of those men became famous, like Gary Fisher, whose name is synonymous the world over with mountain bikes. It remains an uncompro-misingly dangerous sport, but back then the bikes were a long way from having evolved into the kind of machines you can buy today, which are lighter in weight with added advantages like suspension and disc brakes.

What isn't obvious from those early photos is that many of them were taken by a woman. And when she wasn't behind the camera, Wende Cragg would join the men on the Tamalpais trails and down the Repack course.

From its origins, MTB has tended to have a reputation for being a tough and stereotypically 'masculine' sport. It is aggressive, dirty and sometimes dangerous – all the things women have traditionally been encouraged to stay away from. It's true that there are many more men taking part, even today. There have, however, always been women who have helped shape, define and progress the sport over the decades and recast 'ride like a girl' as something fast, fear-less and unapologetically dirty.

In the mid 1970s, when Wende first started fat-tyre biking, she was for some time the only woman among her group of pioneering enthusiasts out on the trails. She still lives in Fairfax, the town nestled at the foot of the mountain, and I talked to her via email about what it was like to be part of this new movement in cycling. She describes the small group she cycled with, which included her now ex-husband Larry and a few local male friends and neighbours, as something more akin to a 'tribe', who felt themselves to be 'the lone explorers of a new world that had just opened up to us'. She liked the fact they were 'under the radar' and doing their own thing.

However, she admits she nearly didn't fall for mountain biking at all. Her first-ever foray on a 25 kg 'behemoth' up the peak in August 1975 left her swearing she would never get back on again. It was hot and dusty, there was a lot of pushing the weighty machine on the uphill and she found the narrow paths down the mountain, or single track, quite terrifying. Unlike the others she rode with, she was at a disadvantage as she hadn't been a cyclist until that point. What got her back on the bike was the extent to which the experience made her feel so connected to the stunning scenery on her doorstep. As she got more adept at handling the challenging terrain, as well as her cumbersome bike, she grew progressively more adventurous, enjoying the 'thrill of discovery' of both self and surroundings. It became something she had to do: 'the perfect fit for my innate desire for fun and adventure. The sense of freedom and jubilation was intoxicating and addicting, and before long, it became apparent I needed my daily "fix".'

The races began as a 'lark', but went on to become highly competitive – participants were always relieved when they reached the finish alive. For the first eighteen months, she was the only woman riding and racing on Mount Tam. Far from putting her off, she says it never occurred to her that she was the 'lone ranger' as the only woman. As a child she had always been more drawn to the games played by her brothers than her sisters and was used to being the token 'tomboy'. This may explain why she didn't find the situation that daunting or unusual, allowing herself to be too much 'in the moment' to give it a second thought. It seemed to her that the bike was an 'equaliser' with the power to 'transform gender and cultural restrictions'.

Wende says it wasn't always about racing downhill as fast as possible. Some days the group would relax and enjoy the scenery, picnicking by the river with their dogs, berry and mushroom-picking along the way. Not that she shied away from the racing side – she still holds the fastest woman's Repack Race time down that 'sinuous and ruthless' 400-metre descent, complete with cavernous ruts and holes, giant rocks, hairpin turns and endless obstacles that caused countless falls, some more serious than others.

Wende ventured further afield with her bike and in 1978 travelled with five other members of the Mount Tam group to Colorado, where she became the first woman to take part in the now legendary Pearl Pass Tour. The event still takes place today and is an infamously punishing 38-mile, two-day route from Crested Butte to Aspen via the 3,872-metre Pearl Pass along an old mule trap road once used to bring ore down from the mines. The Colorado group who had created the tour two years previously had been on the verge of pulling out and leaving it to the Californians and their superior bikes, but when they realised Wende would be doing it too, their machismo stopped them giving in.

Wende describes the ascent up to the pass as more about 'tenacity and endurance' than speed, with many sections of carrying or pushing the bikes, passing over multiple icy streams. The rocky and narrow descent into Aspen the following day was a 'brutal shake-up' and nothing short of 'a true test of fortitude'. This edition of the event has since gone down in legend as one of the pivotal moments in the birth of the sport. The Pearl Pass Tour remains a serious undertaking, not for the faint-hearted; one can only imagine the fortitude it required in 1978 when everything was a lot more rudimentary.

When MTB exploded in the mid 1980s and the races became increasingly serious and regulated, with corporations coming in to sponsor riders, Wende admits it wasn't something she wanted to play a part in. She feels incredibly proud of having been a pioneer in the sport, 'especially as a female on the forefront of a boom that eventually went worldwide and changed the face of the cycling industry for ever'. Her photo archive, now stored at the Marin Museum of Bicycling, is an important record of the birth of the sport and her unique position within it. She tells me she feels a huge sense of joy whenever she sees a girl 'straddling a fat-tire bike'. The sport has changed in so many ways, not least the bikes and the many types of MTB – which include Cross Country, Enduro, Freeride and others – and there are more women hitting the dirt and single track than ever before.

Many of today's female competitors would have been inspired by the incredible women taking part in races as MTB became professionalised in the 1980s and '90s, some of whom rode with Wende in the early days and others who came after, leaving an indelible mark in an overwhelmingly male-dominated sport. Riders like Denise Caramagno, one of the few women who crossed over with Wende at those early races and is responsible for coming up with the now ubiquitous phrase 'fat-tire', which she used to name the magazine she co-wrote, the first devoted to the sport. Or Jacquie Phelan, who stood out on the start line of races for her unorthodox outfits, which included polka-dot tights and a helmet with a rubber duck glued on top. She had switched from road racing to MTB in the early 1980s, winning the first race she entered. Jacquie was a national champion for three years in a row from 1983, back when there were no separate men's and women's races because there were so few female competitors. Another was Juli Furtado, whose brief but stellar career (sadly cut short by a diagnosis of lupus) started with the first UCI MTB World Championships in 1990, which she won in the cross-country (XC) race, and ended with her representing the US at the Olympics in 1996. At the point of her retirement she held a Guinness World Record for the most first-place finishes in MTB (male or female), which at that time exceeded the combined total wins of the most successful man and next most successful woman.

The Missile

One downhill competitor from the 1990s particularly stood out, not only for her formidable skill and domination of the competition, but also for her audacious badass attitude, which saw her catapulted to something close to rock-star status. Missy Giove was definitely no 'dainty lady', she was 'the missile', a punk-rock icon who embodied the phrase 'go big or go home'. Among numerous other major wins, she bagged eleven World Cup medals in downhill, putting her body through all kinds of punishment in the process. She was a highly skilled rider, but hurtling down the toughest and most technical downhill courses in the world at close to 60 mph is guaranteed to result in some spills.

A journalist once described her race style as 'like a nuclear bomb exploded here, here, and here, all the way down the course'. Which may in part explain why her tally of broken bones was so high – an estimated thirty-eight, including both kneecaps and heels, ribs, collarbone and pelvis. She endured multiple concussions and in one terrible accident at the 2001 World Championships she suffered a brain haemorrhage. It's a sobering medical record, and certainly nothing to celebrate, particularly since the effect of the haemorrhage was a big part of her decision to retire in

2003, but it does convey the fearlessness and commitment that so defined her.

'I'm not afraid of death, I wouldn't be who I am if I was,' Missy once told an interviewer. 'I love that experience of flying. It's a very liberating feeling to not be worried about anything but that one moment.' Her philosophy was about seizing the day: 'You're only here once and that's it. You better live it up.' For over a decade there was almost nothing that would stop her getting back on her bike, sometimes straight after a new break. She was unmissable on the start line, with hair that ranged from dreadlocks to short bleached blonde crop or dyed two-tone to match her bike, multiple piercings and tattoos and with unusual lucky charms that made headlines, including the desiccated body of her pet piranha, Gonzo, which hung from a necklace, and the ashes of her beloved dog Ruffian, which she sprinkled in her bra before each race. A huge personality and an outstanding athlete, she was invited on television chat shows with the likes of Jon Stewart and Conan O'Brien, and guest-hosted on MTV – programmes that wouldn't normally take the time to talk to stars of niche sports. At races, legions of teenage boys lined up for her autograph.*

Missy grew up in New York and first got paid to ride a bike delivering Chinese food as a teen. She always found the city suffocating and longed for the mountains, eventually jumping on her bike to relocate to Vermont, where her

---

* If you type 'Missy Giove' into an internet search engine today, the first thing that will come up is her arrest for smuggling a large quantity of marijuana in 2009. It would be odd not to mention it, as it was a story that shocked many in the sports world. I'm not going to go into the rights and wrongs of what she did. The focus here is specifically on Missy's significant contribution to women's mountain biking, which I don't believe is negated by what came later.

grandparents lived. It was there that she got into downhill skiing, winning the junior national championships in 1990 and earning herself a college scholarship in the process. It says a lot about her level of grit that when she was starting out and couldn't afford a lift pass, she would hike up to the top of the slopes to ski down.

As part of her off-season training she discovered mountain biking and immediately fell in love with it. That same year she packed her tent and hitchhiked from Vermont to Colorado for the first-ever UCI World MTB championships, the same event where Juli Furtado won the women's XC. She acquired a race licence and rode in her first downhill competition, where she was spotted by John Parker, manager of Yeti, Juli's team, who immediately handed her a team jersey after recognising that the gutsy and maverick rider would be a winning addition.

Her career went from strength to strength, with spectators always being guaranteed an electrifying and exhilarating performance as Missy shredded the trails at full throttle. A commentator at the 1999 MTB World Cup in Les Gets summed up Missy and her career: 'She's a wild rider, probably one of the wildest in the women's field today. But despite that wildness she's so consistent, usually in the top three.'

Within a few years of joining Yeti she was winning world championships and World Cup medals consistently until 2001. During that time, she moved on to the elite team Volvo-Cannondale, who were throwing a lot of money into the sport and their riders. Missy starred in ads for Reebok, was photographed by Annie Leibovitz and featured in a computer game. The cycling press couldn't get enough of her, filling column inches on her supposed bitter rivalry with the dominant French MTB and BMX racer Anne-Caroline Chausson.

Even with men's racing dominating the media spotlight

so much, Missy succeeded in getting them to pay attention. And she didn't have to compromise to do so. She once told a journalist that she thought it was a 'cool thing' she could be a role model while not having to look like Barbie. Moreover, she has never shied away from being open about her sexuality.

Sport has a problematic history with homosexuality, something it still struggles with. Many athletes in the public eye have felt unwilling to reveal their sexuality for fear it will lose them lucrative sponsorship deals or they will suffer homophobic attacks. None more so than in the hypermasculine world of male football where, according to some reports, the problem of homophobia is getting worse, not better, with homophobic chants still heard at matches. When the UK's Justin Fashanu came out in 1990, he suffered such abuse that it's widely believed it was a significant factor in his suicide eight years later. Since then no other professional footballer in the UK's Premier League has come out. It's a very different picture in women's football today, with Megan Rapinoe, along with around forty other players and coaches in the 2019 Women's World Cup, openly gay or bisexual. It's taken a while to get to that point though.

This is an incredibly nuanced issue that needs a whole book to explore, but it's true to say that sport has been so deeply associated with stereotypes of red-blooded, heterosexual masculinity – those hardmen – that it has struggled to accept anyone seen as deviating from the 'norm'. Athletic women, on the other hand, have long been typecast as gay, because they defy – thankfully now outdated – ideas about what constitutes acceptable femininity. When the teen protagonist in the film *The Miseducation of Cameron Post* is sent to a Christian conversion camp to 'cure' her of being gay, the adults in charge conclude that her attraction to girls was triggered by her love of running.

The conflation of women's sport and homosexuality led to the Rosslyn Ladies and others being labelled lesbians, even when it was untrue. For sportswomen who were in fact gay, to come out risked confirming deep-seated and erroneous prejudices and, more crucially, being treated with hostility. They were also likely to earn less: the tennis star Martina Navratilova estimated she lost $10 million in endorsement deals when she came out in the 1980s. She was one of the first sports superstars to be openly gay and met a fair amount of animosity for it. By contrast, in 2019 a photo of the Swedish footballer Magdalena Eriksson celebrating her team's entry into the quarter-finals of the World Cup by kissing her girlfriend, the Danish footballer Pernille Harder, was seen around the world and widely celebrated. Not that the problem has gone away entirely, but it shows we are now at a point when prejudices around female sexuality and sport might finally be eroding.

Cycling, like many sports, remains in thrall to an outdated hypermasculine and heterosexual ideal of hardmen, a culture that Philippa York, a former professional cyclist who transitioned from male to female having competed at the highest level of the sport, has said means that 'anyone thought to be different has been singled out for ridicule or presented as some kind of danger'. She has been open about her own transition in the hope that the sport will become more progressive, breaking down barriers around gender and sexuality.

Back in the 1990s, homophobia was rampant across many aspects of society, so it's understandable that few people in sports, unlike Martina and Missy, were willing to be openly out. Missy once said being openly gay meant she made less money, but she had no regrets: 'it's important to represent who you are because it gives other people strength'. She was out and proud, talking about her girlfriends and being photographed for gay magazines, showing that there was nothing shameful about being a gay woman doing sport or anything else she chooses. Many have felt that MTB, as a newer discipline, has always been more open and progressive, which may explain why her sexuality wasn't the issue it might have been had she been in a more traditional sport.

Missy thrived in the fast, dangerous and exhilarating environment, never doubting she couldn't ride as hard as those in the men's field. It became part of her DNA and in 2015, aged forty-three, twelve years after her retirement, she made an appearance on the course at the UCI World Cup at Windham. Her wife, who had been diagnosed with cancer, had wanted to see her race at a world championship and so Missy got back on the bike. Though she had barely ridden in the last ten years, she finished sixteenth on the day. She hadn't expected to win but told reporters she hoped to be an inspiration to others. It's good advice from a woman who had never allowed anything to hold her back, and wasn't about to let age get the better of her.

This is something the US ultra-endurance athlete Rebecca Rusch, who didn't even start competing in MTB until she was thirty-eight, would agree with. She has since gone on to win national and world championships in XC and twenty-four-hour MTB races, earning her the title 'Queen of Pain' and a career that is one of the most inspirational in any sport. Meanwhile Missy's former nemesis, Anne-Caroline Chausson, also now in her forties, has survived ovarian cancer and is back on her bike.

Depth of Field

Many in MTB feel that their sport is inclusive and welcoming, less snobbish and rule-obsessed than older disciplines like road cycling, but it's impossible to get away from the fact that it too has far fewer women participants than men, and fewer still from BAME backgrounds. It's difficult to obtain figures on the gender split, but in 2016 one US MTB magazine estimated that its readership was around 15 per cent female, which led it to calculate that as few as two in ten people out on the trails are women; whereas in a sport like running it's equal – in 2015, 57 per cent of all finishers in running races were female.

Sabra Davison, a former professional mountain biker, and her sister Lea (an Olympic-level competitor), were often the only women on their team when they started out in the early 2000s. There were also noticeably far fewer women on the start line at races. When I spoke to her on the phone from her home in Vermont, she told me that they both felt incredibly encouraged and supported by the male riders around them. She admits that her experience wouldn't be for everyone: 'When you are truly just an individual stand-ing on your own, a lot of people find that a hard space to be in.'

As a result, she and Lea created Little Bellas, a non-profit MTB mentoring programme for girls aged seven to sixteen to learn and ride together, to foster a sense of 'community and camaraderie' which they hope will encourage more girls into the sport. Their co-founder, Angela Irvine, only learned to mountain-bike at forty by trying to keep up with her male friends along the trails, so she knew all too well how having a more female-friendly space could help to encour-age greater diversity. Sabra tells me the goal was to make the sport more 'approachable' by creating a space that girls 'feel safe and invited into' since 'it's potentially not a sport that naturally lends itself to that'.

Their organisation has chapters across the country and is so successful they have waiting lists of up to four years in some areas. They offer scholarships to ensure everyone has a chance to join, regardless of family income, as well as sponsors who subsidise the entry fee for each girl to keep costs at a minimum. This is just one of many groups across the US and Europe now helping the sport become more diverse and open by providing supportive spaces for women, BAME and LGBQT+ cyclists – an idea that goes back as far as the 1980s when Jacquie Phelan founded her legendary WOMBATS, the Women's Mountain Bike And Tea Society, a series of camps to encourage women into a sport that was then even more white and male-dominated than it is today.

That sense of being outnumbered in the sport is something Anissa Lamare knows intimately. Twenty-three-year-old Anissa, or Suri to her friends, comes from the north-eastern Indian city of Shillong, part of the mountainous region of Meghalaya, which translates as 'the abode of the clouds'. Nestled between Bangladesh and Bhutan, with peaks that reach 2,000 metres and lush tropical forests in its lowlands, Meghalaya is ideal territory for off-road biking.

The tribes of the province have traditionally operated a matrilineal system, with inheritance passed down the female line – a rarity today in India and elsewhere. Yet despite the region's female-centric stance, in its MTB competitions there is no category for women. The same is true in races in other regions of the country. Which means that Anissa, who first took up downhill MTB when she was seventeen, has been forced to enter in the men's category, first in the junior men's races and now the elite men's. The same was true for Wende, forty years ago, as the only woman taking on the Repack Race on Mount Tam against a field of men.

Like California back then, the sport in India today is very much at a nascent stage, with infrastructure and participation a long way behind Europe and the US. The cost of a bike alone is enough to put it out of the reach of many. Anissa believes she is probably the only woman taking part in downhill races in the country, because she has yet to come across any other female competitors at the events she has attended to date. There is no Indian equivalent of Little Bellas to get more girls and women to the start line, so Anissa stands out as a pioneer, making tracks that others will hopefully follow. She tells me over email that when she signed up to her first competition – riding a BMX bike as that was all she had – she knew almost nothing about the sport. She didn't even own a helmet. But once she'd experienced the overwhelming exhilaration of racing down the mountain, she was hooked. And she managed to get placed in the top ten.

Anissa immediately started saving up to buy a proper mountain bike. The nearest shop was three hours away; since she didn't want to return without a bike, she ended up coming home with one that was far too big. At under five feet, and in a country where there is almost no market for women's MTB, finding one that fitted was always going to be a challenge. The frame was so outsized that in competitions she would resort to borrowing a friend's bike to get down the course, before once again saving for a (second-hand) bike designed for someone her height. She lovingly named her new mount Muse.

Rather than feeling put off by being the only girl out riding and competing, she initially liked being unique. But it wasn't long before the novelty wore off and she started longing to bike with and compete against her own gender. The lack of female competitors made her feel, since she couldn't legitimately compete as a woman, that ultimately there was no future for her in the sport. When she moved to Bangalore, 3,000 km south, to complete a master's degree in political science, she was forced to put a hold on competing entirely since her nearest MTB trails were over 50 km away. The decision, she says, 'hit me hard'; without biking as a release, she feels 'life is just going to be filled with emptiness'. She briefly considered dropping out of her course, but knew that ultimately she couldn't, because of the responsibility she has to support her family financially in the future.

However, she has told her family that she intends to take time out after graduating to focus on competing in MTB again. Her desire to be on the bike, training for competitions, is, she tells me, 'the part of me that will never die'. Anissa hopes that she will make it to Europe, finally to test her skills against other women. Perhaps, by that point, she won't be the only woman in India shredding the downhill trails. Just as Wende was once in the vanguard of MTB in the US, it surely follows that Anissa will not be the lone pioneer for much longer. Perhaps one day she, or those that follow in her tyre treadmarks, will start their own Indian version of Little Bellas for a new generation of girls who will never know what it's like not to have a category of their own.

CHAPTER 12

Can You See Us Now?

For Want of a Yellow Jersey

In a lay-by on a stretch of road heading south towards the Pyrenees out of the town of Limoux in Aude, south-west France, a group of women are pulling bikes out of vans. It's 7.30 a.m. on 20 July 2019, and after several weeks of scorching temperatures it's currently drizzling with a slight chill in the air. Tomorrow this road will be lined with spectators who will watch the participants of the 2019 Tour de France start out on stage fifteen, which this year is a challenging 185 km – with over 4,500 metres of total climbing – ending on the summit of the Prat d'Albis.

The women getting onto their bikes today are going to be cycling that same route. They have completed all fourteen prior stages, each one the day before the men take their turn, and will continue to do so right up to the final kilometres on the Champs-Élysées in Paris. There is no publicity caravan travelling ahead of them to hype up the crowds, no advance motorcade clearing the streets and filming them from every angle, and no press conference at the finish. This isn't the women's Tour de France, because there isn't one. These women are taking on the full 3,479.3 km and 52,000 metres of climbing (the most mountainous in the Tour's history), as a protest against the failure of one of the world's most popular sporting events to allow women to compete.

Among the group are a team of thirteen French cyclists called the Donnons des Elles au Vélo J-1 (which roughly translates as 'give the women the bike') who have been riding every stage of the Tour for the last five years. This year they are joined by ten international riders named the InternationElles. Members of the general public are encouraged to join them on each stage, but today it's just me hanging onto their back wheels as we head towards the mountains.

The first section moves along a fast road following the River Aude before we head gently uphill, passing forests and the ancient Château de Puivert. As we progress, other riders join the back of the group and villagers cheer us on, having heard about these women who are taking on the Tour. I hang at the back with the international team, none of whom has taken part in such an intensive and unrelenting event before, though more than a few are serious athletes with a history of competing in tough challenges such as Ironman triathlons. The Tour, however, is on another level. It's considered to be one of the most punishing endurance events, and though the women aren't racing each other, it is still an outstandingly demanding test. Many have had to take sabbaticals from their jobs and a number have small children back at home, including Pippa, who gave birth to her son eleven months ago and only stopped breastfeeding him three times a day a few weeks before she flew out to Europe from her home in Australia.

Yesterday was another gruelling mountain stage, 111 km that ended with the 2,215-metre Col de Tourmalet, an iconic Tour de France climb, and they then had to travel to the start line for the next stage, as well as get their bikes and kit ready for another long day. At most, the group managed five hours' sleep. Yesterday's clothes are now hanging in the back of the InternationElles support van to dry. It's true to say that no rider in the peloton of the official Tour will have to spend their time out of the saddle worrying about having a functioning bike or a clean pair of cycling shorts – they have teams of support staff, as well as luxurious buses kitted out with multiple washing machines and comfy beds. They also have nutri-tionists and chefs, and onboard masseurs to ease their overworked muscles. Apart from a skeleton support crew of four, these women have few such luxuries. And with no prize money to be won, they are funding the ride themselves.

When we start the climb up Montségur, the first mountain of the day, I find it hard to believe that the group are now on their fifteenth day as I watch most of them power up towards the Cathar castle on its peak. I'm left pedalling behind with a few others who are either feeling a little less fresh after so many mountainous miles or reserving their energy for the rest of the long day ahead. As we make our way up the 14.7 km of grinding ascent, people who've pitched their camper vans and tents at the side of the road, keen to make sure they have a good spot on the iconic mountain to watch the official race tomorrow, shout encouragement. It helps me push onward, as well as giving me a tiny taste of the Tour de France experience from the other side.

The parents of Carmen, one of the InternationElles, have come from the Netherlands to support her and appear near the top to rally her on. At the summit we regroup, refuelling on bananas and energy bars under clear blue skies, before the exhilarating and well-earned descent down the other side. At this point I leave the group to head back in the direction of the start, slightly relieved I won't have to tackle the three brutal remaining climbs, one of which is known as 'the Wall'.

They handled it just fine and over the remaining six days the two groups took on everything the Tour route planners were inflicting on the men the following day. What they perhaps hadn't bargained for was that temperatures in Nîmes would soar to a hellish 46 degrees Celsius, leaving them to resort to cooling off in a car wash. Or that they would ultimately end up riding a longer total distance than the men when an extreme hailstorm in the Alps, the day after the heatwave, caused icy conditions and then a mudslide on stage nineteen, resulting in the men's race being cancelled midway. As they pedalled up that iconic Parisian street towards the finish line, they had more than proved that, if a group of amateur riders were able to handle it, then there is no question the pro women are more than capable.

They aren't the first to protest women's exclusion from this race. It's rumoured that in 1908 a Frenchwoman called Marie Marvingt tried to enter, but, after being refused, rode the entire course before the official race started. There doesn't seem to be any conclusive evidence to back this up, but I don't doubt Marie was more than able to do it. I can't go into all her incredible sporting and other achievements here, which range from swimming the length of the Seine, winning medals at the Winter Olympics, setting women's aviation records, disguising herself as a man to pilot bombing missions in the First World War and working as a resistance fighter in the Second World War; but in short she is one of the most decorated French women in history and has the biography to match. Marie cycled 350 km from Nancy to Paris when she was eighty-eight which, along with everything else, does suggest she would have been more than up to the challenge in 1908.

Fact or fiction, it highlights the extent to which women have been calling out the unfairness of this exclusion for almost as long as the race has existed, but it's far from the only inequality to have persisted in women's cycling. In fact, it's quite a list, including a hefty gender pay gap, fewer racing opportunities and less sponsorship, little or no media coverage, and a lack of diversity in general. Women's professional cycling is now finally changing for the better, thanks in part to a long line of inspirational activists – many professional cyclists themselves – who are calling on the sport to do better. They are disrupting what Nicole Cooke called the 'sport run by men, for men' and pushing for change.

'Cycling Is Much too Difficult for a Woman'

The absence of women from cycling's biggest and most-watched event, the Tour de France, has had a complicated history. In 1984 the Amaury Sport Organisation (ASO), the organisers of the Tour, launched the Tour de France Féminine. This eighteen-stage race offered something as close to the men's race as there had ever been, even if the UCI, the sport's governing body, would only allow a total maximum distance of no more than 1,000 km compared to the men's 4,000 km. The women raced before the men, finishing around two hours ahead each day, in front of the same crowds who were waiting to watch the men go past. This was the same year women's cycling finally entered the Olympics, and although it was just one event, it felt like a significant turning point. The US cyclist Connie Carpenter-Phinney (then just Carpenter), who won gold at that first women's Olympic road race, said she felt that 'we were really going somewhere'. Then the initial optimism around the women's Tour began to fizzle out, because the press were so focused on the men's race. Many remained unconvinced that women should be doing such a thing, not least one former winner Jacques Anquetil, who wrote in one paper that although he had 'absolutely nothing against women's sports', he felt that 'cycling is much too difficult for a woman. They are not made for the sport. I prefer to see a woman in a short white skirt, not racing shorts.' Laurent Fignon, the winner of the 1983 Tour, was similarly unimpressed by women racing: 'I like women, but I prefer to see them doing something else.'

Two years later the women's event was reduced to just two weeks; after another three years the ASO had pulled out. The women's stage race limped on until 2009, being renamed Grande Boucle Féminine Internationale because the ASO saw any use of the word 'Tour' as an infringement of its trademark. It suffered other problems, too: chronic lack of sponsorship, riders not getting paid and the organisers going into serious debt. By 2009, its final outing, it was down to four stages.

The Grande Boucle Féminine was dead, but out of the cold ashes La Course emerged in 2014, a new women's race once again organised by the ASO. This long-overdue rethink was all down to campaigning by the pro cyclists Marianne Vos, Emma Pooley, Kathryn Bertine and the tri-athlete Chrissie Wellington. Its fifth edition took place the day before I joined the InternationElles on their stage fifteen and was won by Marianne.

So if the women have a race, why are these twenty-three women still protesting? Because while the men get twenty-one days of racing and the chance to compete for £2 million, the women get only one day with a total prize pot of £19,000. As a result, the women's race secures nowhere near the coverage of the men's mammoth contest. When Marianne went to the press conference after an exhilarating victory, she arrived in a room full of empty chairs and a handful of journalists, one of whom tweeted, 'Embarrassing that one of the sport's greatest ever riders gets ignored like this.' Mark Cavendish, one of the top men's pro cyclists and someone who has been vocal about the lack of equality in the sport, tweeted: 'This genuinely makes me sad & embarrassed about where my sport is at.'

It can sometimes feel as if the Tour's infamous podium girls, the women who hand bouquets to the stage winners as they plant a kiss on their cheek, are more visible than the women of La Course. In 2013 the pro cyclist Peter Sagan was seen on live television groping podium girl Maja Leye after he came second in the Tour of Flanders – prompting outrage in the media and online, rapidly followed by a public apology from the cyclist – which says a lot about how these women are viewed. This anachronistic tradition has long been called out for its inherent sexism and in 2018, in the face of vocal opposition and petitions, the organisers suggested they would finally end it. This was at the same time that darts and Formula One dropped their controversial 'walk-on' and 'grid' girls. The ASO decided not to follow through; instead it doubled down, announcing that it would continue after all.

The Tour isn't the only race that matters, and there are other opportunities for women to take part in multi-day road races that are more equivalent to the men's. Alfonsina Strada would, I'm sure, be pleased to know that sixty-four years after she made her Grand Tour debut, the Giro finally launched a women's version, initially known as the Giro Donne and now the Giro d'Italia Internazionale Femminile, or Giro Rosa. At ten stages it is currently the longest women's road race (though at one point it was sixteen), and for a few years it was the only multi-stage women's race, or Grand Départ. However, Alfonsina may wonder why its participants can only hope to win a fraction of what the men do: in 2018 the overall winner, Annemiek van Vleuten, was awarded €1,130 which she then had to share with her team mates, while the winner of the men's race scooped €115,668. That same year Chris Froome was paid £1.2 million to take part.

Hard as it is to believe, it's a lot better than it was: in 2014, Marianne Vos received €535 for being overall winner, compared to Nairo Quintana's €200,000. Women's cycling often falls substantially short in prize money compared to many sports. Female tennis players at the world grand slams receive equal money to the men – thanks to the campaign work of former pro and activist, Billie Jean King. In marathon running, athletics and swimming, male and female finishers almost always receive the same. In football, the most popular sport, there is a huge gender pay gap, with players from the FA Super League in 2019 being paid on average 2 per cent of the earnings men command in the Premier League. This led to the USA women's team suing for equal pay after winning their second FIFA World Cup in a row. The US men's football team have never made it to the semi-finals but, had they got to just that stage, they would have been paid substantially more, around $550,000 each, compared to the women's $90,000. While it's grossly unfair, it's much more than anyone competing in the Giro Rosa can hope to earn.

In many other races it's a similar story. In the 2019 Tour of Flanders the winner of the men's race received €20,000. The first woman over the line, Marta Bastianelli, got €1,265. The women's race was just under seventy miles shorter, but that doesn't justify an €18,000 discrepancy. It seems there hasn't been much progress since 1984, when Marianne Martin from the US won the first women's Tour de France and received just over £800 while the men's winner, Laurent Fignon, took home close to £80,000. Marianne later said that taking part had left her out of pocket, though she never regretted it.

In women's professional cycling, lack of prize money and modest – or even no – salaries means that many have other jobs on top of their racing and training to survive financially. It's telling that the Olympic medal-winning cyclist Emma Pooley, who came second overall in the Giro Rosa in 2011 and 2012, told a journalist that she earned more money coming third in a triathlon in the Philippines than she has ever done cycling. Before her retirement the American Mara Abbott had won the race twice, as many times as Vincenzo Nibali has won the men's event, but while he has earned millions, Mara says she lived a fraction above the poverty line. She is also an Olympian, but had to earn money outside of cycling to support herself during her racing career. Nicole Cooke, a Giro winner and Olympic gold medallist, alleged that she wasn't even paid her team salary for three months in the run-up to the 2012 Olympics.

If Women Compete in a Cycle Race and No One Watches, Should They Get Paid?

Iris Slappendel, a retired competitive cyclist from the Netherlands, knows the problems faced by women in professional cycling intimately – she didn't get paid for six years of her career. In 2017 she decided to investigate just how endemic the gender pay gap is and surveyed around 200 female road cyclists on their earnings and work conditions. What she found was that a third of respondents made less than £5,000 a year, and the majority had to work a second job to survive. Over half of those who did receive a salary had to give some of it back to their team to pay for essential expenses.

Like Eileen Gray and other activists before her, Iris realised that no one was going to fight to make changes for women's cycling on their behalf. Far from being sympathetic to the cause, one representative of the men's cycling union asked her, 'Do you really think women are professional cyclists?' So Iris decided she would have to do it herself. Out of this came the Cyclists' Alliance, a union fighting for equality across all aspects of professional women's cycling, along the lines of the Women's Tennis Association set up by Billie Jean King in 1973 to push for the rights of women players.

Iris tells me that, in her experience, 'women's cycling still feels like the last topic on the agenda of many stakeholders'. It speaks volumes that in 2019 the sport's governing body, the UCI, has only two women on its eighteen-member management committee. Emma Pooley, who has been vocal about inequality on the women's side of the sport, once said that she thinks she is viewed by the industry as 'some kind of weirdo, radical feminist' and 'quite unpopular in some parts' as a result.

Iris has pushed hard for her members' rights. So far she has secured an agreement that, as of 2020, teams which take part in the elite series of women's road races known as the women's WorldTour will have to pay their riders a minimum salary of €15,000, which will then rise to match men's Continental Teams salaries of €30,000 by 2023, as well as offering other essential benefits like pensions.

It's definitely a start, but she tells me she feels frustrated that she and others are required 'to be activists just to be treated equally' and that for too long they were expected to 'settle for less and not complain simply because we are women'. She thinks that one of the biggest problems blocking equality in road cycling is that there is so much money tied up in the big men's races. You only have to look at the hefty prize pots of the big races and the fact that the average UCI men's WorldTour team has a budget of around £15 million, compared to an average women's team budget of around £150,000, to see that's evident. She thinks that this is due to the extensive media coverage of the men's races, with so many being televised globally, bringing the sponsors and money flowing in.

Visibility is something that still holds women's racing back; few events are televised. The Giro Rosa, currently the longest women's race, has been notoriously hard to watch outside of Italy, though in 2019 highlights were streamed online after the race. It doesn't help that the race runs at the same time as the Tour de France, meaning that the world's media and cycling fans are almost exclusively focused on that race, which is broadcast live around the world. In an interview with the *Guardian* in 2016, Mara Abbott said that 'it gets depressing' when 'nobody knows what you're doing and you go off to races in the middle of nowhere and nobody's there'. This led her to the conclusion that 'so often money represents significance'. It's a vicious circle since the lack of coverage means that sponsors are less willing to get on board and so there is less money to go round to make a race people want to watch. Road racing differs from stadium sports like football in that it can't sell pricey tickets to fans, which makes it entirely reliant on sponsorship and selling media licences.

The Tour de France has the most exposure of any race in the world and as a result it's the richest. It's also a race which reveals the huge gulf in resources, money and attention between the men's and women's side of the sport at its most extreme level. These are inequalities that Emma Pooley has described as making women look and feel like they are 'second best'. Connie Carpenter-Phinney feels that in many ways women's racing has 'flipped backwards' since the 1980s and that 'women cyclists struggle so much today to be seen'.

Iris believes that the audience is there, but isn't being given the opportunity to view the races. This is backed up by the 2016 Rio Olympics, where the women's road race was the fifth most-watched event in France. And look at the incredible audience figures for the 2019 FIFA Women's World Cup, watched by over a billion viewers worldwide, with more media rights licences granted to broadcasters than ever before. There are few people – not least one of the world's leading flag-bearers for misogyny, US President Donald Trump – who don't know who Megan Rapinoe is. It was a watershed moment which led FIFA to commit to expand the tournament from twenty-four to thirty-two teams in 2023.

Beyond the Road

It's not all glaring inequality in the world of women's cycling. In some disciplines things are much better, even if the gender pay gap hasn't quite closed. In mountain biking, women now get the chance to race in many elite competitions on the same course, for the same amount of time and for the same prize money as men. The women's events are equally popular too: in 2018 the viewership on Red Bull TV for the women's world championship event jumped from 99,000 the previous year to 233,000, putting it on a par with the men's event. Sabra Davison, who runs Little Bellas, tells me that women's MTB cross-country races often attract more viewers than the men's. She thinks this is partly a result of the women's races being more entertaining and unpredictable, since there isn't one woman dominating every competition.

The sport has come a long way since 1990, when Jacquie Phelan was handed the sixth-place prize envelope for the men's competition by mistake. It contained a cheque for $500. The cheque meant for her was just $45. In 2013, when Sabra got involved with the USA's Pro Mountain Bike Cross Country Tour, she was shocked to discover that women would only receive 65 per cent of what the men did. She and her sister Lea approached the sponsor, who responded by increasing their contribution to the extent that the women came away with more money than the men. They all felt this would make a strong statement about the inequality at that time. Sabra tells me that when there is more money at stake, it is harder to make it equal. Men's elite road racing is a prime example, with top cyclists like Chris Froome earning as much as £3 million a year. She believes that when such big figures are involved it makes for 'a more electrified and politicised environment' and one that's harder to change.

Muddy and Equal

Cyclo-cross, which emerged in France and Belgium in the early 1900s, is another sport in which the women's side has now equalised in almost every way with the men's. Races are fast and muddy laps for up to an hour over a short course (one and a half to two miles) which includes a variety of terrain – pavement, wooded trails, grass, steep hills, as well as obstacles over which the rider has to carry their bicycle. The woman responsible for pushing for positive change is Helen Wyman, British national champion 2006–15 and trailblazer for women's cycling.

I met Helen, along with her dog Alonso and two young female cross riders she is training, in a beautiful village in the Languedoc, south-west France, where she lives and trains. It was a sweltering June day and I had cycled twenty-five miles over some big hills from the village where I was living. I guessed she wouldn't bat an eyelid about me turning up sweaty and in cycling clothes to interview her. I was right.

In 2012 Helen was invited to join the UCI's cyclo-cross committee and took that as her opportunity to completely transform the way women were viewed and treated in the sport. The process was 'brutally hard' and she had to fight for the changes she made. Her first significant achievement was getting the women's UCI races moved from a morning slot, when few showed up to watch, to just before the men's race. It cost nothing, so it was difficult to refuse. This meant that journalists who previously hadn't turned up at the women's races were now there at the finish line and giving them media coverage.

The organisers of the prestigious DVV cyclo-cross series in Belgium, in an effort to show they led the way, then committed to put all their women's races on live TV. They were an instant success; audiences have grown rapidly and now represent 93 per cent of the men's viewing figures. Helen tells me that, after her races were televised, she would be recognised in Belgian supermarkets, which shows how far the sport has come from those days when the women's races, in their graveyard slot, were almost invisible. She believes that the audience 'don't care what gender they are watching, they just want a good battle' and that 'arguably 90 per cent of the races this year have been more interesting for the women than the men'.

Another significant change which Helen got the UCI to commit to was to guarantee that by 2021 women's races will be fifty minutes long and every single race will have equal prize money. With men only riding ten minutes longer than the women, it's very hard to make the case that they deserve five times as much cash. Helen feels that women in competitive cycling have too often been 'expected to do it more for love' than for financial reward. While she says it's vital that you love it, 'you also need to live', for 'it doesn't cost more to have a penis'. Now one World Cup cross race will be worth six times what the winner of the Giro Rosa currently has to share with her team. She hopes that women in the sport are on the way to achieving financial parity with their male counterparts.

Like Sabra, Helen believes that change is all down to economics: 'as soon as you show that the women's sport holds a value, that they can get a piece of that pie, then suddenly they are interested'. The DVV now has a sponsor who has come in specifically for the women's race and puts in more money than it costs to run it. She believes this is the clincher for supporting women in the sport: 'when you see that you can't think any differently, they want us because it gets them more'.

After Helen's stint on the commission, women's cyclo-cross is in a strong position and there are now more women taking to the start line at races. She is aware, though, that young women between the ages of sixteen and twenty-three are more likely to leave sport than any other group, so before she left the commission she had the UCI commit to including a junior women's category (for fourteen- to sixteen-year-olds) at all national and international championships, as there has been for men for decades.

Despite announcing her retirement in 2018, Helen remains committed to supporting up-and-coming women riders and recently used crowdfunding to pay the fees for 100 women under the age of twenty-three to enter the UK national cross championships. She also organised the first junior women's race in 2018, the Helen100 Trophy, with a prize fund equal to that of the junior boys.

Helen has competed in many women's road races but feels less optimistic about the pace of change there. She sees it as very much 'an old boys' club', and with the huge amounts of money pouring into men's road racing, she thinks it's almost impossible to change the minds of an organisation like ASO which runs the Tour. Helen has ridden La Course and felt that it was 'basically a little sideshow'. Lizzie Deignan, a pro cyclist who has taken part in the event several times, feels similarly and told me that 'we are there as a token gesture. It's more insulting than complimentary.'

Instead of trying to force the ASO to do the 'morally right thing', Helen thinks it makes more sense to focus on working with organisers who have already demonstrated that they are invested in making the sport equal – though the ASO recently announced that it plans to develop women's cycling within the organisation. She raced in the UK's first Ovo Energy Women's Tour in 2014, which now runs over six days and is one of the most prestigious women's road stage races in the world. Since 2018 it has awarded the same prize money as for the men's race, the Tour of Britain.

She felt that the difference between this and La Course was stark, which she attributes to the way in which the organisers 'set off in the beginning to make it a successful event'. The Women's Tours work closely with local schools, showing pupils that it's normal for women to be racing on bikes by incorporating the women's teams into lessons, from maths to art. This is in sharp contrast to what happened when the InternationElles stopped at a school en route through France and the children showed them their Tour de France artwork, which of course featured only male riders.

There are other races that stand out for equalising prize money and demonstrating that they are invested in women in the sport. The Colorado Classic dropped its men's race altogether in 2019 and doubled the prize money for its women's four-stage race ($30,000 to $75,000 – $5,000 more than the men had received). It also organised free live TV streaming coverage with female commentators. The same year it was announced there would be a new women's race to rival the Giro Rosa, the Battle of the North. This ten-stage race will launch in August 2021 and riders will race across Denmark, Sweden and Norway, presumably for significantly more money than its Italian competitor offers. The organisers have already said they are sure of attracting millions of TV viewers and thousands of spectators along the course. Unlike the Giro Rosa, they won't have to compete for media coverage with the Tour de France.

With other races stepping up to offer women riders better opportunities, why does it matter that the Tour de France currently only runs a one-day women's race? Not least when many female pro riders don't want a road race as long and hard as the French Grand Départ. Activists like the InternationElles aren't asking for a carbon copy of a race that is arguably too long, they want to be offered something that bridges the gulf between women cyclists and male riders.

The Tour de France is one of the most-watched sporting events in the world. It is certainly the most popular cycling event and the only race most of its audience will watch each year. It's possible that the impression they come away with is that women aren't up to it. There is more than enough evidence to prove that's false, but if you're a young girl seeing the race on TV, how are you going to know that?

The day I rode stage fifteen, it was announced that the UCI had held talks with the Tour organisers about committing to a women's stage race. An ASO spokesperson later said, as if they had only just worked this out despite the years of campaigning, 'women cyclists need a race which is to them what the Tour de France is to the men and we need to find a solution for that'.

The phenomenal success of the FIFA World Cup in its home country may have helped convince them that there was money in women's sport, but I like to think that years of pressure from those who have been calling them out on their disinterest in the women's side of cycling has helped with that shift.

Bike Baby Gone

Lizzie Deignan (née Armitstead) was a schoolgirl in Yorkshire when it first occurred to her that a career in cycling might be possible. It was 2004, and British Cycling's Olympic Talent Team, which had come to try out pupils, identified Lizzie as having a natural talent. Lizzie proved them right, winning silver in the 2012 Olympic road race and being crowned World Race Champion in 2015 and British National Road Race champion four times. She has a long list of other palmares to her name in track and road.

I spoke to Lizzie on the phone on a break from her training for the 2019 UCI Road World Championships, which would take place on home soil and pass through her home town of Otley. The run-up to this race, compared to when she won in 2015, has been radically different. Almost exactly a year ago she gave birth to her first baby, Orla. Lizzie and the Italian Marta Bastianelli are likely to be the only mothers taking part in the event, though many riders in the men's race have children. In women's cycling there are only a handful of pro riders who have children and are still racing.

Iris Slappendel of the Cyclists' Alliance thinks the reason for this is largely financial. As well as successfully pushing for higher wages for riders in the top teams, she secured eight months' paid maternity leave clauses for riders competing in WorldTour teams, a benefit that is standard in many job contracts but was absent in women's cycling. There's no doubt that it's a challenge to race and raise children. Iris recalls being away 180 days of the year; had she had children, that would have been impossible unless there was someone taking on the childcare. With the new maternity clause in place, she hopes mothers will no longer be put in a position where they have to choose between their career and their children.

Lizzie tells me that when she was growing up, she assumed that having children would mark the end of her career. With so few women with children in the professional peleton, it's easy to assume that's how it is. However, seven months after having Orla, she took part in the Amstel Gold Race. Two months after that she was overall winner of the Ovo Energy Women's Tour. She hopes that other riders, seeing her return to racing, will no longer 'correlate being pregnant with the end of their career'. Lizzie may have felt similarly inspired by Kristin Armstrong, who, two years after giving birth, won a gold medal in the individual time-trial at the 2012 Olympics. At thirty-nine, Kristin was then the oldest rider to have won the event. When she did it again at Rio in 2016, she made history as the oldest female cyclist to win an Olympic medal and the first rider to win three gold medals in the same discipline.

With new research showing that pregnancy pushes the body closest to the maximum limit for human endurance, it makes sense that women can return to sport stronger than ever. When Lizzie won the 2019 Ovo Energy Women's Tour she was incredibly emotional, describing how the result felt like a 'massive validation' after all the doubts she'd had over whether her return was the right decision. In the months post-birth, when she was juggling a tiny baby, sleep deprivation and getting back on the bike to train – an experience she has described as 'overwhelming' and 'difficult' – she looked to fellow cyclists like Laura Kenny and Sarah Storey, who had successfully resumed their cycling careers after having children. If they could do it, then it wasn't as impossible as it might have felt at 4 a.m. while feeding Orla and knowing she would have to be on the bike a few hours later.

They helped by giving advice about how to manage her pregnancy as an elite athlete, since she found there was little information out there to help her navigate this unknown territory. She admits it's 'not for every woman', but she believes there needs to be a 're-education for everybody' so that women are aware it's possible to exercise more during pregnancy than they are led to believe.

She tells me that she is luckier than many of her peers in that she was able to take time off and not worry about having to rush back to racing. It came as a surprise when the new women's team Trek-Segrafredo signed her up while she was six months pregnant – a decision all the more remarkable in the cycling world, where it's all about being at the peak of physical performance. Lack of financial support for athletes during pregnancy and maternity is widespread throughout the sports world. Nike, a company that has released adverts proclaiming their investment in gender equality, in 2019 was called out for hypocrisy by some of the female athletes they sponsored. These women revealed that the company suspended the pay of pregnant athletes.

When the Olympian Alysia Montaño, one of the top three runners in the world, asked Nike what would happen if she became pregnant, she was informed that they would pause her contract and stop paying her until she returned to running races. She broke with Nike and later released a video which turned their famous slogan 'Dream crazy' – used in an advert where viewers are told to 'believe in something, even if it means sacrificing everything' – against them: 'If we want to be an athlete and a mother, that's just crazy . . . believe in something, even if that means sacrificing everything, like maybe your contract, your pay.' She exposed their positive messaging around women in sport as hollow, just about selling trainers rather than actual investment in equality.

Sports companies often put confidentiality clauses into their contracts to stop athletes disclosing details, but when Alysia left Nike she revealed that the company had the right to reduce an athlete's pay 'for any reason' if a specific performance target wasn't met. They made no exception for childbirth, pregnancy or maternity. When she was eight months pregnant with her first child she ran a major 800-metre race and came seventh. Six and ten months after her daughter's birth, still breastfeeding, she won national championships. She had to use tape to hold her torn abdominals together. Alysia did this partly to prove it's possible to be a mother and still have a successful sports career, but also because her new sponsor, Asics – who said their policy was to pay sponsored athletes in full during pregnancy and after childbirth – had threatened to stop paying her after expressing doubts that she would be ready to come back within the time frame they had set.

Another Nike-sponsored athlete, Kara Goucher, revealed that she signed up to a half-marathon scheduled three months after the birth of her son, because Nike had suspended her pay until she started racing again. When her son got dangerously ill and was hospitalised, she had to keep training instead of being with him twenty-four hours a day as she would have wanted – something she says she will never be able to forgive herself for, though she felt she had little choice. The company also requested she keep her pregnancy secret for four months so they could announce it in a newspaper on Mother's Day as part of their brand promotion around equality.

It's telling that in 2019 all the executives negotiating contracts at Nike are men. But, after the video and a *New York Times* article by Alysia resulted in a Congressional inquiry and a great deal of negative attention for the company, Nike announced a new maternity policy that guaranteed pay and bonuses during and after pregnancy for all their athletes.

Lizzie's new team took a different approach, perhaps because it has two women directors. They are committed to giving 'exactly the same opportunities to women, always considering they are women, so pregnancy could be part of their life'. Lizzie strongly believes that improving rights for mothers in sport is 'all part of the fight for equality' and Trek has been vocal about helping improve parity between men and women, not least hiring the women's cycling activist Kathryn Bertine as an ambassador for equality. Lizzie tells me she felt trusted to do what was best for her, such as missing training camps because she was breast-feeding and choosing when it was right for her to return to racing, something she felt was 'a completely open-minded and new approach'.

Lizzie is aware that every pregnancy and baby is different, and she was lucky that she was able to keep cycling – though not hard – until three days before giving birth. She then took six weeks off before getting back on the bike. She knows that in such a competitive environment many women don't feel able to risk taking time out to have a baby, knowing that childbirth could result not just in the loss of their contract, but also of their peak fitness. But at least the new maternity clause for top-level riders will give them more financial security.

Lizzie is in the fortunate position of being supported by her husband, Philip, who retired early from his own professional road racing career to become a full-time dad. Though she felt she'd been 'thrown in at the deep end' initially, she says that, like any mother returning to work, 'you just manage, you just do it'. She regained her fitness quicker than she expected and, even though her team put no pressure on her, she returned to competing nearly two months ahead of schedule. She says being a mother has rekindled her love of cycling, that before her pregnancy she was winning but not always enjoying it.

She feels her life is more balanced, that being a mother means cycling is now 'just my job and I have to get it done', and as a consequence the wins are more rewarding. She also finds her training rides give her an important 'mental break' from childcare and that she's lucky to have a job that, when she's not racing, only takes her away from Orla for four hours a day. She strongly believes that every woman has the right to choose when she wants to have a baby and to be supported by her employer, even in the world of sport. She hopes that cycling teams will start including paternity rights so that male riders don't risk losing a contract if they too choose to take time out for the birth of their children.

Representation Matters

If you do manage to find women's cycle racing on TV, it's not obvious who might be a mother, but it is plain to see that it's a very white sport. So much so that when the amateur black British track cyclist Yewande Adesida turns up at races, she is more often than not the only black woman there.

I met twenty-five-year-old Yewande in London just before she headed to Newport for a race the following day. She tells me that before she got into cycling she had been a competitive rower, but when she realised she wasn't going to excel as she'd hoped, she decided to look for another sport. She had previously been recommended to take up athletics, which has much more racial diversity. Instead she decided to follow the advice of those who told her she would be a good fit for track cycling. She tells me that the lack of diversity in the cycling world wasn't that much of a surprise to her since rowing is also overwhelmingly white and elitist. Even so, when she first got into track cycling, not seeing anyone else who looked like her at the start line made her wonder, 'Maybe I've picked another sport that I shouldn't really be doing because no one like me does it.'

If she'd read about the experiences of Natnael Berhane, the only black African cyclist to take part in the 2019 Tour de France, then it's understandable she would have felt that way. In 2015 Natnael was racing for Team MTN-Qhubeka, the first African team to take part in the Tour de France. When he competed in the Tour of Austria that same year he was racially abused by a cyclist from another team. If this wasn't bad enough, MTN-Qhubeka said this was far from an isolated incident for their black African team members.

Professional cycling has long struggled to be racially inclusive, as we saw in Chapter 5 with the League of

American Wheelman introducing a ban on non-white cyclists. They took that decision at a time when an African American cyclist, Major Taylor, was leaving his opponents standing, winning national and international champion titles and medals across the US and Europe. As well as being barred from racetracks on account of the colour of his skin, throughout his career he was subjected to vile verbal and physical abuse from fellow cyclists and fans. In one incident he was choked by a rival to the point of unconsciousness. One of the highest-earning athletes in the world in his heyday, he died destitute and forgotten.

As recently as the 1970s, the UK's first black British cycling champion, Maurice Burton, relocated to Belgium because he could no longer endure the racial abuse directed towards him at races in his home country.

Yewande is quick to point out that she's never experienced any sort of racism on the track and that people have always been massively encouraging, but that hasn't stopped doubt creeping in from time to time. She worried more about making mistakes because she felt she already stood out as the only black woman on the track: 'I still had that thought in the back of my mind that maybe I should try something else that someone suggested like athletics.' Joining an all-women's cycling club, Velociposse, helped. They invited her to become a member after seeing her cycling at Lee Valley Velodrome. At that point the idea of joining a cycling club was 'really intimidating', but an all-women club felt like it would be a 'safer environment'. They were able to loan her a track bike, so she didn't have to commit to buying before she'd decided whether to stick with the sport.

Her time with Velociposse helped her grow confidence on the track, as well as her sense of belonging there, and affirmed that she had made the right choice. Two years on, she juggles a PhD in sports biomechanics with competing in mixed-team SES Racing, specialising in sprint events. These tactical races have two riders battling it out over distances from 250 to 1,000 metres. They start extremely slowly, with each rider watching the other's every move, before one initiates the high-speed sprint to the finish.

For someone who initially felt that the track might not be a suitable choice because of the absence of other women who looked like her, Yewande is aware that her participation might make others think that they belong. Self-promotion doesn't come naturally, but she feels it's important to be visible and an active voice in the sport: 'I know what a difference it can make, being able to see someone that looks like you, and so for that reason I don't mind it.'

Though there are times she would rather just get on and ride her bike, by doing interviews and using social media, she knows she is helping to break down barriers about who the sport is for and encouraging more people into competitive cycling. Yewande believes that brands need to step up and show that cycling is much more diverse than the Tour de France would suggest, where the peleton is overwhelmingly white and a large proportion of adverts make use of that same demographic.

In 2019 Yewande was chosen by a well-known company which makes bicycle components, many of which end up on the bikes of pro riders from MTB to road, to front the campaign for its most important product launch for some years. In its images she is seen flying along, crouched over the handlebars and owning the road, the landscape a blur behind her. After the ad went out, she received messages from people who told her it had inspired them to get on a bike. She thinks that other companies should be doing more to use similarly diverse images: 'There are black cyclists out there, people need to open their eyes more and look a bit deeper.'

When Yewande first got into track cycling and was struggling to find other black women in the sport, she was unaware that in the US a cyclist had set out to become the first female African American pro road cyclist. Ayesha McGowan took up cycling in her twenties so she could get to university faster. She instantly fell in love with it and before long was dabbling in track racing before moving on to road, winning a state championship soon after. Like Yewande she looked for a mentor from a similar background, but, not finding one, she decided she would have to become that person for others like her.

Ayesha now competes in professional races and is sponsored by major international brands, but she's yet to achieve her ultimate goal of joining a professional racing team. She has said that 'simply existing in this sport as a black woman is its own form of advocacy', but she goes much further than that and has become one of the most visible and proactive forces for change, pushing the industry to be more inclusive, particularly for women, women of colour and people with disabilities.

Through her popular social media accounts, blog and podcast, as well as media interviews, Ayesha details her journey into competitive cycling, empowering others to do things they might once have thought impossible, as well as turning the spotlight on other women of colour in the cycling world – cyclists like thirteen-year-old Maize 'aMAIZEn' Wimbush from Maryland, who hopes to be the first African American woman to compete in a cycling event at the Olympics. In a film Ayesha made with Nike, she says that while it's obviously about winning, at the same time there's a wider goal of making the sport more diverse: 'It's about showing up and claiming my space and knowing that I deserve to be there. If I don't show up to these pro races then there are no other black women in them.'

When I asked Iris Slappendel of the Cyclists' Alliance about the lack of diversity in cycling, she said the sporting world 'makes a big thing out of everything or person that's not "ordinary" or they're not familiar with'. Justin Williams, an African American from impoverished south LA, experienced this when he entered the elite and rule-obsessed world of professional road cycling. He has described how the experience nearly broke him: 'Being involved in a sport that is primarily white, it was hard not to be alone and it ultimately cracked me.' He has now created his own team, Legion, whose members don't conform to outdated stereotypes of how a racing cyclist ought to look or behave. He hopes his team will inspire the next generation and break down barriers, with riders who 'wear Jordans, listen to rap really loud at races' and who are 'going to be a part of the conversation'.

In Rwanda, a country with no history of women's bike racing, the Africa Rising Cycling Center aims to encourage black women from across the continent into the sport. This non-profit organisation, which has successfully got many black African cyclists into the international men's professional peloton, is helping do the same with black African female riders. One of its most successful is Jeanne d'Arc Girubuntu. In 2009 Jeanne had watched cyclists compete in the Tour du Rwanda and immediately thought that was something she wanted to do. That race is men-only, but it didn't put her off. Six years later she had made it onto her country's national cycling team, the lone female member, travelling to the USA for the UCI World Road Championships, making history as the first black woman from Africa to compete at the event. Jeanne hopes that by becoming a visible force in cycling in Rwanda and internationally, she will help cycling become more acceptable for women in her country, where gender norms are very traditional.

With black African cyclists like Natnael Berhane and Tsgabu Grmay now a core part of the peloton in the big European road races like the Giro d'Italia and Tour de France, black women from Africa are finally making their mark in elite international races. Eyeru Tesfoam Gebru from Ethiopia made cycling history when in 2018 at the Tour Cycliste Féminin International de l'Ardèche she was awarded the title of Most Combative. She is the first black African woman to hold a jersey in a professional race. Like Jeanne, she benefitted from training at the centre in Rwanda and has gone on to become part of new UCI women's team, WCC, which was formed in 2019 with nine riders from around the world. Eyeru now takes part in elite international road races alongside fellow African Desiet Kidane Tekeste.

Africa Rising hopes that, with more support of women's cycling in the continent, which is chronically underfunded, it can continue to expose the incredible talent of African women – women who would previously have struggled through lack of access to training and opportunities to get anywhere near the international elite women's races. In so doing it hopes to change the landscape of the women's international cycling scene for ever.

Where Now?

Lizzie Deignan has said that women's professional cycling is 'at a point now where we cannot go back'. With activists and advocates for the sport like Helen, Iris, Ayesha, Sabra, Yewande and so many others pushing successfully for change, I think she's right. It's been a long time coming and there is still a good distance to go in making the sport as equal, diverse and inclusive as it should be.

For progress to continue in the right direction with the next generation, there needs to be much more exposure of women's racing, because if no one can see it then how will they know what's possible?

If a true women's Tour de France ever does become a reality, the impact will undoubtedly raise the profile of women across every aspect of the sport. French children will be drawing pictures of the likes of Annemiek van Vleuten, Marianne Vos, Lizzie Deignan and Eyeru Tesfoam Gebru. And girls around the world will know that riding a bike, even racing on a bike, is something they can do too.

The narrative of women being the sideshow to the men's main event needs to end and the spotlight to shine bright on the strong, diverse and talented women who are taking to the start line across the sport. Women whom girls around the world can identify with, and think that they can do that too. They also need to be treated like professionals with pay, prizes and races that aren't insulting, as well as working conditions that value them as human beings, in a sport where they are as visible and respected – and by turns celebrated – as their male counterparts. Cycling Queens.

AFTERWORD: KEEP ON PEDALLING

I could easily not have got hooked on cycling. At school I loved exploring the woodlands and open spaces of Bristol by bike with friends. We were often in trouble for roaming further than allowed. But as I progressed through my teenage years I got into punk music, joined a band and my bike mostly gathered dust in the shed. I had never identified as sporty and I remember one school sports report where the teacher wrote: 'I'd like to comment on Hannah's progress this term, but I've not seen her.' Many other women cyclists tell me they too hadn't enjoyed games classes at school, but rediscovering bikes in their twenties changed their perception of themselves. In fact, there are some pro women riders who started late, like Ireland's Orla Walsh, who took up cycling in 2015 to get to college cheaply and quickly. A dedicated party animal until that point, with no prior interest in sport, by 2017, at age twenty-eight, she was on the national cycling team.

I may not be racing, but cycling plays a significant role in my life. It didn't start with commuting (that came after) but with a need to escape – rides that have since become longer and an increasingly important part of my life. Now most of my holidays, here and abroad, revolve around the bike.

That isn't to say my relationship with cycling is uncomplicated. I live with a potentially fatal heart condition which can be brought on by strenuous exercise. I feel fit and able and my ultrasound heart scans have all been normal – and possibly always will be – but people with my rare condition, Marfan's syndrome, are at 250 times greater risk of aortic dissection (a tear or rupture between layers of the aortic wall) than the general population. And it is very often fatal. One cardiologist suggested I cycle only on the flat, but my current doctor is more relaxed and thinks I can judge what might be pushing it. There is no exact measure and there are no guarantees, but I wear a heart-rate monitor and make sure I am never straining or too out of breath.

I need to navigate my way around doing what I love so that it doesn't kill me. I can't ignore my condition, but I can keep pedalling even if I know I won't be challenging anyone to a race up Mont Ventoux. Instead I will be taking it slowly and steadily, which allows me more time to take in the view.

We opened in Cambridge, 1897, with a female effigy on a bicycle being used as a warning to those 'New Women' studying at Girton College to keep out of territories claimed by the male students as their own, particularly higher education and cycling. We end in the same city, but in 2020, where it's abundantly clear the protest ultimately failed. Cambridge is now teeming with women students, like every university in the UK, but what's more unusual is that the proportion of women on bikes is greater than anywhere else in Britain.

Cambridge, with the highest number of bike commuters in the UK, is now dubbed the capital of cycling. If you visit the city, the whir of wheels and ding of bicycle bells might make you think you're in the Netherlands. On the Hills Road alone, a busy artery connecting the train station to the centre, at least 5,000 cyclists pedal the busy stretch each day. And it doesn't take in-depth research to see why cycling is so popular with residents and visitors alike; the city is criss-crossed with an extensive network of safe and protected bike lanes, as well as multiple bridges dedicated to cyclists and pedestrians that cross the River Cam. The city has invested in its active travel infrastructure, prioritising bikes and walking over cars so you don't need to do battle on the roads each day just to get to work or the shops. The superstar classicist Mary Beard has cited her bicycle commute to the university, which includes a scenic path along the river, as guaranteed to improve her mood. She will not be alone: the physical and mental health benefits of cycling have been proven beyond doubt.

Half of those on two wheels in Cambridge are women, which is in stark contrast to the rest of the country where it's 27 per cent on average, and often far less, with similar or worse figures in the USA, Australia and Canada. But wherever you have a good network of bike lanes you get a more even gender split, which is the case in Germany, Denmark and the Netherlands.

Women tend to be more risk-averse than men, for myriad social and cultural reasons, which explains why better cycling infrastructure can shift the gender balance significantly. While in most countries women aren't being told they shouldn't bike – unlike their Victorian sisters – safety on the roads disproportionately impacts their willingness to participate. For example, the League of American Bicyclists reported that in 2011 a street in New York with no bike lane was shown to have only around 15 per cent of women cyclists compared to 32 per cent using the dedicated lane on a street nearby. In Philadelphia the number of women on bikes went up by 276 per cent where cycling infrastructure was installed. To emulate countries that have a greater uptake in cycling across genders, from children going to school to those still pedalling long past retirement, it's obvious more needs to be done to keep everyone safe from cars and lorries.

When the Covid-19 pandemic spread throughout the world in spring 2020, cities around the globe began to experience a new boom in cycling. With reduced traffic on the roads many people unsurprisingly felt safer to bike, including significant numbers of women and children. They have done so to avoid risking infection on busy public transport, to exercise and for pleasure. There have been new converts as well as many lapsed enthusiasts dragging neglected models out of sheds or jumping on street rentals. From New York to Bogotá, newly closed roads and pop-up bike lanes have seen plenty of two-wheeled action, with some cities, like London and Paris, proposing to make the changes permanent even after the pandemic subsides. Manufacturers could not produce bicycles fast enough to meet demand, and repair shops now have long waiting lists for services. This resurgence in popularity has shown that when people feel safer on our roads, they are much happier and more willing to get around by bike.

Renewed pedal-love may help power another kind of societal change; one where we reject congested roads and pollution. We might decide instead that breathing clean air and feeling safe, and travelling in a healthier and more enjoyable way around our cities and beyond, is something worth holding on to. Not many people think that their cities would be improved by more fossil-fuel-reliant vehicles and less bicycles.

We are at a critical point for our health and that of the planet; 2020 saw record-breaking temperatures, with the Arctic recording its first 38 degrees Celsius day and fires raging across Siberia. It is clear that we need to drastically cut our carbon emissions, and making it more attractive for people to journey by bike – or on foot – instead of by car could have a significant impact. Data from the UK government shows that transport is the largest source of greenhouse gas emissions in the country (34 per cent in 2019) and, according to the Centre for Cities charity, an estimated one in nineteen deaths is related to air pollution. We now also know that poor air quality even makes people more susceptible to Covid-19.

At present, 60 per cent of journeys between one and two miles in the UK are done by car. Convert these trips to bike or foot and it would have a hugely positive impact on people's health and the environment. Electric bikes could also play a significant role in this shift, attracting those who might not see themselves as fit enough, or whose commute is too long, for regular biking. Just as adapted bicycles and tricycles help those with varying physical barriers, whether it be age or disability, to continue to cycle.

But if all this makes it sound rather worthy, let's not forget that cycling is also immensely pleasurable. It would be a shame for only a minority to experience all that it has to offer.

I don't have to stop cycling and I hope you don't either. And if you don't cycle already, I hope the stories here might inspire you to start.

Getting on your bike is only the beginning of many new stories and adventures.

ACKNOWLEDGEMENTS

I am immensely grateful to everyone who agreed to be interviewed for this book: Fatimah Al-Bloushi, Yewande Adesida, Wende Cragg, Sabra Davison, Lizzie Deignan, Shannon Galpin, Jenny Graham, Jenni Gwiazdowski, Anissa Lamare, Dervla Murphy, Zahra Naarin, Iris Slappendel and Helen Wyman. Without your generosity this idea would have gone nowhere, you are the beating heart of women's cycling today. I hope I've done justice both to the stories you've told me and your passion for this subject. I would also like to mention the Bike Project, who are doing incredible work and have let me play the most minuscule part in that. Keep doing what you are doing.

Thanks too to my brilliant and peerless agent, Patrick Walsh, who saw enough in my scrappy initial ideas to commit to helping develop them into something much more resembling a solid and persuasive outline for a book. John Ash, also at PEW, played a significant role in this too.

Here I must also give credit to Andrew Franklin, friend, colleague, committed cyclist and experienced publisher, who was the person who instilled in me the belief that I might be capable of writing a book and who, through his unrelenting encouragement, gave me the push I needed to organise my thoughts and take the terrifying step of getting some words down. I do not think there would be a book at all if he hadn't been so insistent I could do it. I'd also like to mention Hannah Westland, who gave much encouragement from the start, and Diana Broccardo, who has been unfailing in her support, not least agreeing to my sabbatical so I could write. Valentina Zanca, Drew Jerrison and Anna-Marie Fitzgerald deserve special mention for being excellent people to work with.

I am hugely appreciative of all those involved at every stage of making this into a proper book; their efforts are immense. My editor Jenny Lord, whose judicious editing and wise guidance, not to mention endless enthusiasm – as well as patience with my inability to anticipate how long it might take to write a book – have been invaluable. Thanks to the rest of the team at W&N who have worked hard to make sure the book happened, including Rosie Pearce, Kate Moreton, Virginia Woolstencroft, Brittany Sankey, Anne O'Brien and everyone else involved in getting the book into the world. Otto Von Beach, the illustrator of the UK edition, deserves special mention here too.

To the friends who read early drafts or even just put up with me endlessly talking about women and cycling, you are all great. As well as everyone who made suggestions, introduced me to people I should talk to, and gave me new ideas – you are too numerous to mention by name, but I'm grateful to each of you.

My parents, John and Sylvia, and siblings, Jon, Nick and Emma, have played a major role in this book coming into being by nurturing in me a love of cycling and the outdoors. You are the reason I can cycle at all and the bike rides I've been on with you are now part of my DNA. I also don't think any present will ever top that time when 'Father Christmas' left a note by my bed attached to a piece of string which led all the way downstairs to a new bicycle.

The biggest thanks of all goes to Mike, without whose

support and encouragement this book wouldn't have seen the light of day. Your readings of the very rough early drafts, and multiple reworkings, were always the most thoughtful and incisive. You also kept me fed and the fires burning – literally, when that was our only form of heating in Villelongue – when I was glued to the laptop too long. You always find the best bike routes and are my favourite cycling, and everything else, partner.

NOTES

INTRODUCTION

'has done more to emancipate women . . .' – Nellie Bly, 'Champion of Her Sex: Miss Susan B. Anthony', *New York World* (2 February 1896)

CHAPTER 2

'rabid disease commonly known as cyclomania' – *Cycling* (1895)

'look sweet on the seat of . . .' – Harry Dacre, 'Daisy Bell (Bicycle Built for Two)', 1892

'the intricate figures performed by the cyclists . . .' – *Munsey's Magazine* (1896)

'a bird, sailing over flower-covered prairies . . .' – Helen Follett, 'Honeymoon on two wheels,' *Outing*, 29 (1896–97)

'at the cost of some thousands of pedal strokes . . .' – Eve Curie, *Marie Curie*, trans. Vincent Sheean (New York, Doubleday, Doran & Co., 1937)

'bus drivers were not above . . .' – Helena Maria Lucy Swanwick, *I Have Been Young* (London, Victor Gollancz, 1935)

'hussy' – Evelyn Everett-Green, 'Cycling for Ladies' in *All Round Cycling* (London, Walter Scott, 1896)

'wild women of the usual unprepossessing . . .' – Ethel Smyth, *The Memoirs of Ethel Smyth* (London, Viking, 1987)

'now and again a complaint arises . . .' – Marguerite Merington, 'Woman and the bicycle', *Scribner's*, XVII (June 1895)

'I rejoice every time I see a woman . . .' – Nellie Bly, 'Champion of Her Sex: Miss Susan B. Anthony', *New York World* (2 February 1896) 'the devil's advance agent' – Charlotte Smith, quoted in Sue Macy, *Wheels of Change: How Women Rode the Bicycle to Freedom* (Washington, DC, National Geographic, 2011)

'bring about constant friction' – R. L. Dickinson, quoted in Patricia Vertinsky, *Eternally Wounded Women: Women, Doctors and Exercise in the Late Nineteenth Century* (Manchester, Manchester University Press, 1990)

'the haze, the elusiveness, the subtle suggestion . . .' – Arabella Kenealy, quoted in Kathleen McCrone, *Sport and the Physical Emancipation of English Women 1870–1914* (London, Routledge, 2014)

'I have seen them rapidly decline . . .' – James Beresford Ryley, *The Dangers of Cycling for Women and Children* (London, H. Renshaw, 1899)

'hardly lets me stir without special . . .' – Charlotte Perkins Gilman, *Herland and The Yellow Wallpaper* (London, Vintage, 2015)

'The woman's desire to be on a level . . .' – Silas Weir Mitchell, *Doctor and Patient* (New York, Classics of Medicine Library, 1994)

'since taking up cycling had been' – quoted in Oscar Jennings, *Cycling and Health* (London, Iliffe & Son, 1893)

'when women began to understand the needs . . .' – 'A Lady Doctor's Views on Cycling', *The Hub* (September 1897)

'there is nothing in the anatomy . . .' – W. H. Fenton, 'A medical view of cycling for ladies', *The Nineteenth Century*, 39 (23 May 1896)

'people are as likely to die early from . . .' – https://www.thelancet.com/journals/lancet/article/PIIS0140-6736(17)31634-3/fulltext

'cycling to the office . . .' – https://www.bmj.com/content/357/bmj.j1456

'cycling was shown to . . .' – Ross D. Pollock, Katie A. O'Brien, Lorna J. Daniels, et al. (2018). 'Properties of the Vastus Lateralis Muscle in Relation to Age and Physiological Function in Master Cyclists Aged 55–79 Years', *Aging Cell*, 17(2)

'Cycling isn't just making us happier' – https://www.bicycling.com/training/a20029339/how-cycling-makes-you-smarter-and-happier/

'men make three times . . .' – https://assets.publishing.service.gov.uk/government/uploads/system/uploads/attachment_data/file/736909/walking-and-cycling-statistics-england-2017.pdf

CHAPTER 3

'not in that dress' – *Pall Mall Gazette* (5 April, 1899)

'abominable. It smelt of spirits . . .' – *Dunstan Times* (2 June 1899)

'use boyish gestures and talk' – *The Lady Cyclist* (March 1896)

'great war' – Elizabeth Sanderson Haldane, *From One Century to Another: The Reminiscences of E. S. Haldane 1862–1937* (London, A. Maclehose & Co., 1937)

'by force of habit . . .' – Florence Pomeroy, *Reasons for Reform in Dress* (London, Hutchings & Crowsley, 1884)

'the pressure on the large vessels . . .' – Victor Neeesen, *Dr. Neesen's Book on Wheeling: Hints and Advice to Men and Women from the Physician's Standpoint* (London, Forgotten Books, 2018)

'one long suicide' – *The Lady Cyclist* (September 1895)

'I can do the work for 16 cows . . .' – Diana Crane, *Fashion and Its Social Agendas: Class, Gender, and Identity in Clothing* (Chicago, University of Chicago Press, 2000)

'a costume that caused hundreds . . .' – 'She Wore Trousers', *National Police Gazette* (28 October 1893)

'a lamentable incident . . .' – *Cycling* (September 1893)

'a caricature of the sweetest . . .' – https://thevictoriancyclist. wordpress.com/2015/02/15/womanly-cycling-part-two

'on her courage in being . . .' – http://www.sheilahanlon. com/?p=1830

'the shocking and painful spectacle' – *Daily Telegraph* (25 November 1893)

'Parisian women are riding . . .' – *Cycling* (June 1894)

'let it visibly announce . . .' – Oscar Wilde, 'The Philosophy of Dress', *New York Tribune* (19 April 1885)

CHAPTER 4

'my beautiful picture . . .' – Frances E. Willard, *Writing Out My Heart: Selections from the Journal of Frances E. Willard, 1855–96* (Urbana, University of Illinois Press, 1995)

'the earthly anchor . . .' – Kathleen Fitzpatrick, *Lady Henry Somerset* (London, Jonathan Cape, 1923)

'born with an inveterate . . .' – Willard, *Writing Out My Heart*

'peculiarities of figure . . .' – *The Lady Cyclist* (March 1896)

'more distressing to the . . .' – *The Lady Cyclist* (June 1896) 'weary and worn out . . .' – *The Lady Cyclist* (September 1896)

'trying to find . . .' – https://www.accesssport.org.uk/News/celebrating-international-nurses-day

'spatial reasoning' – Jamie J. Jirout, Nora S. Newcombe (2015) 'Building Blocks for Developing Spatial Skills: Evidence From a Large, Representative U.S. Sample', *Association for Psychological Science*, 26, 3: 302–310

CHAPTER 5

'cease to be the case . . .' – and all other quotes relating to Kittie Knox, quoted in Lorenz J. Finison, *Boston's Cycling Craze, 1880–1900: A Story of Race, Sport, and Society* (Boston, University of Massachusetts Press, 2014)

'women still only make up . . .' – https://www.theguardian.com/cities/2015/jul/09/women-cycling-infrastructure-cyclists-killed-female

'According to research . . .' – http://content.tfl.gov.uk/analysis-of-cycling-potential-2016.pdf

'women like me . . .' – https://w4c.org/case-study/women-and-biking-case-study-use-san-francisco-bike-lanes

'I have to admit that . . .' – https://www.bicycling.com/news/a20015703/an-interview-with-monica-garrison-of-black-girls-do-bike/

'This is what freedom . . .' – Xela de la X., *Ovarian Psycos*, dir. Joanna Sokolowski, Kate Trumbull-LaValle (USA, 2016)

'We're not about who can ride . . .' – https://www.latimes.com/local/la-xpm-2013-sep-22-la-me-psyco-riders-20130923-story.html

'riding a bicycle often attracts . . .' – 'Women defy Fatwa on riding bicycles', *The Times* (22 September 2016)

'girls deserve to have . . .' – https://www.sidetracked.com/cycling-in-afghanistan/

'I've been telling women . . .' – https://www.arabnews.com/node/1262466/saudi-arabia

'It fills my heart with joy' – https://gulfnews.com/world/gulf/saudi/saudi-women-conquer-jeddah-streets-on-bicycle-1.61705902

CHAPTER 6

'football scrummage' – *Lancashire Daily Post* (14 February 1907)

'a considerable handicap' – Sylvia E. Pankhurst, *The Suffragette Movement: An Intimate Account of Persons and Ideals* (London, Longmans & Co., 1931)

'she would disappear from me . . .' – Pankhurst, *The Suffragette Movement*

'There were usually some slow . . .' – Pankhurst, *The Suffragette Movement*

'the common tragedy . . .' – Pankhurst, *The Suffragette Movement*

'stand up for the oppressed . . .' – Eveline Buchheim and Ralf Futselaar, eds, *Under Fire: Women and World War II* (Amsterdam, Verloren Publishers, 2014)

'Once I ran into a dog . . .' – Simone de Beauvoir, *Letters to Sartre*, trans. Quentin Hoare (London, Vintage Classics, 1993)

'I pedalled on, and . . .' – Simone de Beauvoir, *The Prime of Life*, trans. Peter Green (London, Deutsch, Weidenfeld and Nicolson, 1963)

'I only wanted to eat up the . . .' – de Beauvoir, *Letters to Sartre*

'the moment my legs begin . . .' – Henry David Thoreau, 'Walking,' *The Writings of Henry David Thoreau* (Boston, Houghton Mifflin, 1894)

'I like to have space to spread . . .' – Virginia Woolf, *The Diary of Virginia Woolf*, ed. Anne Olivier (London, Hogarth Press, 1980)

'scarcely make head . . .' – de Beauvoir, *Letters to Sartre*

'Four experiments' – https://www.apa.org/pubs/journals/releases/xlm-a0036577.pdf

'pedalling so indolently . . .' – de Beauvoir, *The Prime of Life*

'intoxicated by the swift . . .' – de Beauvoir, *The Prime of Life*

'leave espionage to those . . .' – de Beauvoir, *The Prime of Life*

'I had lost a tooth . . .' – de Beauvoir, *The Prime of Life*

'a childish sense . . .' – de Beauvoir, *The Prime of Life*

'reduced to a condition . . .' – de Beauvoir, *The Prime of Life*

'saved us from literally . . .' – de Beauvoir, *The Prime of Life*

'back on the road in front . . .' – de Beauvoir, *The Prime of Life*

'pedalled across the railway . . .' – de Beauvoir, *The Prime of Life*

'on a little journey all alone . . .' – de Beauvoir, *The Prime of Life*

CHAPTER 7

'What would become of us . . .' – Henry David Thoreau, 'Walking'

'thirst for longer flights . . .' – Lillias Campbell Davidson, *Handbook for Lady Cyclists* (London, Hay Nisbet & Co., 1896)

'inside the movie, an essential . . .' – Juliana Buhring, *This Road I Ride: My Incredible Journey from Novice to Fastest Woman to Cycle the Globe* (London, Piatkus, 2016)

'some considerable peril . . .' – Mrs Harcourt Williamson, A. C. Pemberton, C. P. Sisley and G. Floyd. *The Complete Cyclist* (A. D. Innes & Co., London 1897)

'the observed of all observers . . .' – 'Martha', 'We Girls Awheel through Germany', *Outing* (April–September 1892)

'prophecies of broken . . .' – Margaret Valentine Le Long, 'From Chicago to San Francisco Awheel', *Outing* 31, no.5 (February 1898)

'has two spare . . .' – Campbell Davidson, *Handbook for Lady Cyclists*

'being stared at . . .' – Elizabeth Robins Pennell, 'Cycling', *Ladies in the Field: Sketches of Sport*, ed. Beatrice Violet Greville (London, Ward & Downey, 1894)

'hers is all the joy . . .' – Pennell, 'Cycling'

'The world is our great book . . .' – Pennell, 'Cycling'

'I am told I made a record . . .' – Elizabeth Robins Pennell, illustrated by Joseph Pennell, *Over the Alps on a Bicycle* (London, T. F. Unwin, 1898)

'a big German frau . . .' – Pennell, *Over the Alps on a Bicycle*

'People may object that I rode . . .' – Pennell, *Over the Alps on a Bicycle*

'immortalise the name and . . .' – Pennell, *Over the Alps on a Bicycle*

'I was doing this thing . . .' – Pennell, *Over the Alps on a Bicycle*

'dine with the fifty . . .' – Pennell, *Over the Alps on a Bicycle*

'wept over the sublimities . . .' – Pennell, *Over the Alps on a Bicycle*

'courage, endurance and enthusiasm . . .' – Fanny Bullock Workman and William Hunter Workman, *Sketches Awheel in Fin de Siècle Iberia* (London, T. F. Unwin, 1897)

'Don Quixotian days . . .' – Bullock Workman, *Sketches Awheel in Fin de Siècle Iberia*

'enabling us an entire . . .' – Fanny Bullock Workman and William Hunter Workman, *Algerian Memories: A Bicycle Tour over the*

Atlas to the Sahara (London, T. Fisher Unwin, 1895)

'not so far advanced . . .' – Bullock Workman, *Sketches Awheel in Fin de Siècle Iberia*

'with much the same awe-inspired . . .' – Bullock Workman, *Sketches Awheel in Fin de Siècle Iberia*

'there seemed to be no chance . . .' – Bullock Workman, *Sketches Awheel in Fin de Siècle Iberia*

'the women stared . . .' – Bullock Workman, *Sketches Awheel in Fin de Siècle Iberia*

'not a pleasant place . . .' – Bullock Workman, *Sketches Awheel in Fin de Siècle Iberia*

'gaunt, wolfish . . .' – Bullock Workman, *Algerian Memories*

'one must look deeper . . .' – Bullock Workman, *Algerian Memories*

'light may fall upon the . . .' – Fanny Bullock Workman and William Hunter Workman, *Through Town and Jungle: Fourteen Thousand Miles A-wheel among the Temples and People of the Indian Plain* (London, T. Fisher Unwin, 1904)

CHAPTER 8

'love of the great-out-of-doors' – https://www.bikeleague.org/content/womens-bike-history-3-days-5-women-250-miles

'I had never known holidays . . .' – Mrs Cattaneo, quoted in James McGurn, *On Your Bicycle: An Illustrated History of Cycling* (London, John Murray, 1987)

'young and fit and ready . . .' – https://www.cyclingweekly.com/news/latest-news/billie-fleming-happy-100th-birthday-121964

'If I went on doing this . . .' – Dervla Murphy, *Wheels within Wheels* (London, John Murray, 1979)

'completely trapped and . . .' – Murphy, *Wheels within Wheels*

'exalted by the realisation . . .' – Murphy, *Wheels within Wheels*

'a hideous bit of business . . .' – Campbell Davidson, *Handbook for Lady Cyclists*

'series of interiors . . .' – Rebecca Solnit, *Wanderlust: A History of Walking* (London, Penguin, 2001)

'seized with sudden envy . . .' – Anne Mustoe, *A Bike Ride: 12,000 Miles around the World* (London, Virgin, 1991)

'the more that doubt . . .' – https://www.youtube.com/watch?v=Y4f4UTmKc1U&feature=emb_logo

CHAPTER 9

'audacious and unprecedented . . .' – Peter Zheutlin, *Around the World on Two Wheels: Annie Londonderry's Extraordinary Ride* (New York, Kensington Publishing Corp., 2007)

'drains your morale, saps . . .' – Buhring, *This Road I Ride*

'nothing to qualify me . . .' – Buhring, *This Road I Ride*

'another being, I just . . .' – Buhring, *This Road I Ride*

'a kind of meditation . . .' – Buhring, *This Road I Ride*

'circus freak show . . .' – Buhring, *This Road I Ride*

'People want to think income . . .' – https://poll2018.trust.org/stories/item/?id=e52a1260-260c-47e0-94fc-a636b1956da7

'34 per cent of American women . . .' –https://news.gallup.com/poll/196487/one-three-women-worry-sexually-assaulted.aspx

'a 2018 study' – https://www.bbc.co.uk/news/uk-scotland-43128350

CHAPTER 10

'a sport run by men, for men' – https://totalwomenscycling.com/news/nicole-cooke-evidence-british-cycling

'no one can have any idea how . . .' – Louise Armaindo, quoted in M. Ann Hall, *Muscle on Wheels: Louise Armaindo and the High-Wheel Racers of Nineteenth-Century America* (Montreal, McGill-Queen's Press, 2018)

'is not, nor can it ever be, a fit thing . . .' – *Cycling* (August 1894)

'if carried to excess . . .' – Pennell, 'Cycling'

'instead of a demonstration of limbs . . .' – http://www.sixday.org.uk/html/1889_sheffield.html

'speediest of all cyclists . . .' – Roger Gilles, *Women on the Move: The Forgotten Era of Women's Bicycle Racing* (Lincoln, Neb. & London, University of Nebraska Press, 2018)

'disgraceful exhibition' – http://nagengast.org/nagengast/Gast/index.html

'far from a pleasant picture . . .' – https://xmasepic2010.wordpress.com/2010/08/01/riding-in-the-26th-century-margaret-gast/

CHAPTER 11

'gouge his eyes out' – 'We're not deviants say the cycling ladies', *Independent* (28 August 2005)

'In the Rosslyn they were all . . .' – Tim Hilton, *One More Kilometre and We're in the Showers* (London, Harper Perennial, 2004)

'injurious to the game . . .' – Albert Lusty, *Cycling* (August 1937)

'stayed home, in her kitchen' – Mariska Tjoelker, 'Mien Van Bree' in *Ride the Revolution: The Inside Stories from Women in Cycling*, ed. Suze Clemitson (London, Bloomsbury Sport, 2015)

'What will the neighbours think?' – Nancy Neiman Baranet, *The Turned Down Bar* (Philadelphia, Dorrance, 1964)

'one of the gang . . .' – Eileen Sheridan, *Wonder Wheels: The Autobiography of Eileen Sheridan* (London, Nicholas Kaye, 1956)

'rocked the racing world . . .' – *Bicycle* (27 February 1946)

'resented the intrusion . . .' – William Wilson, *Marguerite Wilson: The First Star of Women's Cycling* (Poole, CMP, 2016)

'a man to ride a . . .' – Wilson, *Marguerite Wilson*

'never be able to forgive . . .' – Wilson, *Marguerite Wilson*

'wonderfully fresh' – Sheridan, *Wonder Wheels*

'If the men did anything . . .' – Eileen Cropper, 'Sod off, I'm passing you', *Daily Telegraph* (19 September 2019)

'It would have been nice . . .' – https://www.britishcycling.org.uk/road/article/spor20100602-Interview--Eileen-Gray-CBE-0

'more determined to succeed' – https://www.britishcycling.org.uk/road/article/spor20100602-Interview--Eileen-Gray-CBE-0

'carrying, lifting, bending . . .' – Beryl Burton, *Personal Best* (Huddersfield, Springfield Books, 1986)

'Golly, isn't this tough' – Sheridan, *Wonder Wheels*

'Sod off, I'm passing you!' – 'Sod Off', *Daily Telegraph*

'like a nuclear bomb exploded . . .' – https://www.vice.com/en_us/article/wj3nvb/the-champion-mountain-biker-turned-drug-smuggler-missy-giove

'I'm not afraid of . . .' – Missy Giove, 'The Champion Mountain Biker Turned Drug Smuggler', *Vice* (20 November, 2018)

'You're only here once . . .' – https://www.velonews.com/2004/04/mountain/mtb-news-and-notes-missy-on-being-missy_5945

'anyone thought to be different . . .' – 'Philippa York', *Guardian* (6 July 2017)

'it's important to represent . . .' – Missy Giove, *Girlfriends* (July 2003)

CHAPTER 12

'a sport run by men, for men' – https://totalwomenscycling.com/news/nicole-cooke-evidence-british-cycling

'we were really going somewhere . . .' – https://cyclingtips.com/2017/12/learned-connie-carpenter-womens-cyclings-first-olympic-gold-medalist/

'absolutely nothing against . . .' – Isabel Best, 'Remembering the golden era of the women's Tour de France', *Daily Telegraph* (5 July 2019)

'I like women, but I prefer . . .' – Best, 'Remembering the golden era of the women's Tour de France'

'Do you really think women are . . .' – Rachel Sturtz, 'Meet the Billy Jean King of Cycling', *Outside* (24 July 2019)

'Some kind of weirdo . . .' – https://www.bbc.co.uk/sport/cycling/27041315

'flipped backwards' – https://cyclingtips.com/2017/12/learned-connie-carpenter-womens-cyclings-first-olympic-gold-medalist/

'women cyclists need a race . . .' – https://www.theguardian.com/sport/2019/jul/21/womens-cycling-future

'Being involved in a sport that . . .' – *Cycling Weekly* (3 June 2019)

'at a point now where . . .' – https://www.yorkshirepost.co.uk/sport/other-sport/video-lizzie-deignan-delighted-women-are-pedalling-alongside-men-terms-prize-money-480307

AFTERWORD

'a street in New York' – https://www.bikeleague.org/sites/default/files/WomenBikeReport(web)_0.pdf

'transport is the largest source' – https://assets.publishing.service.gov.uk/government/uploads/system/uploads/attachment_data/file/875485/2019_UK_greenhouse_gas_emissions_provisional_figures_statistical_release.pdf

'one in nineteen deaths' – https://www.independent.co.uk/environment/air-pollution-deaths-towns-cities-car-crash-particulate-matter-environment-a9302466.html

'60 per cent of journeys' – https://publications.parliament.uk/pa/cm201719/cmselect/cmtrans/1487/148705.htm

BIBLIOGRAPHY

BOOKS

Atkinson, Diane, *Rise Up, Women! The Remarkable Lives of the Suffragettes* (London, Bloomsbury Publishing, 2019)
——*Suffragettes in the Purple White & Green* (London, Museum of London, 1992)
Atwood, Kathryn J., *Women Heroes of World War II: The Pacific Theater: 15 Stories of Resistance, Rescue, Sabotage, and Survival* (Chicago, Chicago Review Press, 2017)
Bailey, Rosemary, *Love and War in the Pyrenees: A Story of Courage, Fear and Hope, 1939–1944* (London, Weidenfeld & Nicolson, 2008)
Bair, Deirdre, *Simone de Beauvoir: A Biography* (London, Vintage, 1991)
Baranet, Nancy Neiman, *The Turned Down Bar* (Philadelphia, Dorrance, 1964)
de Beauvoir, Simone, *Letters to Sartre*, trans. Quentin Hoare (London, Vintage Classics, 1993)
——*The Prime of Life*, trans. Peter Green (London, André Deutsch, Weidenfeld and Nicolson, 1963)
——*The Second Sex*, trans. H. M. Parshley (London, Vintage, 1997)
Buchheim, Eveline and Ralf Futselaar (eds), *Under Fire: Women and World War II* (Amsterdam, Verloren Publishers, 2014)
Buhring, Juliana, *This Road I Ride: My Incredible Journey from Novice to Fastest Woman to Cycle the Globe* (London, Piatkus, 2016)
Bullock Workman, Fanny and Hunter Workman, William *Algerian*

Memories: A Bicycle Tour over the Atlas to the Sahara (London, T. Fisher Unwin, 1895)

——*Sketches Awheel in Fin de Siècle Iberia* (London, T. F. Unwin, 1897)

——*Through Town and Jungle: Fourteen Thousand Miles A-wheel among the Temples and People of the Indian Plain* (London, T. Fisher Unwin, 1904)

Burton, Beryl, *Personal Best* (Huddersfield, Springfield Books, 1986)

Campbell Davidson, Lillias, *Handbook to Lady Cyclists* (London, Hay Nisbet & Co., 1896)

——*Hints to Lady Travellers at Home and Abroad* (London, Iliffe & Son, 1889)

Clemitson, Suze (ed.), *Ride the Revolution: The Inside Stories from Women in Cycling* (London, Bloomsbury Sport, 2015)

Crane, Diana, *Fashion and Its Social Agendas: Class, Gender, and Identity in Clothing* (Chicago, University of Chicago Press, 2000)

Crawford, Elizabeth, *The Women's Suffrage Movement: A Reference Guide 1866–1928* (London, UCL Press, 1999)

Cunningham, Patricia and Voso Lab, Susan (eds), *Dress and Popular culture* (Bowling Green, Bowling Green State University Popular Press, 1991)

Curie, Eve, *Marie Curie*, trans. Vincent Sheean (New York, Doubleday, Doran & Co., 1937)

Dodge, Pryor, *The Bicycle* (Paris, Flammarion, 1996)

Erskine, F. J., *Lady Cycling: What to Wear and How to Ride* (London, British Library, 2014)

Everett-Green, Evelyn, 'Cycling for Ladies' in Richardson, Sir B. W. (ed.), *All Round Cycling* (London, Walter Scott, 1896)

Finison, Lorenz J., *Boston's Cycling Craze, 1880–1900: A Story of Race, Sport, and Society* (Boston, University of Massachusetts Press, 2014)

Fischer, Gayle V., *Pantaloons and Power: Nineteenth-Century Dress Reform in the United States* (Kent, Ohio, Kent State University Press, 2001)

Fitzpatrick, Kathleen, *Lady Henry Somerset* (London, Jonathan Cape, 1923)

Galpin, Shannon, *Mountain to Mountain: A Journey of Adventure and Activism for the Women of Afghanistan* (New York, Saint Martin's Press, 2014)

Gilles, Roger, *Women on the Move: The Forgotten Era of Women's Bicycle Racing* (Lincoln, Neb. & London, University of Nebraska Press, 2018)

Gilman, Charlotte Perkins, *Herland and The Yellow Wallpaper* (London, Vintage, 2015)

Greville, Beatrice Violet (ed.), *Ladies in the Field: Sketches of Sport* (London, Ward & Downey, 1894)

Guroff, Margaret, *The Mechanical Horse: How the Bicycle Reshaped American Life* (Austin, University of Texas Press, 2016)

Haldane, Elizabeth Sanderson, *From One Century to Another: The Reminiscences of E. S. Haldane 1862–1937* (London, A. Maclehose & Co., 1937)

Hall, M. Ann, *Muscle on Wheels: Louise Armaindo and the High-Wheel Racers of Nineteenth-Century America* (Montreal, McGill-Queen's Press, 2018)

Hallenbeck, Sarah, *Claiming the Bicycle: Women, Rhetoric, and Technology in Nineteenth-Century America* (Carbondale, Southern Illinois University Press, 2015)

Harcourt Williamson, Mrs, Pemberton, A. C., Sisley, C. P. and Floyd, G., *The Complete Cyclist* (A. D. Innes & Co., London 1897)

Hargreaves, Jennifer, *Sporting Females: Critical Issues in the History and Sociology of Women's Sports* (London, Routledge, 1994)

Harris, Kate, *Lands of Lost Borders: A Journey on the Silk Road* (New York, Alfred Knopf, 2018)

Herlihy, David V., *Bicycle: The History* (New Haven, Yale University Press, 2004)

Hilton, Tim, *One More Kilometre and We're in the Showers* (London, Harper Perennial, 2004)

Jennings, Oscar, *Cycling and Health* (London, Iliffe & Son, 1893)

Jordan, Pete, *In the City of Bikes: The Story of the Amsterdam Cyclist* (New York, HarperPerennial, 2013)

Jungnickel, Kat, *Bikes and Bloomers: Victorian Women Inventors and Their Extraordinary Cycle Wear* (London, Goldsmiths Press, 2018)

Lightwood, James T., *Cyclists' Touring Club: Being the Romance of Fifty Years' Cycling* (London, Cyclists' Touring Club, 1928)

Macy, Sue, *Wheels of Change: How Women Rode the Bicycle to Freedom* (Washington, DC, National Geographic, 2011)

Marks, Patricia, *Bicycles, Bangs, and Bloomers: The New Woman in the Popular Press* (Lexington, KY, University Press of Kentucky, 1990)

McCrone, Kathleen, *Sport and the Physical Emancipation of English Women 1870–1914* (London, Routledge, 2014)

McGurn, James, *On Your Bicycle: An Illustrated History of Cycling* (London, John Murray, 1987)

Mitchell, Silas Weir, *Doctor and Patient* (New York, Classics of Medicine Library, 1994)

Murphy, Dervla, *Full Tilt: Ireland to India with a Bicycle* (London, Pan, 1967)

——*Wheels within Wheels* (London, John Murray, 1979)

Mustoe, Anne, *A Bike Ride: 12,000 Miles around the World* (London, Virgin, 1991)

Neeesen, Victor, *Dr. Neesen's Book on Wheeling: Hints and Advice to Men and Women from the Physician's Standpoint* (London, Forgotten Books, 2018)

Pankhurst, Sylvia E., *The Suffragette Movement: An Intimate Account of Persons and Ideals* (London, Longmans & Co., 1931)

Pennell, Elizabeth and Pennell, Joseph, *A Canterbury Pilgrimage* (London: Seeley and Co., 1885).

——*Our Sentimental Journey through France and Italy* (London, T. F. Unwin, 1887)

——*Over the Alps on a Bicycle* (London, T. F. Unwin, 1898)

——*To Gipsyland* (London, T. F. Unwin, 1893)

Pomeroy, Florence, *Reasons for Reform in Dress* (London, Hutchings & Crowsley, 1884)

Purvis, June and Stanley Holton, Sandra (eds), *Votes for Women* (London, Routledge, 2000)

Pye, Denis, *Fellowship Is Life: The National Clarion Cycling Club, 1895–1995* (Bolton, Clarion, 1995)

Ritchie, Andrew, *King of the Road: An Illustrated History of Cycling* (London, Wildwood House, 1975)

Ryley, James Beresford, *The Dangers of Cycling for Women and Children* (London, H. Renshaw, 1899)

Sheridan, Eileen, *Wonder Wheels: The Autobiography of Eileen Sheridan* (London, Nicholas Kaye, 1956)

Smith, Robert A., *A Social History of the Bicycle: Its Early Life and Times in America* (New York, American Heritage Press, 1972)

Smyth, Ethel, *The Memoirs of Ethel Smyth* (London, Viking, 1987)

Solnit, Rebecca, *Wanderlust: A History of Walking* (London, Penguin, 2001)

Swanwick, Helena Maria Lucy, *I Have Been Young* (London, Victor Gollancz, 1935)

Sykes, Herbie, *Maglia Rosa: Triumph and Tragedy at the Giro D'Italia* (London, Bloomsbury, 2013)

Thoreau, Henry David, *The Writings of Henry David Thoreau* (Boston, Houghton Mifflin, 1894)

Vertinsky, Patricia, *Eternally Wounded Women: Women, Doctors and Exercise in the Late Nineteenth Century* (Manchester: Manchester University Press, 1990)

Ward, Maria E., *The Common Sense of Bicycling: Bicycling for Ladies* (New York, Brentano, 1896)

Wellings, Mark, *Ride! Ride! Ride!: Herne Hill Velodrome and the Story of British Track Cycling* (London, Icon Books, 2016)

Whitmore, Richard, *Alice Hawkins and the Suffragette Movement in Edwardian Leicester* (Derby, Breedon, 2007)

Willard, Frances E., *Writing Out My Heart: Selections from the Journal of Frances E. Willard, 1855–96* (Urbana, University of Illinois Press, 1995)

——*A Wheel Within a Wheel* (New York, Fleming H. Revell, 1895)

Wilson, William, *Marguerite Wilson: The First Star of Women's Cycling* (Poole, CMP, 2016)

Woolf, Virginia, *The Diary of Virginia Woolf*, ed. Anne Olivier (London, Hogarth Press, 1980)

Zheutlin, Peter, *Around the World on Two Wheels: Annie Londonderry's Extraordinary Ride* (New York, Kensington Publishing Corp., 2007)

MAGAZINES

Bicycling
Bicycling News
Casquette
Cycling
Cycling Weekly
Cycling World Illustrated
Cyclists' Touring Club Gazette
Lady Cyclist
Outing
Rouleur
The Hub
Wheelwoman

JOURNAL ARTICLES

Fenton, W. H., 'A Medical View of Cycling for Ladies', *The Nine-teenth Century*, 39 (23 May 1896)
Grand, Sarah, 'The New Aspect of the Woman Question', *North American Review*, 158 (1894)
Hanlon, Sheila, 'At the Sign of the Butterfly: The Mowbray House Cycling Association', *Cycle History*, 18 (Spring 2008)
Merington, Marguerite, 'Woman and the Bicycle', *Scribner's*, XVII (June 1895)

WEBSITES

www.bicycling.com
www.bikemag.com
www.cyclingtips.com
www.dirtmountainbike.com
www.dirtragmag.com
https:mmbhof.org
www.pinkbike.com
www.playingpasts.co.uk
www.podiumcafe.com
www.sheilahanlon.com
www.sidetracked.com

www.singletrackworld.com
www.sixday.org.uk
www.sustrans.org.uk
www.totalwomenscycling.com
www.velonews.com

FILMS

A Boy, a Girl and a Bike, dir. Ralph Smart (UK, 1949)

Afghan Cycles, dir. Sarah Menzies (USA, 2018), https://www.afghancycles.com/

Born in Flames, dir. Lizzie Borden (USA, 1983)

Cycling Family, Pathé (UK, 1961), www.britishpathe.com/video/cycling-family/query/Fosters+cycling+family

Housewife Cyclist, Pathé (UK, 1956), https://www.britishpathe.com/video/housewife-cyclist

Hyde Park Bicycling Scene (UK, 1896), http://www.screenonline.org.uk/film/id/785709/index.html

Ovarian Psycos, dir. Joanna Sokolowski, Kate Trumbull-LaValle (USA, 2016)

Racing is Life: The Beryl Burton Story, Bromley Video (UK, 2012)

'The Champion Mountain Biker Turned Drug Smuggler' (USA, 2018), https://www.vice.com/en_us/article/wj3nvb/the-champion-mountain-biker-turned-drug-smuggler-missy-giove

The Miseducation of Cameron Post, dir. Desiree Akhavan (USA, 2018)

Wadjda, dir. Haifaa Al Mansour (Saudi Arabia, 2013)

INDEX